The Making of Language

The Making of Language

MIKE BEAKEN

EDINBURGH UNIVERSITY PRESS

To Kate

© Mike Beaken, 1996

Edinburgh University Press Ltd
22 George Square, Edinburgh

Typeset in Linotronic Times
by Speedspools, Edinburgh, and
printed and bound in Great Britain

A CIP record for this book is available
from the British Library

ISBN 0 7486 0717 X (paper)

Contents

To the Reader

This book is written in an attempt to save language from disappearing – metaphorically, that is. A hundred and fifty years ago the early linguists looked on language as the creation and the property of people, of nations, or of cultures. Linguists since then seem to have been busily trying to shrink the scope of language. This century the study of language has focused on its 'system', or 'structure', in the individual speaker. Then the focus shifted to the speaker's mind, and alongside linguists, psychologists joined in the search for the 'language areas' or 'speech areas' of the brain. Today, the search is on for an even smaller phenomenon – the so-called language gene. With this final reduction of language to the level of molecular biology, the next logical step is for drug companies to start working towards the manufacture of a language pill, to be sold to parents anxious about their children's linguistic and educational progress.

To redress the balance, this work will attempt to restore human beings to a central place in language studies, starting from a view of humans as co-operative sharing people, whose humanity is the result of their collective efforts over time to transform their environment – in other words, human labour. Language has been an essential part of human labour from the very beginning, and we focus on three aspects of labour – activity, social life and thinking – as relevant to the creation and shaping of language. It may seem at first a little surprising that thinking is seen as an aspect of labour. We have to recognise that the key moment in our history was when apes got into the habit of doing things together instead of separately, or side by side. From the moment that co-operation became a habit, labour and language started to develop. These two aspects of social life led directly to the development of a third – human thought, based on the creation of ideas shared between people in the medium of language.

This book, then, is not just about language, but also about human prehistory, human history, social life and social ideas. The scope is vast, unavoidably. Much of this work is a presentation of the ideas of others, but in some areas, such as the origins of speech, and the evolution of syntactic relations in grammar, I have had to struggle towards new ideas to fill gaps in thinking.

I have found it necessary in places to explain concepts from one discipline for the benefit of those from other disciplines. However, I have tried to avoid following a section on archaeology for linguists with one on linguistics for archaeologists, and have tried to avoid on the one hand, too much jargon, and on the other, crude simplification. I hope that readers will not become irritated by explanations of ideas that they are perfectly familiar with – unless, of course, the explanations are wrong, in which case irritation is justified.

In a work like this some speculation is unavoidable. The best we can hope for is the most well-informed speculation possible. I have done my best to keep the speculation rooted in evidence. Readers will be able to judge for themselves the places where this principle has been lost sight of.

This book is a contribution to the debate about language. Its aim, of course, is to inform and persuade, but also to stimulate discussion. It will be fairly clear that the book has been written with a definite viewpoint, one that I would describe as Marxist, though there may be some Marxists who would disagree. If you find the book makes you want to read more, then it has partially fulfilled its aim. If you find it makes you want to argue, then it has totally fulfilled its aim. Get a few friends together and carry on arguing!

1

The Story to Date

For anyone who is interested in the study of language, it should be the most natural thing in the world to want to consider its origins. This was indeed one of the main interests of eighteenth-century writers who addressed questions of language.[1] With the enormous growth of interest in the science of language in the nineteenth century, and the emphasis of philology[2] on historical reconstruction of languages such as Sanskrit, it was inevitable that the question of the ultimate origin of language should remain in the forefront of attention.[3]

The first Neanderthal fossil was discovered in 1856. Darwin's *Origins of Species* was published in 1859; Lewis Henry Morgan's *Ancient Society* in 1877. You would think that the great interest in human origins at this time would continue to stimulate the subject of the origins of language. Strangely, however, just the opposite started to happen. Linguistics in the 1870s and 1880s turned away more and more from the vast general questions involved in the subject.

One reason for this was the multiplication of nebulous theories from quasi-linguists and quasi-philosophers, strongly deprecated by the linguist Whitney in 1873:

> No theme in linguistic science is more often and more voluminously treated than this [origins of language], and by scholars of every grade and tendency; nor any, it may be added, with less profitable result in proportion to the labour expended; the greater part of what is said and written upon it is mere windy talk, the assertion of subjective views which commend themselves to no mind save the one that produces them, and which are apt to be offered with a confidence, and defended with a tenacity, that are in inverse rate to their acceptableness. This has given the whole question a bad repute among soberminded philologists.[4]

As a result, linguistics since the late nineteenth century has tended to treat the subject with great caution, and many have even concluded that it is a subject that can never be known.

However, the neglect of language origins was not simply a case of avoiding cranks. The shift in linguistic study away from language in a cultural setting, to an exclusive concentration on language form, arose from the tasks that came to preoccupy linguists, that is, the understanding of the abstract system of language, its laws, and the regularities of the system itself. The central preoccupation of European linguistics[5] by the 1880s was the history of the Indo-European language family, focusing particularly on the reconstruction of the parent Proto-Indo-European language, by tracing connections between words and grammatical forms in the various recorded European languages and related languages such as Sanskrit, Old Persian, Tokharian and developing laws of sound-change that would confirm or otherwise these connections.

In focusing on words, grammatical forms and sound changes, linguists instituted a trend of attending to the form of languages to the exclusion of those who spoke them.[6] This trend crystallised in Saussure's declaration at the beginning of this century that the primary job of linguists was to study not the history of language but its structure, and that structure (or *langue*) should be studied in its own terms and for its own sake, to the exclusion of its speakers and of the way they use the language in their lives (*parole*).[7] Saussure was as concerned with the study of living languages as that of the dead languages that preoccupied the neogrammarians, but the effect of separating language history (diachronic linguistics) from the study of language structure (synchronic linguistics), resulted in taking language completely out of time, and reducing the study of living language to something comparable to dead text. As Voloshinov observed: 'Linguistics studies a living language as if it were a dead language, and native language as if it were an alien tongue' (Voloshinov 1973, p. 77 fn. 11). When you divorce language from its past, you also divorce it from its present, and you divorce it from its speakers, as Saussure does explicitly with his separation of *langue* and *parole*.

Saussure recognised language as a social phenomenon (Saussure 1974, p. 14), yet his method prevents us from studying it in its social context. This approach to language, known as formalism, abstract objectivism or structuralism has dominated western linguistics for most of this century.

This dualism, – static, synchronic linguistics versus changing diachronic linguistics – and the complementary dualism of language in the abstract (*langue*) versus language in use (*parole*), may originally have had a practical justification. Language interpenetrates with every aspect of human activity. There are many thousand living languages in the world,[8] many more if we consider historical predecessors of today's languages. If we set out to study how life and language are related in all these languages, the task might appear too huge to accomplish. Saussure suggested that what linguists should attempt to do first was a more restricted task – to describe the structure and forms of language. To do this, he considered it necessary for a while to divorce the study of language from the study of its history or its daily use. However, this separation of language from life has become, for recent schools of linguistics, a defining principle of the subject. Chomsky's insistence that the proper study of language should be the abstract rules of syntax, for example, has made into a principle the study of language as a thing in itself.

At the same time, the separation of linguistics from history has led to historical linguistics being treated as a separate discipline of language study, with its own theories and principles, while the area of language study which takes socially organised human beings into account is referred to as 'sociolinguistics', as if it were a subsidiary branch of linguistics proper. Given this self-imposed fragmentation of the disciplines concerned with language, it is hardly surprising that for most of this century, the topic of language origins has continued to be regarded as of marginal interest by western linguists.[9]

Soviet Union in the 1920s and 1930s

For a brief period in the 1920s, when intellectual and artistic work flourished in the post-revolutionary Soviet Union, the work of a group of psychologists and linguists around Vygotsky provided a new starting point for language studies in the Marxist tradition. The group's broad interests covered the questions of the origins and evolution of language, developing the work of Engels (for example, Engels 1954); the nature of primate cognition compared to humans; the evolution of human thought and its relation to language; inner speech and its role in thought; and the development of speech and thinking in children. Another group of thinkers around Bakhtin and Voloshinov was interested in the relation of language to social existence, thought and ideology. Voloshinov attempted to show how the study of language could be furthered in the perspective of Marxist ideas. However, in the climate of bureaucratic oppression of the Soviet Union in the 1930s, Vygotsky and those around him found it harder and harder to develop their ideas. Vygotsky died in 1934, and for generations his work was officially out of favour (Williams, 1977, p. 34). Voloshinov's work similarly fell out of favour with the party bureaucracy, and he mysteriously disappeared in the early 1930s. It is only recently that their work has been rediscovered (see Kozulin 1990; Wertsch 1985).

Marr

In this same period, the work of the linguist Marr won official approval with the Stalinist bureaucracy. The institute he founded, the Japhetic Institute, was renamed the Marr Institute of Language and Thought. He died in 1934, the same year as Vygotsky, but his considerable influence lived on in, for example, the work of Meschaninov and the 'Marrists'. Their ideas, which for many decades appear to have represented the orthodox Soviet view of language, were a strange mixture of dogma, detailed empirical description of languages within the Soviet Union, and speculative fantasies. For example, Marr proposed that the original form of communication was gestural, and that speech was introduced into human life by magicians or shamans, for purposes of professional secrecy. He further held that language evolved in a series of leaps, changing more or less in time with successive stages of society – thus, there were thought to be different forms of language characteristic of primitive communism, of slave society, of feudalism, and of capitalist society. The concepts of base and superstructure were used in a mechanical way to link forms of society with forms of language – without, it must be said, a great deal of evidence or of explanation (see Ellis and Davies 1951; Matthews 1950).

In 1951, Stalin denounced the followers of Marr, and that was really the end of Marrism. In fact there was much that was of value in the work of Marr's followers, such as Meschaninov, and as we shall see in subsequent sections, linguists in the Soviet Union continued to undertake useful work on linguistic history and reconstructions of earlier languages: work that is becoming increasingly known in the West (see Wright 1991).

Reconstructions and the search for Proto-languages
Indo-European

The early linguists who worked on the Indo-European family of languages, combined interests in language, culture and anthropology. One of their interests was in finding out about our Indo-European ancestors, and language was originally seen as one route to this understanding. Only later did the study of language forms become an interest in its own right. Then attention focused on the possibility of reconstructing early forms of Indo-European.

The comparative technique involves matching what appear to be similar words in different languages. After a sufficient number of matches are established, and in conjunction with knowledge of laws of sound-change, it is supposed to be possible to determine first, the degree of relationship between the two languages; and, if they are deemed to be in the same language family, to reconstruct forms of words in the proto-language from which they have both derived.

The reconstruction of proto-languages from correspondences started really with Schleicher, and has a considerable history in the West (see Pedersen 1931, p. 284ff). Marr's work with Caucasian languages gave it considerable impetus in the Soviet Union, and despite the setback of Stalin's denunciation, the work of linguistic reconstruction has been furthered by Illich-Svitych and the so-called 'Nostraticists' from Russia, matched in the West by Bomhard, Greenberg, Ruhlen and others (see Wright 1991; de Grolier 1990).

Many efforts at reconstruction have been criticised; the temptation of delving too enthusiastically into the past are clear in the case of Marr. The more cautious proponents of the comparative method have criticised what they see as a tendency to declare proto-families established on the basis of too little evidence. Greenberg's proposal that all Amerindian languages could be grouped into three large family groups – Eskimo-Aleut, Na-dene and Amerind – has proved controversial, for example (Greenberg and Ruhlen 1992).

In particular, there are arguments about how far back reconstructions can hope to go, in the absence of written forms for any language beyond about 6,000 BP.[10] The cut-off point is usually put at about 30,000 years (Bender 1973, quoted by de Grolier 1989, p. 75). However, modern human beings seem to have existed as long as 100,000 years ago, in Africa or the Middle East, as both. Though Ruhlen claims that the world's original language can be reconstructed (BBC Horizon 1992), there is little chance that such a claim can ever be accepted beyond any doubt.

Language families

But, vague and speculative as the work of reconstructionists might appear, it does seem to find some confirmation in recent work on the genetic similarities of world-wide human groups. Cavalli-Sforza claims that the genetic groupings of human beings established by studies based on DNA and other techniques correspond quite closely to the proposed language groupings of Greenberg and Ruhlen (Cavalli-Sforza *et al.* 1988; Cavalli-Sforza 1991). It appears that linguistic reconstructions may have more validity than was previously suspected.

CHOMSKY'S INFLUENCE ON LINGUISTICS

For all the fragmentation of contemporary linguistics, there is still no doubt that the dominant figure today is Noam Chomsky. Chomsky's work is firmly in the tradition of formalism, for all his attempts to root his ideas in the creative, speaker-oriented tradition of Wilhelm von Humboldt (1767–1835; see Humboldt 1988). Chomsky focuses on form, structure and rules (what he terms the 'competence' of the native speaker), separate from the actual use of language in the form of utterances in context ('performance'). Chomsky's message is that language makes us human. However, the way to discover what it means to be human is not for him the study of human activity, but the study of language, which will reveal the nature of the human mind. Chomsky has done nothing to counteract the continued divorce of the human being from studies of language.[11]

Chomsky's impact on linguistics since the 1950s has been to stimulate research in the study of language structure, encouraging a shift from the detailed study of differences between one language and another to the study of properties that languages share. In particular he gave a tremendous boost to studies of the development of child language. However, his emphasis on syntax as a defining property of language was probably partly responsible for holding back studies of ape language, which were just starting to develop in the 1950s. Chomsky was adamant that chimpanzees were not capable of learning anything like human syntax, and that was for him the essence of language (Terrace 1979a; 1979b).

Chomsky's principal positions are:

(1) Animal communication cannot develop into human language. There is no way that principles of natural selection could account for the extremely abstract principles of syntax underlying the sentences of natural language. The gap appears unbridgeable:

> There is no more of a basis for assuming an evolutionary development of 'higher' from 'lower' stages, in this case [the development of human syntax], than there is for assuming an evolutionary development from breathing to walking; the stages have no significant analogy, it appears, and seem to involve entirely different principles. (Chomsky 1988, p. 167)

(2) Therefore, the only reasonable explanation available is that language must be the result of innate properties of the human mind – in other words the brain. The implication is that mental properties are genetically determined, and are 'hard-wired' in the brain (Chomsky 1979, p. 94).

(3) What has come to be known as Universal Grammar (UG) is in fact the product of a 'mental organ', responsible for the way that children learn the rules of adult language on the basis of only a relatively small selection of adult sentences (Chomsky 1979, p. 230). This mental organ takes the form of a 'language acquisition device' (LAD) that determines the form of grammar that individuals make for themselves as they learn the language around them.

(4) Not only is syntax the product of a mental organ, but so too is the 'semantic component' – another mental module responsible for organising the individual's stock of word meanings – and the 'phonological component', responsible for the rules of pronunciation. Taking the hypothesis a step further, he suggests that other mental capacities are also built into the brain, so that individuals may also be possessed of for example a 'science-forming capacity' (Chomsky 1980, p. 250). The human mind, in other words, appears as an assembly of various mental modules, all with their own inborn properties, rules and principles.[12]

(5) The key to language for Chomsky is the study of syntax. Rather than look at language as an aspect of social interaction, he reduces it to the narrowest possible basis, that of syntax, and not even syntax as observed

in actual utterances, but an abstract, idealised competence. This abstractness is not a problem; for him it is language's essential feature. The move towards greater and greater abstraction seems to take the process begun by Saussure to its logical conclusion. In Saussure, the history of language is cut away. In Chomsky's early work (1965), any connection with society is removed. In his later work, introducing the theory of Government and Binding, all is reduced still further to grammar, and it is a grammar which is shorn of all that Chomsky considers inessential, a core grammar, distinct from a periphery of marked constructions – 'borrowings, historical residues, inventions and so on, which we can hardly expect to incorporate within a principled theory of UG' (Chomsky 1981, p.8). The claimed universal principles of Universal Grammar turn out to be extremely abstract structural principles, and to have little or no connection with the material life of human beings.

Innateness

Chomsky's view that language is the result of innate properties of the mind can be traced back to Descartes and his view that we are born with certain innate ideas. Descartes's dualism, his separation of body and mind, is also reflected in Chomsky's work, where properties of the mind are seen as more significant to language formation than experience. Chomsky has often argued that children create rules of language despite the poor quality of the language they hear around them (Chomsky 1964, p. 134). This approach – based on the individual and the individual's inner mental processes – ignores interactions between individuals, let alone groups of individuals, and the world around them. It is telling that the methodology of Chomsky and his supporters consists of introspection and intuition based on artificial, idealised, decontextualised sentences (Jones 1994, p. 10).

In sharp contrast with his lucid and very practical analysis of world affairs in his political writing, there is in Chomsky's writing on language little relation with the practical details of speakers and their lives, whose impact on language is dismissed as 'performance'. His grammar ends up as a purely formal schema, without speakers, without a history, and without an origin.

The view of language as a property of mind cuts language off from history. If the human mind is based on human biology, it must have always been that way, since humans appeared on the Earth. The question of how the mind came into existence is not answerable, especially as Chomsky does not admit to any antecedent for language in animal behaviour. This sits very uneasily with what we now know about evolution, and it is no accident that Chomsky likes to refer back to thinkers such as Descartes and Humboldt, who were writing before the time of Darwin and evolutionary theory.

THE BIOLOGICAL BASIS OF LANGUAGE

Linguists, dissatisfied with Chomsky's failure to reconcile linguistics with the theory of evolution, have attempted to provide an explanation for language origins that fits with Darwinian evolutionary theory. Two attempts that are influential are by Bickerton and Pinker.[13]

Bickerton and the Bioprogram

Bickerton starts from Chomsky's idea that language is the product of the human mind. The explanation he provides for the development of human beings as a speaking species is a rather crude one – a biological mutation that lifts us from the level of chimpanzees or early hominids straight to humanity. Chimpanzees, like young children at a pre-syntactic stage – that is, before they start combining words into fully formed sentences – are said to be capable of 'proto-language', creating simple utterances by putting words crudely together, without forming grammatical sentences characteristic of human languages. The transition from chimpanzees or ape-like hominids to modern human beings is the result of a biological mutation, to produce beings with the capacity for syntax, and with a mind capable of representing the world in a human way. UG, in other words, was the result of a biological mutation (Bickerton 1990, p. 190). The mutation is a sophisticated genetic programme, a 'bioprogram', governing the development of the individual's language in an emerging sequence. Bickerton suggests that human DNA provides the individual human body with instructions for language growth, just like the physical instructions for standing, walking, becoming sexually mature (Bickerton 1984, p. 143). This bioprogram is said to apply both to children's developing language and in the historical evolution of language. It can be seen in operation in the way that creole languages are formed from pidgins in situations of language contact.[14].

Bickerton does not focus merely on grammar; he also considers thought – the way that we represent the world internally. Language is not at root a system of communication, but one of representation, that 'creates a new and parallel world constrained by the laws of its own nature just as much as the nature of the phenomena it represents' (Bickerton 1990, p. 46). The language organ appears to be not just the producer of language structures, but also the brain function responsible for inner representations.

So, like Chomsky, Bickerton implies that the way we see or understand the world around us is constrained by the structure of our mind. Species-specific innate mental properties prevent us from transcending our own neural limitations. In fact he talks about 'the mode of existence language imposes on us' (Bickerton 1990, p. 231).

What led to this mutation? Bickerton proposes the Darwinian concept of natural selection: language-skilled individuals possess a higher potential for survival; they will produce more offspring than other individuals.

Objections to Bickerton

The following objections can be made to these arguments:

1. Bickerton's explanation of what 'selected' language is inadequate. Exactly why lack of a language organ should see some members of the species fail to reproduce, while the language organ helps others to survive, he does not specify.
2. He views language abilities as a function of individual mental representations of the world – in other words, based on passive contemplation and not interaction with the world. He cannot allow that humans may have made their own language.
3. So he has to propose an unmotivated biological leap or 'saltation' – a new species arising all at once, fully formed, by a fortuitous macromutation. As Chomsky points out, the distance between chimpanzee communication and human language is so great that a single biological event is simply not enough to explain the transition. Such unmotivated leaps have little to do with Darwinian theory. They look more like biblical creations.

Pinker and Bloom and the Language Instinct

Another attempt to solve the problem of the origins of UG comes from Pinker and Bloom (1990) and Pinker (1994). Like Bickerton, they start from the assumption that a 'language organ' exists, though no proof is offered for the existence of this supposed organ. They equate language with complex physical organs such as the eye or the hand, and then attempt to explain how the gene responsible for language gets to be reproduced. It is hardly necessary to point out that the existence of this gene is also unproven: 'Language shows signs of complex design for the communication of propositional structures, and the only explanation for the origin of organs with complex design is the process of natural selection' (Pinker and Bloom 1990, p. 726).

Where Bickerton suggests one mutation, Pinker and Bloom's model depends on a gradual evolution of the language faculty – a series of steps (Pinker and Bloom 1990, p. 711), leading from no language at all to language as we now find it, each step small enough to have been produced by random mutation or recombination.[15]

Unlike Bickerton, who regards the primary function of language to represent the world in our minds – in other words, to think about the world – Pinker and Bloom see language as originating in the function of communication, on the basis of the existence of mechanisms that presuppose the existence of a listener, such as grammatical and intonational features that distinguish topic and comments.[16]

In order to show how natural selection might lead to the evolution of a species innately endowed with UG, Pinker and Bloom argue, like Bickerton

and Newmeyer (1991, 1992), that better grammars give selective advantages. They propose that better communicators will survive and prosper,
either in the outside world or within the social group.

Objections to Pinker

The objections that can be made to these arguments are as follows:

(1) Language is not like the human eye, that evolved from the primate
eye. We are born with eyes, arms, legs, but we have to learn our language.
An anatomical organ has to have an origin, but none can be found for
language. Whereas the human eye can be shown to have evolved from
the eyes of other animals, the lungs from an adaptation in the lung-fish,
human hips from adaptations of the pelvis to upright walking, and so on,
there is nothing we can point to as a predecessor of language, unless we
consider animal communication, such as chimpanzee gestures, as a proto-
language.

More importantly, our eyes work perfectly well when nobody else is
around, but language is essentially a social, not an individual property.
The problem involved in treating language as a biological organ becomes
clear with the question,[17] 'When the first human appeared with the
biological adaptation making language possible, who did he or she talk
to?' If there was nobody around talking at the time, how could the
advantage of speech manifest itself?

(2) As long as we are considering the individual hominid, it is hard to see
how more developed syntax can be an advantage, until the speaker takes
part in a developed social life. An ape with a human language facility will
simply find no use for its new linguistic skills. Indeed, it is only by not
using its newly developed language skills that the individual will be able
to remain part of the social group that, for hominids, is crucial to individual
survival.

Clearly, then, the language organ can only be an advantage if a number
of individuals in the group are endowed with it. It is easy to see that
discussion of alternatives, planning, forethought and so on may contribute
to increased efficiency of food-gathering in a hominid group.

But the human way of life, that is, foraging, that has been the mode of
existence for the vast majority of humanity's time on the planet, did not
burst on to the world fully formed as part of a plan by newly speaking
human beings. All the evidence points to its slow development over a
long period during which techniques developed – techniques of making
tools and spears; carrying gathered food; reading animal tracks; anticipating
where and when trees are fruiting; finding foods hidden in the earth;
using plants for medicinal properties; and so on – none of which is a
biologically programmed behaviour, but is learnt and passed on through
generations, by means of language. Language, in other words, is closely

tied to technology, and does not have to be explained as an independent biological capacity either preceding or following technology. Why should language be any different from the ability to make a fire, to cook, or to make a bow and arrow?

(3) Pinker and Bloom's series of mutations can only work if a convincing factor can be found to select for more advanced language. For Darwinian selection to operate, it has to give an advantage to some members of the species at the expense of others. But there is no evidence that at any period of prehistory before the development of agriculture separate human species were in competition.[18] All the evidence points to a long period of co-operation, of mutually beneficial intergroup contacts rather than warfare. In any case, it would be hard to establish that speakers of a more complex language would truly have a significant advantage over another group, the level of technology and social organisation being equal. Wars are usually won by the side with the larger army and the more destructive weaponry, rather than the one with the more complex grammar, and if we set out to show that one group of humans is getting a better living out of a certain habitat than another, it undoubtedly will be their general level of technology and social organisation that will explain the group's success rather than their sole reliance on more complex syntax.

(4) Pinker and Bloom's argument rests on the assumption that more complex communication is more effective. But it is no easy matter to decide what is 'complex' communication and what is 'simple'. Complexity may be a function of the message to be communicated, of the speaker's purpose or status, of the organisation of social life, of the situational context or of the form of communication. There is no evidence that language complexity invariably confers an advantage. Often the short, simple message is the most effective. The context and the task in hand are the key variables here.

(5) The final objection is whether the 'language instinct' is even necessary in Pinker and Bloom's account. Pinker (1994, p. 365) hedges his bets, suggesting that the instinct for language may have even appeared after language itself was created. In other words, after some hominids started speaking, the habit was genetically 'wired-in' some of us and became part of our genes. Apart from the fact that this seems quite implausible, it is not how selection works. If some of us can communicate without the language gene, then selection will not operate to favour those with the gene for language, because those without the gene will survive just as well as those with it.

Bickerton sees language as primarily for representation. Pinker and Bloom see language primarily for communication. Both are partial views. As Chapter Two will demonstrate, language carries both these functions.

On Sociobiology

One reason why these two accounts of language origins fail to convince is their reliance on the notions of sociobiology, in particular their reduction-ism. Reductionism is best explained by a quotation from Dunbar about what he calls the 'common currency' of sociobiology, that, he suggests:

> allows us to integrate within a single unified framework all aspects of biology and behaviour . . . [W]e can now translate the costs and benefits of different activities or characters into a common currency, so as to be able to make direct comparisons of their relative evolutionary values. (Dunbar 1988; p. 161)

However, it does not help to reduce all phenomena to one level. First is the problem of which is the appropriate level? Is it the level of sub-atomic physics? Chemistry? Biochemistry? Clearly, different levels are appropriate for different phenomena. The second problem is that laws appropriate for one level do not necessarily explain phenomena at a different level. We cannot translate Darwinian evolutionary processes in terms of sub-atomic physics, any more than we can translate sub-atomic physics in terms of Darwinian laws. Similarly we should not expect to account for human behaviour in laws developed for insects. Laws of animal behaviour are compatible with the laws of biochemistry, they have also their own particu-lar laws. Human behavior is similarly subject to its own laws, which are compatible with lower-order laws, but distinct from them, and not reducible to them. The notion that human behaviour can be reduced to the same level as that of insects is the fallacy underlying sociobiology (Wilson 1975).[19]

ANIMAL COMMUNICATION TO SPEECH

Nevertheless, many commentators, often specialists in the study of particu-lar species, are so struck by the apparent ingenuity and intricacy of the system of communication that they are studying that they are tempted, understandably, to draw a parallel with human behaviour.

Richman (1993) emphasises the continuity of singing between primates and humans. He has studied the choral and social singing of geladas, gibbons, siamangs, porpoises and whales. But his parallel between instinc-tive singing behaviour and human music is misleading. The human form of behaviour is qualitatively different from what we know of other creatures – it is controlled, it is learnt, it is cultural.

Staal (1994) compares human mantras with the choral singing of birds and the collective vocalisation of some monkeys. Yet mantras are nothing like the instinctive vocal behaviour of birds or baboons. Mantras are Vedic hymns, communally or individually performed, associated with East-ern religions such as Buddhism, performed by religious groups whose main concern is with forms of mystic life. They only appeared late in human history, and they are a totally human creation. It can be argued that mantras function as a kind of psychological tool, to help individuals and groups achieve mental conditions of calmness, so that contemplation or decision-making can be carried out. Although it is difficult to specify the content or meaning of mantras, there is no doubt that they are totally human products, and not the result of biological instinct.[20]

Another common parallel drawn between humans and the animal world is based on the so-called 'language of bees'. For long it has been asserted that bees can communicate with each other, passing on in a kind of dance what is claimed to be quite specific information about where nectar-bearing flowers are, in what direction from the hive and how distant. These claims are often made as if they had been scientifically proved to the satisfaction of all. However in a series of studies, Wenner has examined claims for bee language, and shown that while an individual bee's dance, or possibly its odour, certainly does stimulate extra activity from fellow bees, it causes them to fly off not just in the direction of the flowers, but in every possible direction. Some bees find flowers, of course, but many others return home empty-handed, or empty-legged. The predominant factor in determining where bees go from the hive is in fact the prevailing wind, not the dance of the bee (see Wenner *et al.* 1990; 1991; Wenner 1994). Yet bees' language is still quoted widely as an instance of the sort of biologically-based behaviour which underlies ape communication and human language.

If we consider animal cries as instinctive reactions to external stimuli, we see that this aspect of behaviour is still present in human beings, but in non-linguistic behaviour, such as crying, laughing, shouting or gasping with pain or with pleasure – vocalisations that are not under our control unless we really train ourselves. These vocalisations have really no connection with language. We can laugh, cry or ouch at the same time as talking. A baby's cry of discomfort does not develop into sounds of speech – it simply continues as crying, until at a certain stage it is suppressed, to reappear only in times of great distress, perhaps in the adult form of swearing.[21]

Pavlov (1957) insists that human language, though related to animal communication, is qualitatively different from it:

> In the animal, reality is signaled almost exclusively by stimulations and the traces they leave in the cerebral hemispheres. This is the first system of signals of reality common to men and animals. But speech constitutes a second signaling system of reality which is peculiarly ours, being the signal of the first signals. (Pavlov 1957, cited by Woolfson 1982, p. 67)

Where Chomsky sees an unbridgeable gulf between animal and human communication systems, Pavlov suggests how the gulf has been bridged. His account of the second signalling system shows how the connections arising on the basis of signs introduce a new, higher principle of neural activity that enables us to reflect on, and therefore control, our instinctive reactions to stimuli. The basic fact about human behaviour is that it has risen above the level of instinct, and proposals to explain facts about language on the basis of animal instinct are bound to lead only to confusion.

THE BRAIN

A number of points need to be made in connection with the sometimes mystifying arguments heard about the relation of the brain and human language.

The idea that human language is the product of the individual human brain, and speech the product of our vocal organs, can be traced back at least as far as Schleicher.[22] Since Broca and Wernicke proposed that there are special areas of the brain, the idea has been pursued with great vigour, but without conclusive results. The parts of the brain known as Broca's area and Wernicke's area are said to be associated with speech, and it is widely assumed that language is governed by the brain's left hemisphere, with different kinds of brain activity governed by the right.

There is no agreement on 'language areas' of the brain

It has long been assumed that the neocortex – the most recent part of the brain in evolutionary terms – is responsible for language activity. However, the more the brain is studied for correlations with linguistic abilities, the more areas are proposed. Even a cursory reading of literature on language areas of the brain reveals a quite bewildering number of areas said to have functions for language.[23]

Ape and human brains differ only in size

Our brain, like our other organs, is essentially similar in structure to that of other higher mammals. It is part of the common mammalian nervous system, with the same chemical transmitters, subject to the same diseases, and composed of the same type of neurons. As Darwin commented:

> On the available evidence, the brains of apes and humans are so similar that one is left at a loss to explain the remarkable, and apparently discontinuous, nature of the mental capacities of humans in comparison with those of our primate cousins. (cited by Donald 1991, p. 21)

We possess, in other words, a typical primate brain, proportioned the way a very large primate brain would be expected to be proportioned (Passingham 1982, p. 109). Campbell comments that it is only the size of our brains – larger by a factor of 3:1 than the nearest primates' – that has lifted humans above the animal into a new order of organic life – a quantitative change that has resulted in qualitative changes of extraordinary significance (Campbell 1988, p. 364). There is, however, no evidence either of special structures in the brain, or that any dramatic changes have taken place in the course of human evolution.

The brain is not an organ

The brain, unlike the heart or the legs, cannot initiate action of its own accord. There is certainly no evidence that it can produce language structures, thoughts, memories, without previous activity on the part of the body it is housed in. An important principle of neurophysiology is that the nervous system does not generate function; it is a system of connections. Its growth in size is a function of the growth in the complexity of the human organism – the number of things our body has learnt to do, especially the hand and arm, mouth and facial muscles. This growth, in our musculature, in our nervous system, in the number of functions controlled by muscles and nerves, has resulted in the growth of the co-ordinating centre for all these activities (Whitcombe 1994), the cortex.

This does not make the achievement of language any the less remarkable, just the reverse. In our first ten years of life we learn techniques of controlling our memory, in just the same way as we learn to control movements of our eyes, arms, fingers, legs, mouth and tongue. An analogy is often drawn between our brains and computers. The analogy is quite a good one, so long as we recognise that the brain is hardware, and the programming we have to do ourselves.

Lack of consensus about brain specialisation

When we look at expert views of the brain, we have to choose between two almost completely opposite views of the development of the brain – on the one hand, that it has become highly specialised, acquiring modules for language, for meaning, thinking, scientific hypotheses and so on; on the other hand, that it has become less and less specialised, consequently increasing its ability to adapt flexibly to a variety of situations and requirements.

It is of course possible that both views have some truth, but the history of human beings suggests that the latter sums up human abilities better. We have shown ourselves able to adapt to life on the savannah, in Ice Age Europe, in the rain forests, the polar tundra, showing evidence of greater flexibility and adaptability than any other species.

We should expect the human brain to show a related flexibility. According to Wallace, the history of the brain is the conversion of an inflexible, strongly hereditary, probably subcortical system, into a productive, labile system under considerable cortical control – that is, a process of reduced specificity and increased plasticity (Wallace 1993, p. 44; Gellner 1989, p. 516).

Nauta and Feirtag comment on the notion of physically identifiable brain modules:

> One is of course tempted to assign a function to each district, as if the entire brain were something like a radio. Yet the essence of the central nervous system – the brain and the spinal cord – is a channeling of incoming sensory information to a multiplicity of structures and a convergence of information on the neurones that animate the effector tissues of the body: the muscles and the glands. The overall system therefore assumes properties beyond those to be discovered in a mere set of modules. (Nauta and Feirtag 1979, p. 78)

The brain as a neural network

Views of brain flexibility underlie models of the brain as a system of neural networks, as proposed for example by Lieberman (1991). Potential links between parts of the brain are present from birth, but the vital factor determining brain structure is experience. The more a pathway connecting two parts of the brain is used, the stronger it becomes (Lieberman 1991, p. 90). A neural network is a huge system of interconnecting networks of millions of nerve cells, drawing on memories, skills and capacities from all over the brain. As Braitenberg and Schüz describe it:

> The statistical picture of the brain's operations is that of a huge network of elements of one kind, the pyramidal cells, connected to each other by a special kind of synapse, residing on dendritic spines. These synapses are very numerous, very weak, excitatory and probably plastic. These four properties make it quite likely that the cortex is a structure which stores memory in an associative way. (1992, p. 89)

The case for a specific, dedicated organ of language is becoming harder and harder to sustain on the basis of physical evidence.

Evidence from aphasia

It is important to note that evidence for the part played by Broca's area in speech is not activity in Broca's area during human speech, but evidence that damage to the area can lead to impairment of speech, a rather different claim. Children who suffer damage to Broca's area and other parts of the brain described above can, in many cases, go on to develop normal language skills. Other parts of the brain that were not considered to be specialist language areas, can in need be made to do the work of the damaged areas. The effect is quite dramatic in hydrocephalics whose brains are a fraction of the normal size, yet can still grow up to become speaking humans.[24]

Remarkably, a recent study of electrical activity in speaking subjects using brain-scanning techniques has shown that different areas of the brain were active in men's and women's brains as they spoke, surely a lethal blow to the notion of dedicated speech areas in the brain (Shaywitz *et al.* 1995).

Language related to manual skills?

If there is any in-built specialisation in the brain, it may in any case not be solely dedicated to language, but may be the result of a link between the fine muscular movements required for manual skills and those required for the production of speech sounds in the mouth and the throat (as Lieberman 1991 argues). Greenfield (1991, p. 537) argues that a common neural substrate (roughly Broca's area) is shared by speech and by the capacity to combine objects manually, including tool use. Among adults, she argues that Broca's area has differentiated into two areas, controlling roughly speech and manual activity.[25]

Growth of the neocortex, and control of behaviour

As Aiello and Dunbar show, there is a strong correlation between the relative size of the neocortex of a species (its neocortex ratio) and the size of its social group (Dunbar 1992; Aiello and Dunbar 1993; Aiello forthcoming). Here we have a strong suggestion that social life is a determinant of the growth of that part of the brain that is associated with control of behaviour. To live in a large group, you have to acquire self-control, which means learning to suppress instinctive behaviour at certain times. Dunbar and Aiello actually focus on 'vocal grooming' behaviour – that is, meaningless noises exchanged between individuals. However, the control of other types of behaviour (aggressive, disruptive behaviour; sulking; quarrelling over food; sexual jealousy) would be just as important if a co-operative life within the herd was to be maintained.

An instinct requires only a small part of the brain, whereas the ability to respond flexibly to different situations requires a lot more neural connections. The neocortex seems to be associated at least in part with self-control. For example, Aiello and Dean suggest that the growth of frontal lobes in the human prefrontal cortex implies an increasing ability to control emotions (Aiello and Dean 1990, p. 181).

In other words, living in a herd, having become an indispensable form of society for survival in a hostile environment, may then produce changes in behaviour as individuals adapt to social life. Hence the tendency of the human neocortex to expand, suggesting increasing control on the part of early humans over instinctive behaviour as social groupings grew larger (Aiello forthcoming).

HOW CHILDREN LEARN TO SPEAK

It is often claimed that evidence for the innate capacity for language comes from the so-called critical period for language-learning in children, from around 18 months to roughly 10 years (Lenneberg 1967; Hurford

1991), and the fact that children all seem to follow roughly the same stages of development. However the fact that children do not start to speak until approaching their second birthday does not mean that the brain is inactive until then. Children start learning from birth, and have to learn a wide range of skills before adults recognise their vocalisations as words. The pattern observed in children is fully compatible with the view that learning starts at birth and gradually slows down over time. Though it continues to grow after birth, the structure of the brain is unchanged, and neither switches on at 18 months nor switches off at 10 years. This section describes briefly how the child's developing brain activity is integrated with social development.

The brain at birth is extremely flexible and impressionable. In the prenatal period, neural material and connections are vastly overproduced, such that up to 80 per cent will die in the post-natal period. Very early learning, then, may have a marked and permanent effect not only directly in terms of the associations which are established, but indirectly in terms of the potential for later associations created or ruled out by selective cell-death (Cowan 1979, pp. 116–17). Cowan comments: 'Although many regions may be hard wired others (such as the cerebral cortex) are open to a variety of influences, both intrinsic and environmental' (Cowan 1979, p. 117).

The newborn infant is helpless, as the various separate systems of the body are not yet co-ordinated. Much of the primary co-ordination of the body's systems, and sensitivity to light, sound and touch, is learnt within the first few days or weeks, and connections are established in the brain that will last for life. Apart from an instinctive ability to suck, the infant has to learn almost every other action from the start.

Babies learn about the world not by passively contemplating or perceiving it, but by interacting with it. This interaction is our original condition. The baby's first perception of the world is an awareness of its own activity (kicking her legs and waving her arms) . Later, activity leads her to awareness of objects (for example, by touching, or grasping objects).

It may be as much as three months before the various brain-and-body activity and neural systems start to be associated in such a way that the child can be said to be in control of her own body movements. Attention starts to come under the child's control. The infant is born with some innate *schemata* – sets of sensory-motor associations, governing vision, smell, touch, movements, and so on (Piaget 1955) – and these come to be integrated with an ever-growing network of associations, forming what Vygotsky calls *complexes* (1962, pp. 61–5) – cognitive organisations of movement and sensation, linked along a neural pathway.

At a certain age primitive words or signs start to appear as part of children's behaviour. The signs may be gestures – pointing, reaching out to be lifted up, turning the head – or may be vocalisations. These signs come to be linked with complexes of sense and movement. At first, the association of a sign with a complex may be quite accidental, a reflection of individual experience. For example an infant might use the sound [ffff] for the sound of blowing out a candle, and later extend the sound to refer to lights of all sorts (Stern 1924, p. 147).

Because her social link with adults is of such vital importance to the child's survival, the word quickly becomes the most important aspect of the complex. Metaphorically, the word is an extension of the neural pathway, linking the complex to the social world around it. And just as a neural pathway is strengthened each time it is stimulated, so the word is strengthened each time it is used to connect the child's cognitive system to that of the humans around. The word simultaneously emerges as the basis of the child's communication, the material of her social life and the organising principle of her thinking. Words also start to be used as a way of regulating behaviour, as in the case of a child who says 'Up' as she climbs up on to a chair, or as a request to an adult to help her up. The development of these complexes depends totally on the response of adults to the child's signs – interpreting them and reinforcing them by action.

Summing up, this description of the development of children's first words (based on Uemlianin 1994) is compatible with a general model of child learning in a social environment, and needs no innate linguistic capacity to explain it.

The Whole Body!

However good a theory of brain functioning we have, language cannot be considered as solely the product of the brain. It is a product of the individual's whole body – the hands, legs, muscles, skin, eyes and ears. Further, language is social behaviour, the product of the individual's part in a collective social unit interacting with the world. Wind has listed over a hundred anatomical and social features of hominid evolution relevant to language, commenting:

> Speech emergence . . . has certainly not been an isolated process or the consequence of a few triggering adaptations. Rather, virtually the whole process of hominisation has to be taken into account. Glosso-genesis, then appears to have been closely interwoven with most, if not all, of the mechanisms that have shaped [human beings]. (Wind 1983, p. 35)

Prisoners in cells

The emphasis on the individual brain and on individual biology to the exclusion of the social bases of human life, leads to a false notion of language. It can leads to what Clark (1978) calls the 'prisoners in cells' notion, where the ideas in our heads are imprisoned, and language is the product of our attempts to let the ideas out. The falsity of this notion becomes clear when the question is asked: where did these ideas come from in the first place? Ideas do not simply grow fully formed in our heads. They arise from our interaction with our environment and with each other. In this world, we exist not by thinking our way through life, but by activity, of which thinking is a part. As Clark puts it, 'communication is that which is involved in the co-ordination of the separate activities of two or more individuals into a single social activity' (Clark 1978, p. 233). To focus on individual neural mechanisms and brain structure is to reinforce the tendency to look for sudden transformations in human biology to explain language origin. Only by looking outside the brain can we find the true alternative.

DIFFICULTIES FACING THE STUDY OF LANGUAGE ORIGINS

This is not an easy subject to study. There is no direct archaeological evidence for the origin of language; in fact all the evidence is indirect. Disagreements abound among the specialists on the significance of cave paintings, of stone tools, of pieces of bone with little notches (Marshack 1989). Unlike Sanskrit and other old languages studied by the early linguists, the earliest languages were not written. We cannot be sure whether they were spoken or gestured. We cannot even be sure which period of time we should be considering. Suggestions that some form of language began with the first apes to start walking upright would mean considering a period of 5 million years or more. Alternative suggestions that language is associated with anatomically modern humans, and that earlier forms of human being were not very effective users of language make the time span little more than 200,000 years – but still quite enough time for plenty of errors to creep in.

Strangely, however, these difficulties may in the long term prove an advantage to the view put forward here. In considering the relevance of evidence for the development and growth of language, we are forced to face up to the question of how language relates to practical life – a question that linguists have so far been remarkably successful at ignoring!

CONCLUSION: A SYNTHESIS REQUIRED

We have seen two different approaches to language studies above: (1) mentalism, the theory that ideas and structures located in the individual mind result in the creation of a language; and (2) Mechanical materialism, the theory that language is the product of our individual genetic structure and of instinctive, even subconscious neural activity, somehow, though mysteriously, connected to meaningful activity.

In 1929 Voloshinov commented on these two traditions, which, while they can apply perfectly well to Chomsky and Pinker, have been around for many years. Language, he says:

cannot possibly be explained in terms of either these superhuman or subhuman, animalian roots. Its real place in existence is in the special, social material of signs created by [humans]. Its specificity consists precisely in its being located between organised individuals, in its being the medium of their communication. (Voloshinov 1973, p. 12)

In other words, to focus on the individual mind, or the individual's genes, is to miss the point about language. Its origins are quite different from the those of the monkey's eye, the peacock's feathers or the tiger's stripes. Language is a social creation, originating not from the individual speaker, but from the interaction between speaker and audience. Therefore when we look for the origins of language, we are simultaneously looking for the origins of the social life of human beings. This is the approach that will be followed in subsequent chapters.

NOTES

1. For example Rousseau, Condillac, Herder and Jenisch. See Hewes 1976.
2. In the sense of the study of language and culture.
3. For a review of nineteenth-century writers such as Schlegel, Rask, Bopp, J. Grimm, Humboldt and Schleicher, see Jespersen 1922.
4. Whitney 1873–4, p. 279; quoted by Jespersen 1922, p. 412. The problem had been addressed in 1866 by the Paris Societé de Linguistique, whose constitution forbade any discussion of the subject.
5. Those following the pioneering work of Grimm, Rask and Bopp in this field – such as Brugmann, Delbrück, Osthoff and Paul (the so-called 'neogrammarians'); see e.g. Jespersen 1922, pp. 93ff.
6. As Brugmann himself warned – see Lehmann 1992, p. 297.
7. Saussure's lecture course in general linguistics was first published in 1916 after his death. See Saussure 1974, p. 14.
8. Comrie (1987, p. 1) considers the question of 'How many languages?' to be virtually unanswerable. There must be at least 5,000 languages with some form of political recognition in the world today.
9. However, this marginal subject still accounts for some 10,000 titles in Hewes' bibliography (1975). Exceptions to the pattern of neglect are Jespersen 1922; Swadesh 1971; Hockett and Ascher 1964; Hockett 1978; Englefield 1977; and throughout the work of Gordon Hewes.
10. B P = before the present.
11. The area of language study that does take socially organised human beings into account is not referred to as linguistics, but as 'sociolinguistics', as if it were a subsidiary topic.
12. A view made explicit in Fodor 1983.
13. Bickerton 1984, 1990; Pinker and Bloom 1990; Pinker 1994. Other linguists working along these lines include Newmeyer 1991, 1992; Hurford 1989, 1991.
14. A pidgin is a form of communication used between speakers who do not have a common first language, usually for simple purposes such as trade, exchange, work. A creole can be said to be a development of a pidgin to the stage where it is learnt by children as their first language, and where it takes on more central social and communicative functions, becoming a 'true' language. The distinction between pidgin and creole is not always easy to make, and there

are many difficult issues involved. Bickerton's work on pidgin is central to many of the controversies. See, for instance, Aitchison 1989; Smerken 1992.

15. But 'there are no conclusive data on any of these issues' (Pinker and Bloom 1990, p. 721).

16. Pinker and Bloom 1990, p. 715. An analysis of utterances that takes into account communication between speaker and listener could divide an utterance into two parts: the topic that is common to both people, and the comment that is the speaker's new material. In most languages both grammar and intonation are used to indicate which material is topic and which is comment.

17. Posed, for example, by Sonia Ragir (1985).

18. However, some have suggested competition for resources between anatomically modern humans and Neanderthals in western Europe in the period 50,000 to 30,000 BP.

19. An example of Wilson's attempt to reduce humans to insects is found in Wilson (1975, p. 554): 'The members of human societies sometimes cooperate closely in insectan fashion, but more frequently they compete for the limited resources allocated to their role sector.' For fuller discussion of the fallacies underlying sociobiology see Rose *et al.* (1990).

20. Buddhist priests take many years to master the use of mantras, for example.

21. Hewes (1976, p. 490) points out that profanity or 'coprolalia' persists even when large areas of the brain are injured.

22. Schleicher (1863) – see Jespersen 1922, p. 74.

23. For example, the Island of Reil (insula reilli) for vocalisation and concept-formation (Irsigler 1989, p. 238); anterior cingulate gyrus (part of the limbic forebrain) for 'isolation calls' of humans, especially in mother–infant commun-ication (MacLean 1988; Newman 1992, p. 315); the arcuate fasciculus which is supposed to link Broca's and Wernicke's area, but which nobody has actually identified (Whitcombe 1994); the corpus callosum (a bundle of fibres connecting the hemispheres) (Tanner and Zihlman 1976a, p. 476); the parieto-occipital-temporal junction (Falk 1980; Falk 1990, p. 763); the hippocampus, a compon-ent of the limbic system – encoding features of our environment in mental representations or cognitive maps (Wallace 1989). Donald (1991) lists 'the cere-bellum; premotor cortex; supplementary motor cortex; thalamus; basal ganglia; superior temporal lobe; hippocampus; angular gyrus; supramarginal gyrus; insular and opercular regions, and inferior frontal cortex'. Yet, says Donald, we cannot identify the critical area of the brain that he calls the 'Linguistic controller', i.e. we cannot say which areas have to be destroyed in order to stop language production (Donald 1991, pp. 261–7). Mehler *et al.* (1984) discuss the difficulties of relating neurophysiological data to psychological processes.

24. hydrocephalus is a condition where the normal brain is displaced by fluid. After treatment the brain does not always return to normal size, yet in many cases patients learn to speak, even though their speech is not quite normal. They may display 'cocktail speech', speech that is apparently grammatical and sociable, yet is superficial and irrelevant in content (Bloom and Lahey 1978, pp. 295–6).

25. Holloway (1976, p. 346) also makes the point that 'there are very great similar-ities between the cognitive operations involved in language production and stone tool-making'. It is also worth mentioning Calvin's (1983) ingenious arguments that stone-throwing increased the complexity of the brain and the co-ordination of movement involved in speech, though these look less convinc-ing in the light of Kortlandt's observation that chimpanzees can throw just as accurately as humans when they need to (Kortlandt 1986, p. 120.

2

Language and Labour

We have seen in Chapter 1, that linguists, in the hopes of capturing the essence of human language, set out to isolate it in various ways. Some have attempted to explain it as a result of mental activity; others in terms of human biology, focusing all the time on the individual speaker/hearer. Their attempts to explain the origin of language have relied on abstract, intellectual factors, such as intelligence, cognition, perception, and so on.

However, there is a long tradition of attempts to explain language as the product of human labour, a tradition that pre-dates Marx and Engels, appears in Vygotsky and Voloshinov, has influenced the functional grammar of Halliday, and partially underlies the recent revival of interest in the topic of language origins in anthropological circles,[1] in the thinking of, for example, Kendon. This chapter presents the view that humans created language and consciousness, just as they created pots and pans, and bows and arrows, in the course of co-operative activity. In so doing, they created the means to transform the world around them, and to transform themselves.

WHAT IS MEANT BY LABOUR?

Labour refers not simply to techniques of obtaining food (foraging, agriculture, industry, etc.), but also the social relations, the organisation of society, that make possible production and reproduction. Put simply, labour is the social production of the means of life, and the highest development of social behaviour. The study of labour necessarily involves the study of history too. The Kalahari forager, the Arctic herder of reindeer, the Greek slave, the medieval serf, the late-twentieth-century computer programmer, all these forms of labour live in specific social circumstances. The details of their lives are the result of a number of factors – the development of technology; the way that society is organised; the way that families come together and raise children; and which people have political power at the time. Labour is both a result and a cause of these factors, a product of past history and a contributor to the forces that will shape future history.

Among apes are some of the preconditions of human existence: a gregarious species, with a well-developed ability to solve problems on an individual basis. Engels shows how the emergence of human society from apes ensued from factors that can be regarded as further preconditions for co-operative labour. First, the development of upright gait freed the human hand, making possible the development of manual skills, the basis of labour and technology. The consequent freeing of the mouth made possible at a later stage the development of speech. The gregarious nature of the ape, combined with a life that gradually extended the range of food eaten and activities undertaken to obtain food, led to a gradual increase in cases of mutual support, co-operation and joint activity. Habits of sharing food led to co-operation in obtaining food, and to situations where more and more challenging problems could be tackled. Finally '[humans] in the making arrived at the point where they had something to say to each other' (Engels 1954, p. 232).

Relevance to language origins?

We have of course no record of the thinking or the language, spoken or gestured, of the first humans.[2] All that we can find are bones and artefacts, records of their activity. Those who regard language as primarily a way of expressing thoughts, or of communicating ideas, can only make guesses about the significance of these records. However, an approach that sees language as emerging from activity has a better chance of interpreting them. If labour and language were intimately associated from the very start of humanity, then the records of the activity of human beings are also, even if indirectly, records of their developing social life, and indirectly of their communication and their language.

The Origins of communication in labour

Conditions leading apes to communicate can be created in ingenious experiments, but simply are not there in the life of apes in the wild, who therefore communicate very little. What is lacking to them is shared attention on external objects. The factor that created such joint attention, we argue, is what humans have in abundance, relative to apes – problems. If the individual's object of attention (say, food) is part of a problem that requires co-operative action in its solution, then the various parties must communicate with each other – or the problem will remain unsolved. Co-operative action does not spring out of nowhere – a point that observation of chimpanzees proves abundantly.

The sign, a solution to a problem

We adopt a working definition of language as *the exchange of symbolic meanings in the context of activity* (see Halliday 1978). Meanings arise from interaction between human beings in their collective attempts to solve problems, in a context made up of the physical environment, the technical problem, relations between speakers and other contributory factors, all combining to produce an utterance shaped to carry out a specific function. We note that this description of contextual factors, taken together, also constitutes a definition of labour.

If we try to reconstruct the circumstances surrounding the earliest exchanges of meanings, between our ancestors, they may have had these elements:

1. A problem confronts a number of individuals.
2. The solution of the problem requires both (a) joint attention on some phenomenon – object, animal or person; and (b) co-operative activity in relation to this phenomenon (moving it, catching it, hitting it, and so on).
3. Some material form – it may be an action, a sound, an accidental association with an object – is accepted as a way of referring to the object of attention, and comes to be associated with the action required to solve the problem in (1). Thus a sign[3] is created by the individuals concerned, that has a meaning related to their joint experience in solving this problem.
4. The sign and its meaning enter the memory of individuals. It is now possible for any one of them to use the sign as a way of referring to or representing some aspect of the problem and the action that solved it. The sign is a collective, social achievement.

This may seem like a lot of words to express a situation that is to us an everyday experience – getting help from another person – but in terms of the route from ape to human it has a great significance.

This emphasis on the *problem* as the precondition for communication explains how the creation of signs is possible. The learning of signs described above is not the slow tortuous learning of a person undergoing instruction – the second-language learner, for example. Nor is it the mechanical stimulus–response reinforced model of learning favoured in behaviourist psychology. It is the instant learning that we notice ourselves when a problem has long been worrying us; then suddenly the solution becomes clear, in a flash, as it were (the *aha!* phenomenon). The next time this problem arises, the solution comes back to us almost instantly, without our having to go through any trial-and-error learning. This kind of learning is noticed by Köhler in his studies of apes (see Chapter Three), and is also seen among infants learning their first words. The problem sets up the solution. And the solution to the problem is an elementary concept, with the property that it can be labelled with a sign.

The creation of this elementary meaning-sign has a number of consequences:

as an organiser of action for the collective group, who may use the sign socially, to repeat the action in future;

as a social memory of the experience for the group, who may use it to refer back to the accomplished action;

as an internal record for each of the individuals involved in the original action, as an individual memory;

for each individual, as a way of recalling the action, and therefore as a guide to action when repeating it on an individual basis.

These functions – social memory, social organising function, individual memory and individual organising function – are all aspects of what we term 'consciousness'. Even this list still does not exhaust the functions of the sign, or all the aspects of consciousness. We have only considered the social aspects of consciousness, not touching for the moment the question of the conceptual, or meaning, content of the sign. What should be clear from this example is that labour is inextricably connected with communication, and therefore with consciousness and with thinking.

Labour, language and consciousness

Consider in a little more detail the connection between labour and thinking. Not all forms of thinking require language, as we see in chimpanzees' ability to solve a variety of physical and social problems (see Chapter Three). Some types of human thinking are independent of language – for example, we can mentally rehearse physical movements before undertaking them, or conjure up the taste of food, without words. Conversely, language may exist separate from consciousness, as in young children and certain pathological conditions.[4]

What distinguishes humans from apes is not in the first instance cleverness, ingenuity in problem-solving, or intelligence,[5] but the ability to think in signs, or better, in meanings. Consciousness as we have described it, though it has a biological foundation in individual cognitive processes, is a social achievement: the result of creating and exchanging meanings in the course of activity. Its content, its meanings, are available to us as individuals, and as we learn to speak we enter the world of social consciousness, a world created by others long before us, to which our own consciousness can now contribute. As Voloshinov puts it: 'Individual consciousness is not the architect of the ideological superstructure, but only a tenant lodging in the social edifice of ideological signs' (Voloshinov 1973, p. 13)

Consciousness is the creation of a community. It is the sum of its actions, each action giving rise to an associated meaning, that exists in this collective consciousness of all its speakers. This means that each speaker has access, through the system of signs and their meanings, to all the experience, knowledge and wisdom of the other speakers of the language.

The sequence described here starts in collective activity, and ends in forms of thinking and consciousness.[6] Equally important, however, is to appreciate that signs, the product of labour, are also part of the labour process. From the earliest stages, language has organised socially-based work, serving as a form of interaction between the members of the group, a means to communicate practical ideas and to put them into effect.

Once a system of signs, a simple language, becomes established among a group of individuals, then it becomes possible to manipulate the signs, both in public, social utterances and in internal thinking, to start to create a system of relations between phenomena – structures of syntax at first and, at a much later stage, structures of logic.

Over time, the system of signs that originated in activity develops to the point where it starts to generate its own internal laws and regularities. Language shakes itself free from activity, but in so doing, takes on the appearance of a phenomenon that is autonomous, and more powerful than the humans who created it.

Language and Technology

Biological evolution often involves a species in a whole complex of adaptations. In the early stages of human evolution we witness advances in both anatomy and behaviour. Prehistoric humans not only developed physically from ape to human, but also developed technically and socially. In more recent prehistory, anatomical development becomes of less and less significance, and advance is primarily technical and social.

Leroi-Gourhan describes it as follows. First, the organism adapts physically to its environment. After a certain stage of development, adaptation is in external forms – behaviour and social organisation. The final step is in the creation of external objects – tools, language, social institutions:

> The whole of our evolution has been oriented toward placing outside ourselves what in the rest of the animal world is achieved inside by species adaptation. The most striking fact is certainly the 'freeing' of tools, but the fundamental fact is really the freeing of the word and our unique ability to transfer our memory to a social organisation outside ourselves. (Leroi-Gourhan 1993, p. 235)

Significance of tools

The clearest and most durable evidence for the beginning of human labour is the record of stone tools. We have to be careful how we interpret this record, however. Looking at the individual shaped piece of stone, it is easy to focus on the individual tool-maker and his or her tool. But a tool is a collective, not an individual product. Even at the lowest level of social co-operation, among chimpanzees, mothers teach their children to make and use tools. Without this minimal level of social life tool use dies out.[7] Tools and technology are often taken as the yardstick of hominid development, but it was social organisation that made possible the development of tools beyond the simple techniques of apes.

In fact, other types of technology may have played a more central part in early human development. Contrary to earlier views of our ancestors as hunters from the beginning, it is now believed that the early tools of *Homo* were not weapons, and probably not even for hunting, but for food-gathering (Tanner 1981; Zihlman 1978). Tanner (1981, p. 268) and Lee (1979, p.493) both emphasise the importance of carrying technology at an early stage. When individuals live together in a herd or troop, moving around and foraging for food together, carrying is relatively unimportant, since food is eaten where it is found. As infants with larger brains are born at earlier stages of maturity, in a condition of greater dependence, the need for food to be gathered and brought back to a fixed location grows more pressing. This need is met by the development of methods of carrying, a new technology that increases the capacity to feed children and nursing mothers, and leads to the establishment of a division of labour within the group. The material of carriers is not durable, and leaves little or no record, but we can deduce that the technology must have existed from evidence of the practice of carrying food back to an agreed assembly point (see Lee 1979: Appendix; Tanner and Zihlman 1976b; Zihlman 1978). We cannot argue that tools and technical advances in themselves lead directly to language,[8] but that the collective activity associated with technical developments is the necessary precondition for communication.

Division of Labour

Kendon (1991) argues:

> until two or more individuals need to share a common goal, communication about concepts is not needed. For this to arise, a change in social organization is required in which there is both a consistent differentiation and a complementarity between the activities of different individuals within the group – in other words division of labour.[9]

'Division of labour', at its simplest, means the ability of an individual to share in collective tasks, at first by performing the same action as others, but eventually performing an action complementary to that of others, as in lifting one end of a log while someone lifts the other end. In other words, (a) to perceive the actions of another individual, possibly imitating them; and (b) to understand the viewpoint, and anticipate the needs of that individual.

Ilyenkov makes the point: 'Where there is no division of labour, not in elementary form even, there is no society – there is only a herd bound by biological rather than social ties' (Ilyenkov 1982, p. 90). This emphasis on the division of labour makes possible a deeper understanding of the necessary preconditions for communication. The implication is that while life as an undifferentiated member of a herd may encourage closeness between its members, it does not permit the development of individual activity, inclinations, wishes, initiatives, thinking. We see that these features that are often supposed to form an innate part of the human character, rely on labour for their development, indeed for their social creation.

Ilyenkov suggests that the division of labour opens the way for individuals to become unique creative personalities because every other individual interacting with them is also unique and creative, rather than a being performing stereotyped, standardised actions, driven by instinct (Ilyenkov 1982, p. 90).

What evidence would indicate the timing of the development of a division of labour? Surely it would be evidence in the archaeological record of co-operative behaviour, of males and females caring jointly for children, the passing on of skills, the care of the sick, the sharing of meat. Anatomical features such as sexual dimorphism (the difference between males and females) are also important clues to the development of social co-operation and the division of labour (see Chapter 5). Language depends absolutely on forms of social behaviour that favour co-operation and minimise conflict.

FORMS OF THE IDEAL

If the first forms of communicative behaviour were tied closely to activity, how is it that communication and consciousness are now free of this connection? Burke Leacock expresses the problem this way:

> The very impressiveness of mankind's mental achievements, however, has obscured the fundamental significance of labour. Furthermore, the separation of planning for labour from the labour itself, a development of complex society, contributed to the rise of an idealistic world outlook, one that explains people's actions as 'arising out of their thoughts instead of their needs'. (quoted by Woolfson 1982; p. 77)

The key to understanding this separation lies in the concept of ideality, introduced first by Hegel and developed by Marx and more recently by Ilyenkov, in their analysis of money.

The ideality of money

The concept of ideality is important in a consideration of the relations between forms of social life, thinking and language. This rather difficult concept underlies phenomena in our lives that are apparently abstractions, but still take on very concrete form and have very concrete effects. Phenomena such as laws, social conventions, values, kinship relations, even names, are forms of ideality or 'ideal forms', the most characteristic of which is money.

Money, as Marx explains (Marx 1887, pp. 47ff), originates in the exchange of commodities (barter). What starts out at the stage of barter as
a simple, negotiated transaction develops later into money, an external,
concrete phenomenon. But the essence of money is not its physical form
– gold, paper or plastic – but the fact that its value is socially agreed.
Money as an ideal form is social in origin; ideal in form, material in
effect.

In barter, an individual exchanges, for example, a coat for a roll of
cloth. At this stage, the exchange is apparently a purely private transaction
between two individuals, and the goods exchanged are for use, not for
further exchange. There is, however, an underlying value to the commodities – put simply, the value depends on the amount of labour that went
into producing them. Over time, in the course of thousands of similar acts
of exchange, the value of these commodities comes to be socially fixed, in
an expression of the cost of the labour involved in producing them. Eventually, one commodity comes to be accepted as a general unit of value.
Marx's example is a roll of cloth, though in different societies this unit of
exchange may take different forms – cowry shells in Africa; bundles of
yams in the Trobriand islands (Malinowski 1966, vol. 2, p. 91).

Finally, one commodity emerges above all others as the established
unit of exchange – gold. This may not be because of any intrinsic quality
of gold. In fact, gold was the ideal unit of value precisely because it had
few other uses – it was a relatively worthless metal, with few practical
applications, but was scarce enough for the purpose, and was long-lasting.
As Marx says of money: 'a social relation, a definite relation between
individuals, here appears as a metal . . . as a purely external thing' (1857,
p. 239). Once gold was established as a currency, it then took on a life of
its own, and made possible further developments in the economic system.

What was in origin the creation of human beings, came in a rather
mysterious-seeming process to dominate humans' lives, and has now
become the organising principle of our system of social organisation, built
upon the accumulation of wealth. The very real economic laws of this
system now have a life of their own, beyond the control of any individual
or group of individuals. The products of human labour, as Marx puts it,
are thus alienated from human beings.

Comments on ideality

Marx showed that gold became money because of social processes. In its
use as money, its value derives specifically from human labour. More
generally than that, however, its value is the expression of a relationship
between people – at its simplest between those who make and those who
use products. Therefore money can be said to be concrete (pieces of
metal) and abstract (the expression of a relationship) at the same time.
Perhaps the term 'abstract' is a little confusing here, and a term like

'relational' may be more revealing, as in Marx's comment: 'Man carries his social power, as well as his bond with society, in his pocket' (Marx 1857, p. 240).

For a number of reasons (because money was never invented, but gradually evolved; because money takes a very real, concrete form; because money can now stand alone as a symbol of wealth; and a great many other complicating factors), the origins of money and the original connection between labour and money are now obscured.

Ideal forms exist in social consciousness. Though this consciousness appears to us as individuals to be located in our own minds, we find soon enough that the products of consciousness – ideal forms – are beyond our power to alter. They appear more powerful than the individuals on whose consciousness and individual brains they depend for their continued existence.

Language as an 'ideal form'

Ilyenkov (1982, p. 90–1) sees the ideality of money as a characteristic case of ideality in general. All ideal forms such as money, gods, law, duty, language, originate in the exchange of meanings between individuals. These ideal forms are not simply word meanings, but have real values and, in fact you could say, real power. Where do these values and this power come from? Again, from the activities of human beings in society. Our language is an entirely social product. Words, like the value of the dollar, have no material existence outside social consciousness and social activity. Their form is ideal, but their effects are entirely concrete as organisers of human life.

Saussure saw that language was a totally social phenomenon. He also perceived its independence from control by its speakers. But the historical process by which this state of affairs came about can only be explained by reference to Marx's concept of ideality.

Just as kinship, myths, customs, taste in food, all appear to us from childhood as facts of life, so too do words, their meanings, their pronunciation, their ways of combining in sentences. It is noticeable how children pass through stages in their social development where they take different attitudes to language. At one stage they are extremely literal, insisting on the truth of words. A word at this stage is experienced as an integral part of the phenomenon it describes. Later, children perceive that there is a difference between object and word, and start to enjoy puns, riddles, focusing on the form of language for its own sake.

Ideality accounts for the power of language in our lives, and underlies practices such as taboo, magic and so on. This process Marx refers to as fetishism or ideological inversion (Jones 1991, p. 22). Before money, language .was probably more powerful than we now appreciate, playing the role of currency of exchange, and the regulator of social life. To the member of a foraging group, a verbal promise to help in case of bad times, consolidated by a social form of alliance, is as good as, if not better than, money in the bank.

CONCEPTS, KNOWLEDGE, LANGUAGE

Implied in the advance of technique is the historical accumulation of knowledge. Without language, knowledge cannot be passed on, cannot develop beyond a very crude stage. In this sense, language is an aspect of technology.

But what is the precise relationship between language and accumulating human knowledge? Knowledge is often said to be handled in the form of concepts. But this formulation is not as straightforward as it seems. Bickerton (1990) lists a number of 'concepts': *ghost*; *soul*; *angel*; *neutrino*; *phlogiston*; *gravity*; *atom*. His argument is that for every one of us today 'there are some you do and some you don't believe in'. All these terms originated as educated guesses as to what the world might contain; they are, or were theories of the world (Bickerton 1990, p. 37).

As we can see, some of these concepts are sustainable by scientific proof; others are figments of the imagination. But if it is up to the individual to decide which to believe in, we can never be sure that we see the world as it really is. Bickerton implies that our innately determined internal representations get in the way.

Nevertheless, despite the unevenness of human history, we can see over time, a tendency for humans beings, with human cultures and languages, to achieve greater control over the world around them. There must be some factor in the human condition that can help us to distinguish genuine information from misleading representations of the world. Once again, this factor turns out to be human activity.

Notions and Concepts

What might be useful here is the distinction made by Ilyenkov (1982) who divides meanings into *notions*, the simple material of social consciousness, and *concepts*, a higher order of knowledge.[10] When we express our own or others' experience of the world in speech, we transform individual experience or observation into notions. A notion is a superficial correspondence to the observed general features of a phenomenon.[11] In their simplest form, notions may be no more than names or labels, but they may also be more general inclusive categories, classified on some immediate impressionistic basis, as when we classify people by the colour of their skin, or divide living creatures into *animals*, *pets*, and so on. Though these are general categories, they are not yet concepts; merely their prerequisites.

The process from notion to concept represents an advance from an immediate impressionistic experience of the world, simple observation, to a higher stage of logical assimilation and understanding of the world (Ilyenkov 1982, p. 44). Concepts represent an analysis of experience that goes beneath the surface, and matches the highest possible understanding of world experience at a historical point in time. We can express it most clearly in the formulation: every concept is the solution to a problem. The highest level of analysis that a concept can attain is that of the scientific concept, which is universally true,[12] but there are many other practical concepts with which we operate in daily life. For Ilyenkov a concept:

> is not therefore a monopoly of scientific thought. Every [human] has a concept, rather than a general notion expressed in a term, about such things as table or chair, knife or matches. Everybody understands quite well both the role of these things in our lives and the specific features owing to which they play a given role rather than some other one, in the system of conditions of social life in which they were made, in which they emerged. (Ilyenkov 1982, p. 98)

Concepts are not simply abstractions, though that often does characterise them, but rather a reduction to essentials. 'Scientific abstractions reflect nature not only more deeply and correctly than living contemplation or notion but also more fully (thus more concretely).'[13] It is in practice that we test out notions, those educated guesses that Bickerton talks about, and historically arrive at concepts, which enable us to transform the world. In the last few hundred years this process has become institutionalised in what we know as science.

Of course, experience teaches a lot, and can be handed on, but simple experience cannot deepen our knowledge to the same extent as active attempts to change or to transform the world – whether solving our own individual problems, or participating in large-scale social enterprises. Human existence depends on this ability to see beyond appearances, to see in a dry stick the potential for fire or the material for constructing a shelter; to see in shrivelled seeds a source of a future harvest; to see in a lump of mud the potential for a pot.

The concept of Seed

We can illustrate the difference between notion and concept in relation to the meaning of *seed*, as it might be understood by people at different social-historical stages.

In a foraging society seeds will be perceived essentially as food. People may have words which we recognise as standing for *seed* – the seed you eat (nuts, berries); the seed you crush (grain); the seed you cook (beans); the seed you discard (pips, stones). However until the historical advent of agriculture, the labels for various types of seed are no more than notions. Foraging people are confined to a mere contemplation of seeds in their various forms (and after contemplating, eating). They may have a practical classification of seeds on the basis of which are edible, poisonous, and so on. The concept of *seed* as a source of further food, is unlikely to be grasped, until the practice of sowing seeds arises.

A subsequent socioeconomic practice, horticulture, depends on the understanding that certain grains, or tubers, can be sown, to produce future crops – but what horticulturists recognise as *seed* is still limited to those seeds that are of value to farming. Other seeds – of wild flowers, nuts, pips – may not be recognised as such. Still, some general concept of *seed*, as part of a plant, and part of a cycle of life, has been formed. Doubtless, too, as today, different names would be given to seeds used in different ways – as we still talk about nuts, pips, stones.

With the scientific study of botany comes a fuller, richer concept of *seed* – as an essential part of the cycle of life of all plants, and hence of all living things. The concept derives not only from theoretical study, but also from practical experimentation, the breeding of new strains, and so on, linked to agricultural practice, organised in a new, capitalist way.

The scientific concept of *seed* is today fully developed. The reality to which the concept relates is accessible to all, though we may apprehend it in different ways in different situations. Children can understand *seed* in different ways – as a detail of a plant, or a piece of fruit – pips, nuts, grains, beans (still as a notion), or as an element of the cycle of life and death, a deeper, more concrete understanding. In our daily lives, the concept is not always used in the most scientific way. We use it as a metaphor (ideas 'germinate', people are described as having 'gone to seed'). In certain activities we apply only part of the knowledge that lies behind the concept. In cooking fruit and vegetables, the seed is something to be cooked or thrown away – the element of life-giving is not relevant. In gardening, we are more aware of the cycle of life. We extend the term to, for example, 'seed potatoes'.

Historical development of concepts

Thus, the development of a concept is not a steady progression from simple label or name to scientific concept. Nor is it simply a progression from concrete to abstract. Practical considerations determine the nature of a concept at every stage. In the past there were certainly periods when, from today's point of view, false concepts were held. For example, the ancient Egyptian concept of the universe was based on the view that the stars and planets went round the earth. This false concept, however, did not prevent Egyptian astrologers from making quite accurate predictions of the positions of the stars. The Eyptian's concepts were the best available at the time, and the ones that worked the best in solving problems of astrology. One of the features of language in its living, social context is a constant dynamic struggle over the use and development of terms. Our language today is full of terms which are the focus of both ideological and practical struggle (Voloshinov 1973, p. 23). *Race* is a good example of an ill-defined notion, which is treated by some scientists as a concept, though it is without scientific basis. The notion entered European languages for a very specific economic reason – the slave trade – and it will only be removed from the languages of the world by the activity of those opposed to its ideological value and its practical social effects.

It has been observed that at certain stages of human development, in the languages of foragers and simple horticulturists, concepts – concrete abstractions – are relatively few. This is not a case of inability to handle concepts in thinking, and not necessarily an indication of a low level of technical skill or of practical understanding. It may rather be the result of absence of any need to use the concept – because planning, analysis, experimentation, are not yet institutionalised as social practices. The relative scarcity of these functions in the daily life of foragers may simply be a reflection of a low level of development of social and political organisation, matching low levels of production.

In day-to-day interaction, human beings move from notion to concept and back again. However the sum of human knowledge is constantly accumulating, and more and more concepts are therefore becoming available to us. So what we see in language evolution is a historical expansion of the cognitive content of human languages – on a world-wide scale, since no language exists or has ever existed in isolation. As Vygotsky points out, this means an increase in the proportion of conceptual knowledge in our language, and as a result an increasingly widely shared skill in abstract reasoning (Kozulin 1990, pp. 17ff). The requirement of our modern languages to handle abstractions, arises both from conceptual content, and from the increasing range of social tasks required of these concepts. The effect of this increasing range of tasks on the form of language is examined in Chapters Eight and Nine.

LANGUAGE AS AUTHORITY

We have seen that language and other forms of social consciousness are the creation of individuals organised in collective activity over countless years of history, gradually advancing in ability to understand and transform the world. At first sight this appears as an unlimited benefit to children learning their parents' language.

However, looked at in another way, the language of our parents and ancestors could be seen as the dead weight of history and other people's experience, getting in the way of our ability to see the world as it really is. Forms of social consciousness (from forms of political organisation, morality, down to grammatical rules, words) structure from the outset our experience (Ilyenkov 1982, p. 41). If as Saussure observes, our language is given to us, and nothing we do can change it, then our view of the world is totally determined for us from the time we start learning language.

Painting the situation in the bleakest possible light, you might describe language as a prison, from which there is no chance of escaping.[14] As in Bickerton's list of 'concepts' on p. 32, the question arises of whether we can ever really know the world we live in, and therefore whether we can ever change it in the direction we want.

Words as controllers: linguistic determinism

Linguistic determinism takes many forms. It dates back to nineteenth-century linguists such as Steinthal; can be found in the ideas of Sapir and Whorf; in the so-called post-structuralists; and also, somewhat surprisingly in the work of Halliday, an otherwise enlightened linguist, and one of the few to make coherent connections between life and language (Halliday 1978). It is worth considering Halliday's views, since he is an influential linguist who makes perceptive and coherent connections between social life and language. Yet he seems to see the general connection between these two phenomena back to front. That is to say, instead of recognising that social life influences the form of language, he suggests (in Halliday 1992) that the form of language creates or 'construes' our social reality, and hence distorts or refracts our view of the world, and hence determines our social life.

The problem lies in 'the cryptotypic patterns of the grammar which typically remain beyond the limits of our conscious attention'. Language is something of a conspiracy; 'there is a syndrome of grammatical features which conspire . . . to construe reality is a certain way; and it is a way that is no longer good for our health as a species' (Halliday 1992, p. 84).

One example of this conspiracy is what Halliday calls 'growthism'. It is because our language values growth – large things in preference to small – that rain forests are being destroyed and whales slaughtered. Because our language classifies air, coal, iron, oil as uncountable (implying 'unbounded'), we are in danger of abusing the raw materials that the planet supplies. Similarly, because agents in human grammar tend to be animate beings (humans or animals), inanimate Nature cannot feature in our thinking. The language makes it hard for us to take seriously the notion of forests, rivers, oceans as active participants in events. The implication is that the wasting of our planet is not the fault of any group of human beings, or of the particular economic system that dominates the world, but the result of grammar, or perhaps the people who allow grammar to influence their view of the world.[15]

The implication is a pessimistic one: our language is out of our control; it is making people behave irrationally; it prevents us from seeing what is going on around us. It follows we cannot do anything to stop it. This bleak picture should be countered by two considerations. First, the alienation of language, unpleasant though it sounds, is not an unmitigated disaster. The divorce of language from activity has undoubtedly given us an ability to draw back and reflect on the world. Alienation is also objectification. Our image of the world had to acquire an apparent life of its own, in order for us to be able to contemplate it, similar to the process that goes on for us individually when we write down ideas; when we tell them to a friend; when we draw a picture, a diagram. Thereby we make objective our inner experience.

Secondly, other systems of human symbolic activity are alienated, in the sense of having become independent of their source – music, drawing, mythology, religion, commodities, even technology. These organs of the human brain created by human hand seem to have a life of their own. However, few people would argue that the development of these phenomena has hampered human progress, except perhaps for those who entertain the fantasy that computers will one day take over the world.

Two-sided nature of word

Concepts are two-sided – on the one hand they dominate our thinking; on the other, they enable us to transform our world, and thus to transform ourselves. Language can be seen as potentially both imprisoning and liberating.[16] We certainly do not spend all our lives repeating the experiences of our parents. New experiences can be expressed in our language, even though we may have to negotiate their meanings with our fellow humans, and may at first fail to express them adequately.

Today the problem of knowledge is acute. We are surrounded with information, the product of past activity, of which we can never possibly comprehend more than a small part. Nevertheless the possibility for each generation of understanding and therefore transforming the world is greater than ever before. This does not mean that the world is better now than our grandparents' – but simply that we have greater opportunities to make it so.

LANGUAGE AS TOOL

Vygotsky had a special interest in the way language functioned in the mental and social life of individuals as a 'psychological tool', to help individuals cope with practical tasks. The essence of a psychological tool is that a system of commands for others has the potential of becoming a command for oneself.

From the very early words of the infant, helping herself climb with an utterance like *Up!*, humans accompany their own activity with language. Vygotsky's studies of inner speech have shown how the external social forms of language that children learn become internalised, in the form of inner speech (Vygotsky 1962), as a vehicle of thinking for the individual, and Luria shows how inner speech develops as a regulator of children's self-activity (Luria and Yudovich 1959).

Memorising

Speech and gesture have a much shorter life than written records, and the ability to memorise is much more important in pre-literate than in literate societies. Luria and Vygotsky describe the 'auxiliary memory tools' of people living in pre-literate societies – tools which make possible memorisation of long messages, or of vital technical information. They regard these memorisation skills as ways by which people started to control their memory before the development of writing rather than allow memory and other forms of mental life such as dreams to dominate them. An example is the use of knotted strings or *kvinus* as a memory aid for the bearers of messages in Peru (Luria and Vygotsky 1992, pp. 56–9).

Knot-tying

The relation between language and technique has been much debated in connection with the record of stone tools. Some archaeologists argue that skill can be divorced from language, that, for example, the ability to make a stone tool can be passed on from generation to generation simply by imitation. Clearly, though, there must come a point where technique can advance no further without language. The problem is to ascertain where is this point. Many technical operations are possible without language, but it is also true that such operations are much easier to remember with language than without. For example, it is much harder to teach someone how to tie a knot by instruction without demonstration, than by demonstration it without instruction. On the other hand, to get someone to remember the skill, instruction is much more effective than demonstration. This is why the most effective technique is to combine practical demonstration with memorable words. I can still recall how to tie a reef knot, thanks to the formula 'left over right, right over left'. I am not so clear about the running bowline, though I can remember the instruction about 'chasing the rabbit round the tree' to this day.

Language as a means to self-control

A particularly clear illustration of how the use of signs can free an individual from instinctive behaviour and enhance self-control, comes from an experiment involving chimpanzees (BBC Horizon 1993, p.22). I give here the complete description of Sarah Boyson's study with two chimpanzees, Sheba and Bob:

> the animals are given a choice between two amounts of candy and the rule is simple: if you pick an amount it goes to your partner and you get whatever's left over. So if you are aware of the rule, then in order to get the most you should pick the smallest amount – then you get the remainder. But they can't do it. Try as they might, presented

with two piles of candy, they always pick the largest. But once the animals were taught the use of numerals [i.e. taking away the candy and putting numbers in their place, but still giving candy at the end] – they are completely released from their automatic, contextually imposed choice of picking the largest, and use of numerals allows them to use this cultural, symbolic rule. When they went back to candy, the same result as before. (BBC Horizon 1993, p. 22)

In this experiment the chimpanzees overcome instinctive behaviour by the use of a symbol – putting a distance between the problem and themselves, thereby making it possible to consider the problem objectively.

It can only have been through use of some form of language that we were first able to overcome our fear of getting burnt, to grab a burning stick and carry home fire (Bickerton 1990, p. 141). Sign-mediated behaviour makes possible self-control, as well as a more objective assessment of the situation and what is required.

Decision-making

Vygotsky included in his list of psychological tools, the use of language for decision-making: such practices as casting lots, dice, bones, interpreting dreams and so on (Kozulin 1990, p. 144). Lee shows that for the Ju/'hoansi divination and prophesy had fairly practical functions as psychological tools helping people to come to decisions. Ju/'hoansi hunters count 'oracle discs', which they use to help decide where to hunt, as part of their hunting equipment along with bow and poisoned arrows (Lee 1979, p. 149).

SOCIAL ACTIVITY AND REGISTER

This section finally addresses the question of linguistic form – usually the central question in works of linguistics. It will be clear from the above sections that theories of formal grammar cannot explain the origins of their central subject matter – grammar. Functionalist approaches, that seek to explain the form of grammar on the basis of the way it is used (e.g. Halliday 1985; Givón 1979; Voloshinov 1973), offer better possibilities: 'The internal organisation of language is not accidental; it embodies the functions that language has evolved to serve in the life of social [humans]' (Halliday 1978, pp. 42–4).

A functionalist approach to language can provide a framework for the development of language form as follows: human society is organised on the basis of work, and historically can be shown to have passed through different work-based socioeconomic stages – roughly speaking, foraging, agriculture, urban civilisation, feudalism, capitalism – in which social life is characterised not simply by the production of the necessities of life, but by different forms of interaction such as kinship, child-raising, political decision-making, social gatherings, and so on. These interactive contexts vary according to the socioeconomic basis, and from the very beginning, language plays a key organising role.

Characteristic forms of interaction, defined by all their circumstances (Halliday calls these circumstances the 'context of situation' (1978, pp. 32–5)), are associated with characteristic forms of communication, conducted according to social and linguistic rules, governing what can and cannot be said, who can speak and how they should speak. Such varieties of communication have been variously labelled *register*, *discourse*, *genre*, *style*, *field*, *frame* or *function*. This work will use the term 'register', though its usage will extend rather more widely than usual. Shaped by its various contextual factors, each register is characterised by its own often unique, linguistic (semantic, syntactic or phonological) forms, which we have to learn as we learn to take part in the social situation.

Register is obvious in the case of technical vocabulary and jargon, such as the specialised vocabularies of law, science, medicine, the weird language of magic mentioned by Malinowski (1966, vol. 2, pp. 223–5), and so on. Some registers may have been part of human interaction from the very earliest stages of social life. What Englefield (1977) calls simple imperative communication (commands and requests for action), may well have been the very earliest type of communication.[17] It is certainly found in every linguistic community, and among the earliest utterances of children. This register has a very specific grammar in English, and probably in most languages (a specific form of the verb in Latin, for example). While 'imperative' is a formal label for a verb form, we find in practice that many imperatives are not verbs at all. Utterances like *Up!*, *Out!*, *Back!*, *Higher!*, *Left-hand down!*, and so on, are outside the classic formal description of the structure of a sentence (neither verb phrase, nor noun phrase). In a familiar context, imperative communication can be fulfilled with ready-to-hand materials – gestures, pointing, pantomime action. This would certainly have been true of the very early stages of language (Englefield 1977, p. 34).

A complete contrast with imperative communication is provided by the register of scientific writing. The context of such writing is a universal and unspecified 'ideal' readership. Since nothing can be taken for granted about such a readership, content must be detailed, with the maximum specification of premises, procedures and conclusions. The form of the writing is highly structured. Sentences are formal, with heavy modification of the initial, subject, noun phrase. There is hardly any need to give examples here, and I hope few will be found in this book.[18]

Another example of register is to be found in Labov's analysis of natural narrative in American speech (1972, p. 380). Within this register he isolates different functional components, the main ones being orientation, complicating action, resolution and evaluation. For each function in the narrative, there are specific and characteristic linguistic forms.

A final example of the way that function determines form is given here, to emphasise the universal applicability of functional approaches to language – inner speech, which was extensively studied by Vygotsky (1962), and which he regarded as a development of egocentric speech observed in young children. Inner speech is not usually thought of as a register, but it is composed of the same material as external speech (signs), and like other registers, has its own characteristic form. If utterances are considered as being composed of two elements, the *argument* (or topic) and *predicate* (the comment you are making on this topic), then the utterances of inner speech are composed predominantly of *predicates* without *arguments*. In inner speech you are talking to yourself. Since the argument of your thoughts is known, your thinking is almost entirely in predicates, comments on the topics that move through your consciousness. This form of language is not usually accessible; it is externalised in children's egocentric speech, and can be glimpsed in the speech of adults in times of unusual stress. In Joyce's *Ulysses* there is an excellent imaginary reconstruction of what inner speech might sound like, in the interior monologue of Leopold Bloom.

Registers and linguistic change

Now, if new forms of social life give rise to new registers, with new forms of language, how do such changes affect the established language? Will a new register, especially an influential one, affecting a large part of the community, influence the established language? We should expect it to do so – and over time, we should expect changes in the established language to spread back into other registers. The relationship of register to language is clearly that of part to whole, with a constant interplay between them.

This view is expressed here as a corrective to the standard view of grammar as a phenomenon that can be codified, written up in completed form in an authoritative Grammar. Such a grammar would be an artificial construct, because as soon as it was written, new forms of grammar would have arisen in connection with new activities. Language cannot be reduced to a logical consistent form. Its essence, if we have to characterise it, is constant dynamic variation, an inevitable consequence of its task to adapt flexibly to ever-changing situations.

But this is still a one-sided view, as we see when we consider children's learning of their community's language. Children clearly do not learn a separate form of language for each situation they find themselves in. As Chomsky (1964) points out, they regularise the forms they learn, quickly construct rules, and within a few years have internalised a complete grammar, this being the most efficient way to cope with the learning task. The result is what appears to be a new integrated grammar for each generation, slightly different from that of the previous generation, and reflecting changes in the activities and social life of their community since their parents learnt their language.

Language at any point in time is in a state of dynamic tension as the result of the interaction of these two tendencies – the innovative tendency that creates new forms of language in association with new social activities and functions, and the counteracting tendency to consolidate and regularise these disparate forms in a single, unified, learnable language code.

CONCLUSION

To summarise the argument in this chapter: language is not to be seen as the primary force in human history. That role should be ascribed to human labour, expressed in the social relations surrounding different historic forms of collective activity. In the course of this activity human beings created their own language. Nevertheless, the central role of language in human activity, as an organiser of labour, and as an embodiment of notions, concepts, ideal forms, has to be acknowledged. Without the creation of language, human labour and social consciousness could not have developed.

The freeing of language from the activity in which it originated and from its links with the immediate context, enabled human beings to reflect on their activity, but also gave rise to the alienation of language; an illusion that language was in some way a power governing human existence. Alienated forms of language enabled human beings further to transform their environment, to overcome instinctive forms of behaviour and to transform their own natures. The expanding range of human activities has given rise to new ideal forms and new human abilities of abstract relational thinking. Social activity – whether it is the activity of groups of people or the internal, mental activity of individuals – requires language to perform varying functions, giving rise to linguistic forms appropriate to these functions. The creative, generative force that enables language to adapt to new communicative and cognitive functions is forever counteracted by conservative, consolidating forces.

NOTES

1. Most notably in journals such as the *Journal of Human Evolution*, and *Current Anthropology*.
2. The term 'human' rather than hominid or hominine will be used as far as possible for early forms of the genus *Homo*, using the term *hominid* to distinguish early species from modern humans where necessary.
3. The term 'sign' is used as a more general form of 'word', a term that normally implies speaking.
4. Some pathological conditions are discussed by Lieberman 1991, pp. 119ff.
5. Contrary to Burling (1993).
6. The relation between activity and consciousness is explored in detail in Leontiev (1978).

7. It would, for example, be particularly difficult to argue for a tool-making instinct, in the light of the fact that the Acheulean biface (a stone tool made by chipping stone from two faces) appears twice in the record – see below, p. 89.
8. Although there are convincing suggestions that brain functions appropriate for tool-making are also used in many linguistic operations – Gibson 1991; Greenfield 1991.
9. Kendon (1991, p. 212). A point also made by Burke Leacock (1981, p. 229) and by Ilyenkov (1982).
10. A lower level of thinking in sets or 'complexes' is also necessary to explain aspects of consciousness among children and certain facets of human languages. See p. 145 below.
11. In Ilyenkov's term, 'verbally expressed contemplation' 1982, p. 43.
12. Alongside scientific concepts are universal logical relations such as cause, result, possibility, necessity – the categories that Kant proposed in *Critique of Pure Reason*.
13. Ilyenkov (1982, p. 47) uses Lenin's expression 'concrete abstractions'.
14. As does Michel Foucault, for example; see Foucault (1970, p. 298).
15. Halliday does not always view the relation between language and reality in this one-sided fashion. Elsewhere in the same paper he recognises the two-way interaction between the two: 'language is at the same time a part of reality, a shaper of reality, and a metaphor for reality' (Halliday 1992, p. 65).
16. Halliday himself acknowledges this point (1992, p. 65).
17. In fact, they are present in a non-linguistic form among chimpanzees.
18. The register of science is discussed in more detail in Chapter Nine.

3

Apes, Humans and Common Ancestors

One of the problems this book addresses is the gulf between animals and humans. There is no doubt that human language is qualitatively different from animal communication. Most examples of animal communication are unmistakably based on instinct rather than learning. However, apes show an ability to learn, far in excess of any other creatures. It is therefore misleading to treat their behaviour as governed by instinct, simply because they are not human. To do this is to miss out on the extraordinary range of abilities they show, the subtleties of their social life, and the lessons that they can teach us about our ancestry. Chimps can do some of the things that humans do, in a scaled-down way. Accurate observation of their life in the wild, coupled with experimental manipulation of their behaviour has uncovered many remarkable abilities.

This chapter, then, is about what the study of monkeys and apes, particularly chimpanzees, can teach us about language. Though other apes – gorillas and orang-utans, for example – have undoubted abilities to communicate,[1] there are special reasons for focusing on chimps.

First, they are our closest living relatives, sharing 95 per cent of our genetic material (Gould 1988, p. vii). The split of chimpanzees and humans from their supposed common ancestor is reckoned to have taken place less than 6 million years BP (Campbell 1988, p. 35; Savage-Rumbaugh 1986; p. 5), and despite the possibility of some changes in behaviour since the split, such as the adoption of knuckle-walking by chimps, we can assume that chimpanzees continue to live a life similar in most respects to our joint ancestors, in or at the edge of tropical forest (Foley and Lee 1989, pp. 903–4). It is generally agreed nowadays that the bonobo chimpanzee *Pan paniscus* is closer in behaviour to humans than the more common *Pan troglodytes*. The bonobo shows a greater range of language-related skills, and is in many ways less specialised than its cousin (Savage-Rumbaugh, Wilkerson and Bakeman 1977; Zihlman *et al*. 1978; Susman 1984).

Secondly, while chimpanzees' material existence and social life are considerably simpler than humans, there are still good grounds for supposing that their way of life is closer to that of our ancestors than present-day gorillas or orang-utans. Gorillas live on the ground, leading a life of 'mild and amiable serenity', with plentiful food supply and no predators to fear except humans (Campbell 1988, p. 156), while orang-utans lead a relatively solitary life in the trees, coming together in monogamous pairs for breeding (Campbell 1988, pp. 155–6). Chimpanzees, on the other hand, lead a complex and active life which is intensely social. They are inventive, they make and use tools, and occasionally take part in organised social activities such as hunting. If it proves possible to establish relationships between their way of life, their way of 'thinking' and their use of symbols,[2] then these relationships may throw light on the connections between human activity and human language.

<h3 style="text-align:center">CHIMPANZEES' LIFE IN THE WILD</h3>

Jane Goodall (1988) has given a detailed picture of the life of common chimpanzees (*Pan troglodytes*) in the Gombe National Park in Kenya. The chimps spend about half their time foraging for food on the ground and in the trees, and the rest of the time in social interaction – grooming, playing, squabbling and making up. Social structure is quite flexible and free, with constantly changing associations of individuals – some all male groups, some solitary males, some females and youngsters, some mixed (1988, p. 21). In the dry season groups are large, and in the rainy season more often small units of two to six (1988, p. 61). Male dominance is not a permanent feature of social life. A chimp who has meat does not usually give it up to a dominant male, but shares it with those who beg for it (1988, p. 171). Males do not fight over females, patiently waiting their turn to have sex (1988, p. 84). Females who are ready for sex – 'in oestrus' is the usual term – may move to another neighbouring group to find male partners (1988, pp. 188–9). Females take the initiative in sexual encounters, and will mate with a number of males. Baby chimpanzees are quite dependent, and young chimpanzees spend most of their early years with their mothers. They reach maturity between their tenth and fourteenth years, by which time they have learnt a wide range of social and practical skills. Although violence and even warfare have been reported between neighbouring groups of chimpanzees, these incidents are often connected with disruptions to their normal life, such as artificial feeding methods or incarceration in zoos. Otherwise, chimpanzee social life appears well balanced and harmonious when food is abundant and life is undisturbed. Occasional aggressive incidents between individuals usually end in reconciliation (1988, p. 117). Naturalistic studies confirm that chimpanzees live in fluid open groups, with no sign of dominance, where sharing not competition is the rule.

Chimpanzees can use tools to obtain food, and mothers will pass on the skills of tool use – such as the use of a twig to obtain termites – to their infants (Goodall 1988). Boesch's studies (1991; 1993) confirm the wide-spread practice of mothers teaching skills to children.

Studies of chimpanzee life in different habitats show that they adapt their behaviour to different environments. Kortlandt (1986) notes regional differences in uses of stone 'hammers' by wild chimpanzees, and differential skill in climbing, relating these differences to the separation of chimpanzee populations in West, Central and East Africa. At sites in Sierra Leone and Ivory Coast, chimps show greater manual dexterity than elsewhere in Africa (Kortlandt 1986, p. 77), and in the Tai forest, which has escaped climatic changes affecting most other parts of Africa, chimps appear to be very specialised in arboreal climbing and arboreal tool use. We could describe these differences as cultural adaptations. The picture is of a flexible intelligent creature developing skills in response to differing environmental challenges.

CHIMP INTELLIGENCE

Köhler's experiments set out to explore the problem-solving abilities of a group of captive chimpanzees (Köhler 1925). He set them a variety of tasks, some of which they solved with ingenuity and resourcefulness, some of which were quite beyond their capacity. Bühler (1934) noticed that the problems the chimpanzees successfully solved seemed to require two related cognitive abilities:

1. Going a roundabout way to achieve a goal.
2. Using a tool to get to goal.

These two problem-solving techniques he related directly to chimpanzees' life in the trees. (1) reflects the chimpanzee's ability to work out a route through the branches of trees to get to food. (2) reflects the ability to use a stick to get at fruit, or to pull a branch bearing fruit down until the fruit is within reach.

By contrast, problems involving the removal of an obstacle were extremely difficult for the chimpanzees, reflecting the fact that in the forest they would not normally have to remove an obstacle, being able to go round or over it. Luria and Vygotsky (1992, p. 21) note in this behaviour what they call 'transfer of structures', whereby cognitive abilities learnt in one situation are applied to problems in another.

Donald (1991) relates chimpanzee behaviour and social organisation to a level of consciousness and culture that he labels 'episodic'. By episodic he means the capacity to apprehend a connected sequence of actions or episodes carried out by another or to repeat a connected sequence carried out by the self in an appropriate situation. Donald suggests that apes' life is a result of their thinking, a factor which, by implication, is part of their biological inheritance. However, Vygotsky, with Köhler, puts it the other way round – that the material life of apes has led to their developing a behaviour and hence a mentality that are action-oriented, related to their way of life, specifically their method of gathering food among the trees.

To the two manifestations of chimpanzee intelligence above we can add a third. This is the social skill to manipulate others. Byrne and Whiten (1988) have devoted an entire book to the study of what they term 'Machiavellian intelligence'. A good example is provided by Savage-Rumbaugh and MacDonald, in an incident where a young chimpanzee, Austin, stops a bigger chimp, Sherman from bullying him:

> by going outside and making unusual noises which sound as though someone is scraping or pounding on the metal. After making such noises Austin runs back indoors and looks outside as though there is something out there to fear. Sherman then becomes fearful, runs over and hugs Austin, and stops the bullying. (Savage-Rumbaugh and MacDonald 1988, p. 228)

This type of behaviour relates to chimps' social life. Chimps are dependent on each other, and as they grow up into the life of their group they need to be able to form friendships and alliances, to learn to cope with competition and occasional hostility. It is important for them to be able to understand and anticipate the reactions of others to their own behaviour; to have, as Premack (1988) puts it, a simple 'theory of mind'.

We see that the habits of thinking that result from material life lead to a specific mental orientation, rather than the converse – mentality producing an orientation on material life.

Egocentrism of chimps

We have seen three features of ape mental ability that can be said to underlie human abilities. We need also to examine a crucial difference between ape and human behaviour – social orientation. Savage-Rumbaugh has described chimpanzees as 'egocentric', using a term that Piaget originally applied to a stage of children's cognitive development (1959, p. 9). Like young children, chimpanzees can work and play side by side with others of their species, but without showing much sign of co-operation with them, working 'in parallel', but not together (Köhler 1925, pp. 174–6; Kendon 1991, p. 218). They may show each other objects, but find it very hard to share them. This is not selfishness, in the way that we apprehend the term. They have no sense of 'self', and therefore no sense of the 'other'. As a result, it is difficult to train a chimp to regard another chimp as an audience, and turn-taking in conversations does not come naturally (Terrace 1986, p. xviii). Like children, chimps behave as if others in the situation know what is in their mind, and therefore do not need to be informed (Savage-Rumbaugh 1986, p. 337). Immediate sensory impressions dominate. chimpanzees' perception – sound, smell, touch, but particularly the visual sense. Observers report a number of cases in which chimpanzees seem to show grief at the visible suffering or death of another chimpanzee, but as soon as the sight of the suffering chimp is gone, the pain is apparently gone too (Goodall 1988; Köhler 1925).

It is only fair to say that in experimental conditions Savage-Rumbaugh's chimps have been taught to take turns in conversation, to share food, and to help each other in tasks where the objective is shared (Savage-Rumbaugh 1986, p. 378–9). We should remember that these social skills do not come naturally to human children, but have to be learnt. It is possible that human children without socialisation may not rise above the level of chimpanzees in the wild (as cases of 'wolf children' apparently demonstrate). The issues of nature and nurture are as much interlinked in chimpanzee life as in humans'.

STUDIES OF CHIMPANZEE COMMUNICATION
Chimps and syntax

Chimpanzees have shown remarkable abilities, in experimental situations, to use symbols to communicate. Studies of chimps in the 1970s, influenced by the emphasis of linguistics at that time on the centrality of syntax, started by asking the question, 'Can chimpanzees produce sentences in the same way as humans?' The answer was generally a fairly clear 'No!'. Terrace's (1979) negative conclusions at the end of a long study with the chimpanzee Nim led to some disillusionment with the possibilities of research into chimpanzees' linguistic abilities, and the study of ape language took a while to recover from this setback. More recent studies have addressed the subject asking the rather more open-ended question: 'What kind of communicative abilities have chimpanzees got?', and producing more interesting and positive results. That chimpanzees communicate is beyond doubt. The interesting question of course is: 'What communicative abilities have apes and humans in common?'

It was discovered some time ago that common chimpanzees, *Pan troglodytes*, could not be taught to speak more than an insignificant number of words (Hayes and Hayes 1951, p. 105). Experimenters who devised other ways of communicating with them, by American Sign Language (Gardner and Gardner 1969), plastic symbols (Premack and Premack 1972) or an electronic keyboard showing lexigrams (Savage-Rumbaugh 1986), found that their subjects were capable of a wide range of linguistic skills. Savage-Rumbaugh sums up the findings:

> They can learn words spontaneously and efficiently, and they can use them referentially for things not present; they can learn words from one another; they can learn to use words to co-ordinate their joint activities and to tell one another things they otherwise would not know; they can learn rules for ordering their words; they make comments; they can . . . announce their intended actions; they are spontan-

eous and often inventive in their signs. In sum, they are communicative and they know what they are about. (1986, p. 379)

Additionally, it is clear that there is a critical period for young chimpanzees during which they can learn symbols fairly rapidly and easily, but beyond which learning is much more difficult (Savage-Rumbaugh *et al.* 1993; p. 42; Gardner and Gardner 1992, p. 258). This resembles the 'critical period for language acquisition' which has been claimed as a species-specific feature of human development, though it starts and finishes somewhat earlier. The early experiments with chimpanzees were not only trying out new techniques, but in some cases started with chimpanzees who were fairly old (Sarah was 5 years old when her programme with David Premack started (Linden 1976, p. 173)). Chimps may be capable of even greater communicative abilities than was first thought, and future studies may reveal other unexpected abilities. Particularly interesting results have been obtained by Sue Savage-Rumbaugh from bonobo or 'pygmy' chimpanzees (*Pan paniscus*). One bonobo, Kanzi, has learnt to use lexigram[3] symbols without instruction, to comprehend spoken English, and even to start making what are admittedly indistinct sounds in response to human speech.

Limits to symbol use

However there is a limit to chimps' cognitive skills. Though they can use names for food to obtain food, they do poorly at tasks which require simple naming of the same foods in a task unconnected to eating (Savage-Rumbaugh *et al.* 1993, p. 15). They have not reached the stage which human children reach around the age of 18 months, of pointing to and requesting names for objects around them, often using a fairly arbitrary vocalisation such as [da]. It seems that the activity of 'naming' is not important to chimps, that it is of no interest to them as an activity in its own right.

Various observers have recorded chimpanzees' spontaneous use of symbols, outside the experimental situation, where they were interacting with other chimps or with humans. The type of communication that predominated in these situations was 'make a request of another' – mainly for food or for action (see, e.g. Savage-Rumbaugh 1986, pp. 271–5).

Other speech acts were occasionally observed, like 'announce what you're about to do' (Sherman uses the symbol *funny face* before pulling his lower lip down over his chin (Savage-Rumbaugh 1986, pp. 334–5)) – and comment on visible objects (e.g. Sherman's reaction to a sparkler indoors is to sign *straw give scare*, *outdoors* and then hurry to the door to be let out (Savage-Rumbaugh 1986, p. 284)). Though these uses of symbols are novel combinations, and go beyond simple requests, they are still tied to the here and now, and are relatively infrequent. It takes a lot of training and practice to get chimps to talk about objects and events outside the immediate context. Planning, remembering, thinking about things not present – all of which are summed up in the term 'displacement' do not seem to be within the chimpanzee's repertoire of skills. This linguistic profile puts the trained chimpanzee at about the same level of linguistic skills as a human child of between 1 and 2 years. Savage-Rumbaugh comments:

> it appears that the chimpanzee is inclined to remain at the level of communication with which it was naturally endowed – namely, an ability to indicate in a general fashion that he desires another to perform an action upon him or for him, when there exists a sole unambiguous referent (as in the case when one chimpanzee has meat and the other has none). (1986, p. 28)

Of course the whole question of what is the chimpanzee's 'natural endowment' is open to debate. Apparent limitations on apes' abilities often turn out to be consequences of experimenters' methods.

The ideational and the interpersonal

It appears that the chimpanzee's life has two separate aspects, which are combined in the human – the *ideational* function, dealing with information, judgements, evaluations, and so on, and the *interpersonal* function, encompassing greeting, persuading, commanding (Halliday 1978).

The ideational language function may be rooted in the chimpanzee's considerable problem-solving powers, based on its visual and manual skills. Köhler's experiments showed that the ape can truly think about problems of a certain type, reflect on them and solve them, without language. If two or more chimpanzees are working on the same problem, they may both try to solve it, each building on what the other has done, but the final solution is not the result of co-operation, but of an accidental coincidence of aims. Ideational skills, we might say, are not connected in any way with interpersonal skills; the chimpanzee can think about a problem, but cannot talk about it with a fellow chimp.

Interpersonal relationships also present problems to be solved, and the many recorded cases of Machiavellian intelligence show that chimpanzees solve interpersonal problems in a variety of creative ways.

Human experimenters have presented chimpanzees problems which require them to demonstrate abilities in both these spheres. Menzel's (1988) test involved hiding food in a field. One of a group of chimpanzees was shown the location of the food, and then released into the field with others who had not seen the hidden food. The informed chimpanzee was able to lead the others to the food with a high rate of success. These chimpanzees had not been taught symbol use, and the human observer could not tell how information was being communicated.

One of Savage-Rumbaugh's experiments (1986) requires a chimpanzee to ask another for a tool in order to get access to food for the two of them. The food is on the other side of a hatch, that can be opened with one of a set of tools – spanner, screwdriver, key, and so on. One of the apes has access to the hatch, and the other ape has access to the tools. Their abilities and resources in this situation are different, yet both are indispensable to the task. It cannot be solved by either of them separately, only by the two together.

What was noticed about the apes in this situation, was that for the first time they learnt the names of the tools with no trouble. Previously they had learnt names of foods easily, as you would expect, since food is of intrinsic interest, but the names of tools were not so easily learnt, until they became relevant to obtaining food, when they were learnt without difficulty.

Clearly, Savage-Rumbaugh's experiment pushed these two chimpanzees beyond the limit of what they could communicate without symbols. When the experimenters, as a control, turned off the lexigram board the chimpanzees were using to communicate, they could not continue with the task, grew irritated and perplexed. They could not communicate, and behaved as though they knew it (Savage-Rumbaugh 1986, p. 202).

CHIMPANZEE GESTURES IN THE WILD

Observers of chimpanzees in the wild have recorded a wide range of apparently meaningful gestures used to other chimpanzees. Examples include: infant raises its arm in the air as a signal to mother that it wants to be groomed; arm stretched out to beg; pointing; reassuring touches on the groin; arms raised as sign of disclaiming responsibility; arm stretched out in invitation; shaking head in refusal; gestural communication between two bonobos to negotiate copulation position; male chimpanzee waving his arm as a threat.[4]

These and many other examples appear to represent exchanges of meaning, apparently carried out under the control of the chimpanzee.

The following observations can be made about chimp gestures:

They appear to develop from purposeful actions – for example, the infant who raises its arm to ask for grooming is adopting the usual position for grooming; the aggressive male's threatening gesture of waving away uses the same action as hitting; the action of invitation repeats the movements of pulling someone towards the signer. These actions become meaningful gestures as soon as the audience understands them to be so.

In this sense, the meanings are iconic and can be easily retrieved from the context in which they are made, both by human observers and apparently by fellow chimps. Without knowledge of the context, though, chimp communication and human interpretation would probably break down.

They are in the main appeals or demands for action by another individual, and are thus carrying out both ideational function – indicating an action

– and interpersonal function – requesting that the action be carried out
– at the same time.

These features, it will be noticed, describe the register of 'simple imperative
communication' noted in Chapter 2. As Burling suggests (1993), this seems
to represent the very first (tiny) step along the road to language.

However, though it is agreed that chimpanzees make meaningful gestures, it is clear that such gestures are not crucial to chimpanzee society
and the survival of the species. Even the rare cases reported of chimpanzees
acting in concerted fashion have not appeared to depend on the use of
gestural sign to organise them. For instance, the simple co-operative hunting
observed by Goodall, during which one chimp chased the quarry, a young
colobus monkey, through the trees, while others guarded trees to cut off
the quarry's escape route (Goodall 1988, p. 199; also Teleki 1973, p. 33),
was unaccompanied by any gestures or sounds until the monkey was
caught. The use of a stick to catch termites was copied by a young
chimpanzee, without any sign passing between him and the adult chimp
(Goodall 1988, p. 168). Learning here was a case of simple observation
and imitation. Boesch (1991) observed a mother chimpanzee teaching
youngsters to use a stone to crack open palm nuts, again, without gesture
or sound.

Vervet monkeys

Here it is worth referring briefly to the often-quoted study of vervet
monkeys by Cheney and Seyfarth (1990). The authors distinguished three
types of vervet call, corresponding to predator on the ground ('snake');
predator in the air ('eagle'); predator approaching along the ground ('leopard'). Some commentators have viewed these calls as instinctive responses
to stimuli. Others have argued that the three calls have distinct referential
meanings, as in human language. This is to mistake the nature of primate
communication at this primitive level. Whether the monkey makes the
call or not depends on what is in the environment, not what is in the
monkey's mind at the time. Vervet monkeys can modify their calls to
meet changes in the environment (Leakey and Lewin 1992, p. 242), but
cannot apparently be induced in experiments to repeat the calls in the
absence of a predator or predator-type stimulus (Wallman 1993, pp. 44–5).

These calls should not be compared to human language. The closest
aspect of human behaviour they can be compared to are sounds such as
the reaction of disgust, 'ugh'; of surprise, 'oh'; the reaction to a sharp
pain, a rapid intake of breath 'ouch'. Now the point about such utterances
is that they are not words. They come close to instinctive reactions, the
product of physiological reactions discussed by Darwin (1872). We can
learn to control and imitate them, but their origin is in our system of
reflex responses to external stimuli, and therefore not analogous to the
system of meanings that humans have created for themselves.

If we found ourselves in a situation where the sound of a fellow-human's 'ouch' could be interpreted as an indicator of some phenomenon to be avoided, say a swarm of wasps, while 'ugh' could be interpreted as a threat from a different source, say a swarm of large repulsive cockroaches, then our reactions would probably be similar to the vervet's – differentiated forms of avoidance. But we should not be justified in saying that 'ouch' meant wasp, or 'ugh' meant cockroach. There is a world of difference between instinctive response and meaningful reference.[5]

WHY CAN'T CHIMPS SPEAK?

Given the undoubted intelligence of chimpanzees, their highly sociable nature and the fact that they are our closest cousins, the question of why it has not proved possible to teach them human speech is an intriguing one.

Hearing

It is certainly not because of poor hearing. Studies of chimpanzees' hearing show great sensitivity to the entire range of sounds that are required for human speech, with a maximum sensitivity at 2 kHz. As Wallace suggests (1994, p. 44), life in a forest habitat would give an advantage to creatures with auditory sensitivity to sounds such as the snap of a breaking twig, the creak of a dead branch, the rustle of leaves. Human senses – vision, touch, hearing, smell – are still very close to those of the monkeys. Evolution has hardly altered our senses in these respects (Campbell 1988, p. 153).

The vocal apparatus of chimpanzees is not suitable for speech

It is clear that there are significant differences between humans and chimpanzees in the anatomy of nose and throat. The only problem is, people cannot quite agree which aspects of the chimpanzee's vocal apparatus are deficient.

Studies by Lieberman (1991) and his colleagues show that the chimp's vocal tract is quite distinct from the human: the larynx is high in the throat, and as a result the pharynx is relatively short. Chimpanzees' jaws are longer than humans', and the roof of the mouth and the tongue are long and flat in comparison with the human arched palate and rounded tongue. The shape of the chimpanzee airway is a gently downward sloping tube, while the human airway bends sharply. The human tongue can be positioned to divide the airway (the oropharynx) into different shaped sections each producing a clearly distinct vowel – what Lieberman calls the 'quantal vowels' [i], [u] and [a].[6] The chimpanzee airway and tongue may not be able to do this.

Duchin (1990) disagrees with Lieberman about the importance of the length of the oropharynx. She claims that the main restriction on the chimpanzee's production of consonants is that the muscles of its tongue will not allow it to reach the various parts of the mouth that the human tongue touches in the production of consonant sounds. The chimpanzee is said to be unable to raise its soft palate to shut off the nasal cavity, so that if it could speak all its vowels would be heavily nasalised and therefore rather indistinct (Lieberman 1991, p. 57).

Finally, examination of the chimpanzee's larynx, the source of sound for human speech, shows that it differs from the human larynx in a number of respects. It is relatively large, in comparison to the rest of the vocal tract; it is positioned higher in the neck, and it is linked to air sacs, which may be important for conserving air supply during energetic movement. It is adapted to vocalisation on both inward and outward airflow, unlike the human larynx which responds best to outward airflow. (Chimpanzee 'pant-hoots' are uttered on alternating expiration and inspiration (Kelemen 1948, p. 328).) Kelemen comments, 'in spite of its high mental qualities, this animal is unable to imitate human speech, as its own voice is made up of entirely different phonetic elements' (Kelemen 1948, p. 255). Wind (1983, p. 17), on the other hand, plays down these differences and emphasises the great variety of sounds that the chimpanzee can produce. For him it is neural control of the musculature of the airway that is different in the chimpanzee.

Whereas humans can control the movement of larynx, tongue, pharynx, soft palate and lips, such variation as is heard in chimpanzee calls is produced mainly by variation at the larynx, and in the shape of the oral cavity and the lips. Chimpanzees, to put it another way, can produce a variety of vowel sounds, a variety of voicing types, and a variety of pitch patterns, but they do not seem able to produce more than a fraction of the consonant sounds that humans can make.

Chimps' brains are structured differently

Neurological studies suggest that the chimpanzee's brain is structured differently from humans. Human speech areas are thought to be located in the neocortex, the area of the brain that developed most recently. The calls of chimpanzees are said to be controlled by the older, subcortical part of the brain, or limbic system. Hewes adds that the association areas of the human brain, linking auditory input areas, the limbic region and motor speech centres in the left hemisphere do not appear to be developed in monkeys or apes (Hewes 1973, p. 67), suggesting that one of the factors differentiating chimpanzee and human may be simply the co-ordination of the movements of different parts of the vocal tract.

It is often suggested that chimpanzee vocalisations are governed by 'emotion' – instinctive reaction to external or internal stimuli – and that chimpanzees will vocalise even when it is not to their advantage to do so (Lieberman 1991, p. 52). Certainly chimp calls do not appear to have directly communicative intent, in that they are broadcast whether others are present or not (Hewes 1973, p. 67). If chimpanzee calls are relatively involuntary, and under the control of the limbic system, then explanation of the origin of human language has to account for the liberation of non-human primate vocal communication from limbic control (Steklis and Raleigh 1973, p. 77).

Chimps use noise in a different way from us

Compared to humans, chimpanzees are capable of a great deal of noise. Chimp calls, especially their characteristic pant-hoot, can carry through the forest over distances in excess of a mile, and may result in continued exchanges between individual chimps or groups (Boehm 1992, p. 337). They produce a wide variety of sounds – pant-hoots, pant-grunts, pant-barks, screams, pant-screams, grunts, 'wraas', 'whaas', cough-threats, whimpers, laughing, lip-smacking (Boehm 1992; de Waal 1988). Noise clearly plays an important part in chimpanzee life, but perhaps more in interpersonal than ideational functions. Long-distance calls play an important part, probably in defining a group's territory. Intensity of noise is an essential aspect of displays, by which chimpanzees defend themselves against outside threat and establish their social ranking within a group. An example is provided by Mike, a young male chimpanzee at Gombe, who discovered that banging a tin can make a loud noise. He used this to his advantage, putting on a terrifying display of rushing through the middle of a group of chimps banging the can and sending others running in fear. After this he was for some time recognised by the others as a dominant male (Goodall 1988, p. 112).

In social interaction within a group, however, sound is much less important than touch and gesture. Kortlandt's description of a scene in the Congolese forest illustrates this well:

> About 200 yards away was a hamlet where human children were playing; while watching my chimps, I could always hear the hullabaloo of the children. The chimp youngsters played almost exactly the same games as the human ones – running around, doing gymnastics, mock-fighting, playing tag and king-of-the-castle, dangling on low branches etc. – but without a single sound. Social intercourse in the chimpanzee group was achieved chiefly by silent facial expressions, arm and hand gestures, and bodily postures. From time to time, however, some of the adults (particularly the males, the childless females, and the ovulating females) would burst out in a deafening pandemonium of hoots, screams, and yells, i.e. the accompaniment of their brief intimidation displays and sexual riotings. (Kortlandt 1973, p. 73)

We see that grooming is important to the chimpanzee – but that sound may not be so important in this function as physical contact and action.

Both Goodall (1988) and Köhler (1925) describe chimpanzee dances that combine vigorous physical activity with hooting and screaming.

GAINING SELF-CONTROL

If chimpanzee studies give a pointer to the importance of iconic gestures in the emergence of language, they also indicate that the path to 'the liberation of primate vocal communication from limbic control' is perhaps not so hard to understand as was previously thought.

An anecdote from Goodall (1988) starts by repeating the common assumption that chimpanzees have little control over themselves:

> Chimpanzee vocalisations are closely tied to emotion. The production of a sound in the absence of the appropriate emotional state seems to be an almost impossible task for a chimpanzee. A chimpanzee can learn to *suppress* calls in situations when the production of sounds might, by drawing attention to the signaler, place him in an unpleasant or dangerous position, but even this is not easy. On one occasion when Figan [a male chimpanzee] was an adolescent, he waited in camp until the senior males had left and we were able to give him some bananas . . . his excited calls quickly brought the big males racing back and Figan lost his fruit. A few days later he waited behind again, and once more received his bananas. He made no loud sounds, but the calls could be heard deep in his throat, causing him almost to gag. (1988, p. 125)

Goodall's interpretation is that chimpanzees have a hard time controlling vocalisations, because they are dominated by emotion or instinct. But look at the story again, remember that Figan was an adolescent at the time, and you can see a young chimpanzee learning between the first and second incident – 'a few days later' – to control himself. In a later incident reported by Goodall (1988, pp. 141–2), Figan glanced briefly at a hidden banana that had not been noticed by other chimps in the group, and calmly walked away from it. Later he returned to get the food when the larger chimpanzees had left. In this third incident he seems to have mastered volitional control of vocalisation pretty well!

Other reports of chimpanzee 'deception' indicate that they can successfully suppress vocalisation in a situation that might otherwise call forth an uncontrolled response. Two examples given by de Waal (1989) show chimpanzees controlling vocalisations associated with fear and with sexual pleasure:

1. Two adult male chimpanzees, who have been vying with each other for some time, finally face each other in physical confrontation. Neither shows any sign of fear, but later, out of sight, they both discharge their fear by screaming (1989, p. 133).
2. A female chimpanzee screams aloud during sex with a dominant adult

male, but screams silently during sex with a less impressive male out of sight of the large and possessive adult (1989, p. 49).

There are sufficient of these anecdotes to indicate that chimpanzees can control their vocalisation, if their physical or social situation requires it. Controlling vocal communication seems perfectly possible under conditions of social life, where the importance of maintaining the individual's place in the social system imposes a measure of self-control that may not be observed in experimental conditions. Again aspects of the individual ape's behaviour should be seen as the product of social life, rather than the converse – social life as the outcome or sum of individual instincts and emotions.

As far as the voluntary production of vocalisation is concerned, researchers may again be too eager to write off chimpanzees' abilities (see also Steklis 1988). While it may be true that attempts in laboratories or researchers' houses to train common chimpanzees to modify their vocalisations have not been very successful (Lieberman 1991, p. 53), they do seem to be able to achieve more control when in a group. Kortlandt (1973, p. 74) reports a group of wild chimpanzees putting on a display of hooting and drumming to frighten away and eventually demolish a (stuffed) leopard. If this had been an emotional reaction, based on the limbic system of each chimpanzee, surely each individual – no match for a leopard – would have run away, screaming in fear. In a group, however, it is apparent that chimps can organise a collective response to drive away the predator. This is not to suggest that the collective response would be entirely under voluntary control in a situation of relaxed calm. It may be fairer to say that the group, faced with a choice between flight and fight, replaced its flight response with its fight response. In so doing each individual in the group gained some control over their own behaviour.

Interestingly, Jolly (1988) reports that lemurs, a much less brainy species of primate, bravely mob a four-legged predator such as a leopard, but scream 'instinctively' with fear when a hawk goes overhead. Why the difference in behaviour? We have what appears to be the strange situation of 'instinctive' bravery in one situation and 'instinctive' cowardice in another, very similar situation. Of course, instinct cannot explain these reactions adequately. They have to be seen as examples of learning. Could it be that experience has taught the lemurs that mobbing a leopard works, but that there is nothing they can do to stop a hawk carrying them off?

Recent reports on the bonobo Kanzi suggest that he is able not only to understand and respond to spoken requests delivered in normal spoken English, but even to start to make muffled vocal responses – admittedly not very like English sounds, but markedly different from the normal range of bonobo chimpanzee vocalisations. That is, to say, he appears to be making genuine attempts to imitate human speech (Hopkins and Savage-Rumbaugh 1991).

CO-OPERATION AMONG CHIMPS

It is interesting that scientists can look at chimpanzee behaviour and come to two almost opposite conclusions – one, that they are aggressive, competitive, anti-social creatures, who by some amazing achievement of nature manage to live together without killing each other;[7] the other, that they are co-operative, sociable, creatures, who may get aggressive when provoked but are otherwise fairly amiable (e.g. M. Power 1994).

There is evidence for both views in studies of chimpanzees. But what is the reality? We suggest that chimpanzees are really not that different from their human cousins, and that the circumstances of life play the key role. Circumstances that allow you to survive, in an environment that is predictable, will give rise to a rational system of social life, adaptations to the circumstances that will enable people to combine their skills in an efficient and rational way. Circumstances that are unpredictable, where survival is precarious and under constant threat, may lead to the breakdown of social life and a tendency for individuals to compete with other.

The aggression shown by animals in zoos is now recognised to be a product of the latter factor – an unpredictable and, from the animals' point of view, totally irrational environment, that in its extreme forms can send animals mad. Nevertheless, in Arnhem Zoo, de Waal observed that when chimpanzees engage in co-operative tasks, the patterns of dominance established by aggression, competition and occasionally deceit, temporarily disappear. He noticed cases where co-operative activity was initiated by one or more male chimpanzees with the apparent intention of restoring social stability, and of 'working off their frustrations' (de Waal 1989, p. 203). Dominance patterns also disappeared when an individual chimpanzee had meat to share (de Waal 1989, p. 202).

WHAT HAPPENED IN HISTORY?

Chimpanzees' abilities to use symbols have been amply proved by experimenters. They have been seen to be able to control their facial expressions, their bodies and their vocalisations. If chimps are to be taken as the model of our ancestors, what would it take for them to set out on the road to humanity and speech? Ultimately, chimpanzees do not fail to talk because of any physical or mental deficit, but because life in the forest provides them with no incentive to do so. The material existence of chimpanzees in the wild (food-gathering and a close but relatively uncomplicated social life) presents no situations where one chimpanzee is dependent on another for information. When an individual chimpanzee solves a problem, the solution may be copied by others, but it does not appear therefore to be shared – to become a part of social consciousness. Chimpanzees' actions are not co-operative; they are parallel, and chimpanzees' egocentrism is the cognitive equivalent of their parallel communal life.

Until situations arise where there is a shared objective and shared consequences, chimpanzees will have no need to talk to each other. Savage-Rumbaugh's tool experiment and Menzel's hidden-bananas experiment have both shown that when a situation is devised by humans, where the outcome depends on the knowledge that one of them possesses, chimpanzees can communicate effectively. Chimpanzee society appears to have in it the embryo of co-operation and language. Exactly how gesture may have developed through joint labour and how ape vocalisations may have developed into speech will be explored in more detail in the following chapters.

NOTES

1. See Patterson (1981) for a study of Koko the gorilla; and Miles (1990) for a signing orang-utan.
2. Tanner (1981) uses the term 'culture' for these aspects of behaviour, as does Donald (1991).
3. A lexigram is an electronic keyboard whose keys represent not letters but arbitrary symbols with the meanings of English words such as *lettuce*, *chase*, *tickle*, *more* and so on.
4. Examples from Kendon 1991; Goodall 1988; Callaghan 1993; de Waal 1989; Savage-Rumbaugh, Wilkerson and Bakeman 1977; Boehm 1992; Plooij 1978. There are also reports of spontaneous use of gestures among zoo gorillas (Parker 1994, p. 363).
5. To make the example more up-to-date, many people go 'ugh' when Noel Edmonds appears on television, but this does not mean that 'ugh' is a meaningful reference to Noel Edmonds.
6. The vowels in *tea* [i], *too* [u] and *tar* [ɑ]: Lieberman 1991, pp. 51–2.
7. E.g. Byrne and Whiten's (1988) view of Machiavellian intelligence; de Waal's (1989) account of murder in Arnhem Zoo.

4

Gesture and Origins of Meaning

Looking at animal behaviour, there appear to be two possible routes by which we could have arrived at today's spoken modern languages, one from the calls of primates, leading to speech; the other from animal's actions. Both these forms of behaviour have some part to play in the subsequent development of human speech, but neither can be regarded as direct antecedents of language, because both are based on instinctive individual responses to stimuli. Human language, by contrast, was from its very origins a creation of collective rather than individual behaviour. It was a new, specifically human behaviour – labour – that created language.

Interaction between individual animals, whether it is the physical grooming of chimpanzees or the collective vocal activity of baboons, will remain at the level of grooming,[1] unless there is meaningful content – something to talk about. Once a message has to be communicated, a form of communication will be found by its sender and its receiver, using the available material, whether this is gesture, speech, pantomime or depiction.

This chapter examines the argument that gesture was the medium of our ancestors' first communications.

THE GESTURE THEORY OF LANGUAGE ORIGINS
The theory itself

Communication starts when two or more individuals co-ordinate their separate activities to produce a single social act, solving a socially relevant problem. The earliest version of communication takes the form of an iconic version of the joint activity – a truncated action, and therefore a gestural sign. The individual's initially unintentional meaning becomes intentional when the other individual responds to it. Englefield (1977, p. 13) describes this process as one whereby the executive act (i.e. the act of doing something – lifting, pushing, carrying, hammering, etc.) becomes a communicative act. For this to happen, the response to the gesture is as important as the gesture itself. The creation of meanings is a dialogue from the very start, and communication is shaped by its function of exchange of meanings.

From initially iconic forms, with a direct connection between the representation and the action, a variety of forms develop. The establishment of the sign in social life depends from the start on agreement between two or more individuals – a convention. What may have originated as fairly elaborate pantomime gets shortened, iconicity is lost, and conventional or arbitrary signs predominate.[2] The context of gestural sign use is initially quite restricted, limited to a few essential social activities. Over time, more and more activities are organised with gesture, and as part of this process general all-purpose forms, something like grammatical forms, start to develop. This focus on gestural sign does not imply that early humans did not use sound in a variety of social functions, such as keeping the group together.

History of the theory

The idea that gesture preceded speech has a long history – tracing as far back as Plato.[3] Hewes concludes a long review of the theory with the comment that there is not much room for completely original views – everything seems to have been said, pro and con, many times over (Hewes 1976, p. 488).

Evidence supporting gesture theory

Some of the arguments in favour of gesture theory derive from studies of apes. Chimpanzees display embryonic forms of co-operation; they also display embryonic forms of gesture: gestural actions that appear to be under their control; but their vocalisations do not seem to be under control, and would appear to be linked to instinct. Other evidence in support of gesture theory will be presented in the following section.

Existing gesture languages

Gestural signing has in the past been thought of as a somewhat inferior version of language. The history of deaf education shows a prejudice against gesture over almost a century, with great cruelty shown against deaf signers by hearing teachers who believed that speech was the only suitable medium for deaf children to aspire to (Kyle and Woll 1985).

After a period of neglect, it is increasingly being recognised that gestural languages have both a long history and a widespread use around the world, and that such languages are as worthy of study as spoken languages. There are numerous examples of modern day gestural communication.

The American Plains Indians developed a system of gestural language that served as a lingua franca between North American tribes over thousands of years (Skelly 1979). Kendon (1989) has shown that gesture language is widespread among native Australians, and instances are reported in many places in South America, in New Guinea and among the Khoisan people of the Kalahari (Alan Barnard, personal communication), and so on. Luria and Vygotsky (1992) suggest that every foraging society at one time used both gestural and spoken languages.

In general, gesture can be used in any situation where speech is not possible or permissible. In contemporary western society we see traces of this principle, in the restricted gestural systems used by bookmakers on racecourses; soldiers on army manoeuvres; by scuba-divers; in recording studios; and by workers in noisy factories. It is clear that deaf signing is not exceptional, and gesture languages do not represent a separate linguistic code, simply a different linguistic medium.

Children's language development

Children do not start to speak their first words till the age of about 9 months, and their first sentences at about 18 months. Before 9 months parents understand their children's needs and intentions from their actions, rather than words. Because of babies' dependency on adults, and the resulting close bond that develops, parents can read meanings from babies' eye movements, body movements and facial expressions. Studies of children's development at these early stages show that their interaction with the world progresses from touch, to action, to gesture, then gesture and sound, and finally to speech (Clark 1978). This progression depends crucially on parents attending to what children are trying to do, and interpreting their behaviour.

Perhaps the most typical babies' gesture is the pointing action which almost invariably precedes and often accompanies their first words. This is a development of early reactions to objects that interest them. First babies reach out to try and grasp an object. If parents understand and respond to this reaching action, babies discover that reaching alone is sufficient to achieve their desires, and the action consolidates into pointing. At a subsequent stage they accompany the pointing gesture with a vocalisation. This may at first be an indeterminate sound, becoming a more structured syllable, for English babies something sounding like [da], and interpreted by adults as 'That?' Adults are almost guaranteed to respond to this behaviour by speaking the name of the object pointed to. Thus the original accidental, almost instinctive reaction of grasping for an object, becomes a meaningful gesture and a social tool, as a result of this pre-linguistic dialogue between baby and parent.[4]

Language pathology

With patients suffering impaired speech functions as a result of brain damage or illness, it has been found that a simplified gesture language can be used in place of speech. This suggests that gesture may be in some sense more basic than speech. It is probably the more direct, less arbitrary connection between gesture signs and the actions, objects or shapes that makes the system easier for such patients to handle (Skelly 1979; Jones and Cregan 1986).

Here we have to tread very carefully, because the inference can easily follow, that gesture is more primitive than speech. This is implied by Donald in his scheme of the development of consciousness, the second 'mimetic' stage of which is characterised by gestural communication. To explain this development, Donald (1991) proposes a module of the mind, the 'Mimetic Controller', but this is to put forward a biological explanation for a process which has a perfectly rational explanation, once the significance of labour, as collective activity, is grasped.

The Characteristics of gestural language

Gesture has intrinsic characteristics which make it much more likely to have been the first medium of communication than speech. These characteristics can be seen in natural gestural communication by which is meant, not the sophisticated communication of deaf signers, learned by children as their first language, but the gesturing of two or more people who do not share a common language, and are forced to invent a visual system of communication for the exchange of essential messages. The American Indian lingua franca based on gestural signs may have originated as a system of this type, easily understood and learnt, composed of iconic gestures of natural actions (Skelly 1979), supplemented with facial expression, posture, pointing to or touching objects.

Gestures are in origin a natural medium, derived from human actions and perceptions of the world, and therefore iconic, whereas spoken languages have only a small proportion of natural signs – mainly onomatopoeia, imitations of natural sounds – but the proportion of iconic material is never more than about 10 per cent.[5] Iconic gesture meanings are by nature universal in comparison with the restricted usage of spoken words. For instance, every language has a different word for the concept *sleep*, but the gesture of laying the head on the hands to one side while closing the eyes would be understood immediately anywhere in the world.

Gestures are based on physical properties of the world – shapes, movements, but most of all on actions. Natural gesture seems to excel at the expression of concrete, visual meaning. The meanings of natural gestures depend on the immediate context in which they are used. Since interpretation depends on context, meaning is relatively easily recovered, and the signer can use contextual features to elucidate meaning, for example, by pointing to objects, people, places in the vicinity. However the ability of signers to talk about matters beyond the here and now is limited. Gesture meanings may be complex or simple, according to the situation. There may be many elements of meaning in just one gesture. One sign corresponds to *sleep/sleeps/sleeping*, or even *I am sleeping/I was asleep*, and so on. The sign for *drink*, a cupping of the hands together, can also mean *a cup*, *a drink*, *water*, *thirsty*, and so on.

Since each gestural sign has a wide range of meanings, the load on memory is light, though ambiguity and misunderstanding may be frequent. It may be that as few as 300 to 400 would provide a communicative system adequate for social interaction and simple co-operative tasks. (Skelly's manual gesture code for aphasics is based on 256 signs). The upper limit on memory for manual signs is probably in the order of 1,500 to 2,000 (Hewes 1973, p. 71). Gesture is possible at a distance, and can also reach a large number of people at once, provided they are attentive. It is possible in noisy conditions, and conditions requiring silence.

All these features are in certain circumstances advantages for communication. As anybody who has travelled to a country without knowing its language will attest, a surprising amount of information can be communicated without any common spoken language. Interestingly, there are still today some things that can be better expressed through gesture than speech – describing the dimensions of an object, shapes, movements, indicating direction, specifying objects and persons in the immediate context (deixis), and so on.

Learning time

Englefield makes the point that a functioning vocal language requires a large number of spoken words, to be learnt quickly and thoroughly by all the members of the group: whereas a gestural sign system can function with a small number of iconic signs, each sign carrying a large functional load (1977, p. 87).

As we know, while early hominids had a longer learning time than chimpanzees, it was still a lot less than modern human children have. Children today take as long as 6 to 7 years to learn the basics of their language, and have only just mastered them by the age of 9 or 10. *Homo erectus* on the other hand was mature at 14, and their period of rapid brain growth or brain plasticity may have finished by 6 or 7. This short growing period must have placed a limit on learning. Therefore natural gestural signs, easy to learn and to remember, would appear to be the likeliest original communicative medium.

THE FORM OF EARLY GESTURAL LANGUAGE

The first gestural communication systems would probably have been rich in signs for actions connected with elementary labour (gestures for lifting, carrying, cutting, indicating directions, imitating animal movements) and for social interaction (gestures for mating, sharing food, attending to the young). Judgements of value would also be important, stemming from the fairly vital distinctions between good (to eat) and bad (to eat), good (behaviour) and bad (behaviour). Note that the modern chimpanzee, Washoe, was able to express judgements on aspects of her environment – and even to swear in sign language (Linden 1976, p. 7).

Communication may have been slow, and in a situation of any complexity would have resembled pantomime more than present-day deaf signing. However, over time commonplace, habitual ideas would have come to be expressed quickly and simply, stylised into more conventional signs, providing more rapid communication for a familiar audience (Englefield 1977, pp. 56–82). This move from iconic to conventional representation is a common developmental feature of all human languages.

It is often suggested that the earliest stages of language would have been dominated by action words, hence 'verbs'. However, while the emphasis would probably have been on action, to talk of verbs is mistaken. Utterances would have been of one word or sign only, without any clearly developed syntax – rather like children's first utterances. The difference between agent, action and patient of action may not have been distinct. The gesture of cupping the hands for a drink, for example, could convey the idea of agent (the person who drinks), action (drinking) or patient of action (water), as well as the property of wetness, the sensation of thirst, the object that holds water or the object that is used to carry it.

'SEMANTIC PHONOLOGY' AND THE ORIGINS OF SYNTAX IN GESTURE

Armstrong, Stokoe and Wilcox have proposed that the origins of syntax can be found in gesture. They see in a gestural sign a sentence in embryo, containing the elements agent, action and frequently goal or patient. So the American Sign Language (ASL) sign for 'catch', involves one hand (in the role of agent) moving across the body (an action) to grasp the forefinger of the other hand (the patient). Gestures of this type, they suggest, form the basis for a syntax that develops as signers over time analyse the gesture, gradually decomposing it into the separate semantic roles or meanings contained in the original unitary sign: '[gestural] signs have a potential that vocal signs lack for being decomposed into meaningful agent/action sub units' (Armstrong, Stokoe and Wilcox 1994, p. 356).

Armstrong *et al.*'s ideas provide a welcome new perspective on language origins studies. They are truly concerned with seeing how language might have originated. Instead of starting from today's language and working back, with all the idealist baggage of modern linguistic theory, they start at the beginning and work forward. Instead of describing signing in terms of speech, they view speech in terms of gesture, with interesting results. Rather than divide language into two irreconcilable forms, spoken and gestured, they enable us to see it as one unitary but varying form, and spoken words as 'complexes of temporally ordered muscular gestures rather than as semiperfect representations of abstract formal categories' (Armstrong, Stokoe and Wilcox 1994, p. 352).

Their suggestion that within the gesture are all the elements of the utterance – the agent, the action, the patient – implies that syntax develops in the process not just of building, but also by way of analysis and decomposition of signs. The various elements of the utterance slowly emerge from the sign, as it becomes necessary to differentiate agent and action, action and its patient, and so on. However, two critical comments need to be made on their proposals.

First, their view of gestural signers is one of passive viewers of the world rather than active participants in it. While they hint that communication is action, they do not carry through the implications of this approach. For them, the historical effect of syntax was not that it enabled humans to further transform themselves and the world around them, but that it:

> transformed naming into language by enhancing the ability of hominids to comment on and think about the relationships between things and events, that is, by enabling them to articulate and communicate complex thoughts. (Armstrong, Stokoe and Wilcox 1994, p. 354)

Contemplation of the world does not of itself lead to an analysis of events in terms of agent–action–patient. There are alternative semantic relations that might result from different ways of looking at the world, and a 'contemplative' analysis of sentence structure needs to explain why these alternatives do not show up, and why human languages are dominated by the semantic relationships of agent–action–patient.

The second problem is that Armstrong *et al.* show some confusion between syntax and semantics in their system of 'semantic phonology', even in their fundamental definition of a sign as 'an agent-verb construction' (Armstrong, Stokoe and Wilcox 1995, p. 12), and later in the blending of the two levels of description of the sign: 'the pattern is syntactic (subject–verb–object), but its elements, as agent, action and the optional patient, are semantic terms' (1995, p. 14).

This is not just a quibble, but a vital distinction. It is not syntax that is implicit in the action-gesture, but semantic relations, often termed 'case relations' or argument structure. Grammatical, syntactical relations are more abstract. Very often in a modern sentence an agent is not a subject, and a verb is not an action. For example: *The path led up the mountain*; *His action caused a sensation*; *I got infected with hepatitis*.

Armstrong *et al.*'s failure to make this distinction is related to their failure to understand the significance of action as opposed to contemplation. This becomes clear in relation to the question: where do these primal semantic relations come from? To Armstrong *et al.* they are simply an intrinsic component of gestural signs, and therefore, since they see gestural signs as the source of syntax, it is probably not very important whether they regard them as expressing real relations from the real world, or abstracted relations of syntax.

But when we look for the origin of these relations outside the act of communication, in the real world, and not in the heads of the speaker or signer, then it is vital to distinguish semantic and syntactic levels. Semantic

We need to show how others – not
just SVO are represented in gesture

relations are quite directly connected to human activity in the world, while syntactic relations are on a more abstracted plane, at one remove from activity, and therefore freer from it, able more flexibly to express ideas about that activity.

The function of a verb is not simply to express 'action'; its role in a sentence is to express a relationship between the subject of the sentence and the rest of the world. Sometimes the verb involes an action, but even the most apparently concrete verb still expresses a relationship. It is a common observation that different people viewing the same event can interpret it differently. A clear example is: *he fell*; *he was pushed*; *he jumped*. Here the same event is expressed in three different interpretations, each of which involves the imposition by speakers of different relationships between the participant in the event (the subject), and the world around. Similarly the syntactic category 'subject of a sentence' is not a person or a thing, but once again a relationship: a way of connecting one element of the speaker's experience with another.

The failure of Armstrong *et al.* to make this distinction is related to their failure to understand the significance of action as opposed to contemplation. This becomes clear in relation to the question: where do the primal semantic relations agent–action–patient come from? There are alternative possible underlying semantic relations to the characteristically human pattern agent–action–patient. We might, for example, on the basis of (admittedly few) sentences such as *Come dancing*; *Let's go eat*; *Why not try shouting?*, argue that here an underlying semantic relation is action–action. No grammarian, it has to be said, has ever argued this. But is that because the semantic relation is impossible? No, it is perfectly possible; it just does not occur in human language.

Kanzi's 'grammar'

However, in the mini-grammar of the bonobo Kanzi, described by Savage-Rumbaugh and Rumbaugh (1993), we find alongside the human semantic relations agent–action; action–patient, and so on, some utterances that would fall outside a human model of grammar, including action–action utterances like *tickle bite*, and some sentences, such as *food blackberry*, whose semantic structure is quite idiosyncratic, and can only be described as food–food. Action–action sequences actually form quite a large proportion of Kanzi's utterances. Of 724 two-element utterances, the category of action–action utterances is the third largest – 92 utterances (1993, p. 101).

Now if you consider for a moment the peculiar life of Kanzi, a chimpanzee in a human experiment, who spends much of his life in actions that seem to have no apparent purpose for him, and whose prime interests are games and food, his preference for these semantic relations makes sense. Many of his actions are indeed merely for the purpose of further action – chase in order to tickle, tickle and then bite. It can be argued that his particular form of social existence (there is no doubt that chimpanzees before Kanzi never lived a life like his!) may have given rise to this particular form of expression.

Life and syntax

The difference between humans in their social lives and Kanzi in his artificially created situation is that our actions are generally purposeful and goal-directed. They are frequently the result of a conscious agent initiating an action that has a clear goal. We can argue therefore that human semantic relations are not simply present in the world, waiting for us to discover them, but are the creation of human beings interacting with the world. It is surely because these are the relationships that are crucial to human beings acting on and interacting with the world, the relationships underlying the process of labour, that they feature so prominently in human languages, and not because this is the nature of gesture. To attribute these relationships to the intrinsic nature of human gestures, is to suggest that linguistic form determines the way we analyse the world, rather than the converse, that our interactions with the world lead us to an analysis of experience that shapes our language.

In so far as Kanzi is involved with the work of humans around him, his syntax expresses human-type semantic relations. But his peculiar form of interaction with the world also produces his peculiar form of syntax, based on semantic relations that are relatively unimportant to humans. Bruner puts it this way:

> The initial structure of language and, indeed, the universal structure of its syntax are extensions of the structure of action. Syntax is not arbitrary; its cases mirror the requirements of signaling about action and representing action. (Bruner 1981, p. 50)

THE DEVELOPMENT OF EARLY GESTURES

We would expect the first gestural signs of prehistory to be relatively undifferentiated with respect to agent, action or patient. But what happened when the original undifferentiated gesture started to decompose. Did it tend to become thing-noun? or action-verb? We know that eventually both these forms must have emerged, in order for syntax to form. But which came first?

It is often argued that language developed through deixis – pointing, specifying objects and people around, which leads eventually to naming them.[6] It is also claimed that early language must have been dominated by actions, at the expense of attention to objects. The two views are in contradiction with each other and it is worth considering the issue: which came first, emphasis on objects (hence naming, hence nouns), or emphasis on action (hence verbs)?

If the logical content of an utterances is analysed in terms of the components *argument* and *predicate*, the earliest utterances would surely be ones where the predicate predominates.[7] The fact that communication had not escaped from its context means that the argument would always be present in the situation. The argument in this situation is given to both speaker/signer and addressee, so is not specified. Predicates would predominate – as they do in inner speech. The implication is that emphasis on action would historically precede emphasis on agents or patients.

The register that predominates at this early stage must therefore be simple imperative communication, and the content must be dominated by physical and social activities – *run*, *lift*, *go-come*, *sleep*, *eat*, *drink*, and so on. In chimpanzee life these activities may have no purpose; in the context of human labour, activities have a purpose, and therefore an implicit goal. This stage of elementary message formation is a prerequisite for the later stage of naming, when gestural signs develop into two forms, one for the action and the other for either the agent or the patient of the action.

In fact it is not hard to see that naming is a fairly advanced function of language, presupposing a level of attention on objects and other phenomena that requires a certain level of social development. It is observed among children that while naming is an important development in language learning it is not the first. Uemlianin (1994) argues that children become aware of their own activity, before they become aware of objects around them.[8] Their first act of meaning is the action of pointing rather than reference to objects. It is in the response of adults to this action, the 'original word game' (Brown 1973), that learning of names proceeds.

In conclusion, there is no difficulty in understanding how individual gestures could be created from actions, once collective action required communication. The material of gesture is ideal for the creation of a simple communicative system, and today is still better for some communicative tasks than speech.

DISADVANTAGES OF GESTURE?

A number of supposed disadvantages of gesture relative to speech have been proposed.

Differential access to information

No less a thinker than Vygotsky urged the importance of reading and writing in the education of deaf children, on the basis that otherwise they would be cut off from vital sources of information and from contact with the wider culture of their society. Is it fair to suggest that by comparison with speech, gesture restricts the availability of information?

It is certainly true that modern-day gesture cannot by itself carry out all the tasks of communication that its users require. Deaf signers have to rely also on forms such as finger spelling that derive from the spoken tradition. Kendon (1988) makes the point that gestural languages of aboriginal Australians are dependent in their form on characteristics of associated spoken languages. But these are not inherent deficiencies in gesture. Rather they are a reflection of the dominance of spoken language today. If gesture is today not adequate for all communicative needs, then it is also true that speech is not adequate – we rely more and more on written forms of language. So the question is really, can speech do so many more things than gesture?

There really are not that many things. Suggested activities that depend solely on speech include (a) attracting attention, including calling from a distance; (b) co-ordinating activity; (c) the intimidatory use of noise. The significance of such activities will be examined in Chapter Six in relation to the origins of speech. They do not establish that gesture is in any way deficient or inferior to speech as a communicative medium.

Abstract and concrete ideas

Some have proposed that gesture is more suitable for concrete notions, and speech more suitable for abstract notions. When we think of natural gesture, and its use as a lingua franca, the notion seems attractive. But we must remember that abstract notions are not the result of the medium of speech; they are the result of a certain level of social and technical development, such that thinking can be separated from the immediate activity and immediate sensory impressions. The proof of this is the fact that modern deaf signing can cope perfectly well with abstract and general concepts.

Iconicity v. Arbitrariness

Pulleyblank proposes a variation of the idea – that speech is arbitrary whereas gesture is iconic, and that gestural signing is therefore restricted by its inability to invent new terms (Pulleyblank 1983, p. 402).

This characterisation – gesture is iconic, speech arbitrary – again ignores the evidence of gestural signing today. Deaf signing is not generally iconic; its forms are in many respects as much a matter of convention as are spoken words. Conversely, while many follow Saussure (1974, p. 67) in insisting on the arbitrariness of sound-meaning connections, there are a great many connections between sound and meaning, in sound symbolism examined on p. 105 below.

In other words, while it is correct to argue that language forms show an evolution from more iconic to more arbitrary, it would be a mistake to identify 'iconic' with gestural sign and 'arbitrary' with spoken word.

Nor has a gestural signing community any less capacity to form new words than a speaking community. Thanks in part to the quality of gradience in signs, deaf signers can produce exactly as many meanings as are needed for their communicative purpose – whether they are dealing with a Shakespeare play or the day's financial report. For example, the variation expressed in the series *slow*, *slow-ish*, *quite slow*, *very slow*, *extremely slow* and *dead slow*, can all be expressed by varying the speed with which a gestural sign is executed.

Gestural sign systems can easily make the transition from iconic to arbitrary form, and one of the strengths of gesture theory is that it provides a convincing explanation of how language might originate in iconic form, and then make the transition to the arbitrary form of today's languages. The general picture of the development of gestural form is that a gestural sign originates as iconic representation, with a direct and natural connection with the aspect of the world that it represents. Over time, with increasing complexity of communicative needs, the form of gestural signs moves away from this natural connection towards conventional arbitrary form. Communicative needs demand that the meaning of a sign be restricted in some way if it is not to be ambiguous. Using Englefield's illustration (1977, p. 20), footprints can be read for many different kinds of information – about the maker's direction, weight, speed, the time they passed, and so on. A footprint made for the purpose of passing on a message is read in quite a different way. In this case only a small part of the range of meanings can be intended, and this has to be the result of previous agreement or convention. The latter sign meaning is derived from the natural meaning, but can only correspond to a part of it (Englefield 1977, p. 20).

Historically it was necessary for messages to become independent of context, separate from reliance on a direct connection with the world around. The associated development from iconic to arbitrary signs was a prerequisite for the later establishment of the almost totally arbitrary system of spoken language.

Speed of processing information

In his discussion of supposed differences between modern humans and their ancestors Lieberman (1991) emphasises the speed of processing of information that is characteristic of speech – suggesting that in speech, we process between fifteen and twenty-five phonetic segments per second (1991, p. 37), whereas non-speech sounds cannot be handled at a rate no better than seven to nine items per second (1991, pp. 37–8, quoting Miller 1956). The implication is that speakers handle 'information' more efficiently than non-speakers (such as gestural signers).[9]

But anyone who watches deaf-signing interpretation of television programmes or public performances will immediately be aware that the signer processes information at just the same speed as speakers. What they are processing of course is not the distinct phonetic segments, but information contained in word meanings, or propositions. Klima and Bellugi conclude: 'though signs are produced at half the rate of words, the rate of producing propositions does not differ in the two modes' (Klima and Bellugi 1979, p. 194).

In other words, we seem to be processing not individual speech sounds or phonemes, but meanings – and in these terms information processing is no different from that in any other realm of human activity. We have to insist that deaf signing is a fully-formed human language, as highly structured, as expressive and as rapid in transmission as any spoken language, and equally capable of carrying out the communicative tasks of human society.

Overload of information

The suggestion comes, surprisingly from Armstrong, Stokoe and Wilcox, that gestural signing may suffer from an overload of information: 'as social organisation and exploitation of the environment evolved, vision and the upper body became overburdened and began to share more of the task of communication with the much less iconic and deictic vocal medium, always an important part of the primate heritage' (1994, p. 364).

However, as we know, and as Armstrong *et al.* would be the first to point out, being confined to gesture does not prove a barrier to communication for deaf signers, who do not complain of being 'overburdened' with visual information.

NATURAL SELECTION OF SPEECH

In some discussions of a possible transition from gesture to speech, we find suggestions that because of all the presumed advantages of speech, there must have been in operation some Darwinian selective mechanisms, selecting speakers, and operating against gestural signers. This is implied in some accounts of the demise of the Neanderthals – they failed, or disappeared, because their speech was slow, cumbersome, just not arbitrary enough, somehow. Lieberman suggests that the ability to produce distinct unnasalised quantal sounds (i.e. sounds within the modern human phonological repertoire) was the biological factor that enabled humans to survive but condemned Neanderthals to extinction.[10]

Once again, in this account, language is viewed as the factor that determines human history. But to repeat the point made in Chapter Two, it was not language that made us human, but us humans that made language. As Chapter Seven will demonstrate, the Neanderthals had a technology as advanced in its day as any made by anatomically modern humans. For thousands of years anatomically modern humans and Neanderthals lived side by side, and while some features of Neanderthal anatomy are not seen today, there is no certainty that they did in fact become extinct.

This story of how things might have happened does not in any case fit the Darwinian theory of selection of the fittest to survive in a given environment. For natural selection to operate in this area of human activity, we should need to establish that the ability to produce syllables consisting of consonants and vowels (cv) gave a primary material 'advantage' to individual hominids. This is clearly not tenable. The ability to articulate the names of hares, antelopes and leopards does not give better chances of survival in the savannah, nor does it make for better food-gathering techniques, or enhance the survival chances of the infants. It is not even easy to demonstrate that articulacy gives an advantage in survival to groups of hominids, let alone to the individual members of the group. There is no way to demonstrate this without considering the social life of the group – and, once again, we see that deaf signers can cope perfectly well in constructing a social life.

In fact gesturing, because it can be immediate, visible, easy to learn and easy to remember, may well have given an advantage to hominids in the early stages of our development that speech could never have conferred. So those who seek biological explanations for the survival of our species, based on linguistic abilities, need first to explain how gesture, from being an advantage to our species at one point, later became a positive disadvantage!

Suggestions are often made that compared to gesture, speech makes possible finer analysis of concepts, makes possible syntax and grammatical morphology, thus greater differentiation and greater complexity. It is also argued that forms of communication based on gesture would be more conservative than those based on speech, and hold back innovation – and that this might explain why *Homo erectus* remained virtually unchanged for a million years or more in the Acheulean Period (e.g. Corballis 1994). It may be true that certain forms of gestural communication – what we have called 'natural gesture' – are syntactically very simple, lacking for example in morphological endings characteristic of speech, but, as Kendon (1993) observes: 'systemic, code-like properties in gestural communication expand in proportion to the range of communicative demands it is employed to meet' (p. 59) – that is, linguistic properties of code are properties which result from communicative function. This point is particularly important, because if there was an increase in syntactic complexity at a certain point in our history, it was not due to a change from gesture to speech, but rather to an increase in the range of communicative demands made on language, and this can only have been due to an increase in the range of activities in social life.

Thus we have to find a different explanation for the shift from gesture to speech. Many forms of speech, for example, imperative communication, are very simple today. More importantly, we have to caution against pinning too much significance on language, on ideas as the movers of the world. Wonderful as words are, they cannot change the world in themselves. Language can neither promote progress nor hold it back, except as part of more general social developments.

GESTURE TODAY

The final point to make in support of gesture theory is that gesture has not withered away as speech has advanced. Gesture today is still a very important part of our communication – whether in manual gesturing or, as McNeill has suggested, in a translation of original gestural movements to the level of intonation and other forms of prosodic behaviour accompanying speech, such as loudness, voice quality, and so on.[11]

NOTES

1. Aiello and Dunbar's phrase (1993) for the collective vocal activity of primates is 'vocal grooming'.
2. Conventional signs predominate in modern deaf signing, for example, and in the gesturing of monks in silent orders (Englefield 1977, p. 48).
3. The case for an original gesture language has been put forward by such writers as Voltaire, Condillac, Wundt, Marr and Paget: see Hewes (1976) for a comprehensive survey.
4. This sequence is encapsulated in the title of A. Lock's (1978) collection of articles, *Action, Gesture and Symbol*.
5. de Grolier (1990, p. 145). Interestingly, though learners of deaf sign language are struck initially by the iconic nature of some signs, it is estimated that languages of the deaf such as ASL, BSL (British Sign Language) have no greater a proportion of iconic material than spoken languages (Skelly 1979, p. 5).
6. As Rolfe (1992, p. 30). Hewes (1976, p. 482), traces the idea that deictic gesture is the first step to naming, as far back as Augustine's *Confessions*, AD 400.
7. Agent and action are semantic categories; subject and verb are syntactic relations; argument and predicate are logical or propositional relations, relating to the division of an utterance into what you are talking about – the argument – and what you are saying about it – the predicate. Arguments often do coincide with agents, and subjects, while predicates often coincide with actions, or verbal phrases, but not always.
8. Donald also sees the first evidence of mimesis in children's pointing behaviour preceding first words, *c.* 14 months, following a period when children have learnt to direct their gaze and focus attention where their mother or parent is focusing (1991, p. 171).
9. Notice that not all spoken languages are as fast as each other. It is widely observed that a pidgin language, spoken as a second language is much slower than the same language spoken as a native language – when it is said to be a creole.
10. Lieberman (1991, pp. 76–7). Chris Knight refers to the 'speech defect' theory of evolution.
11. McNeill (1985) identifies linguistic gesticulation of three types: (a) iconic gesturing, related to meaning of utterance, e.g. expressing shape, movement; (b) metaphoric gesturing relating to more abstract conception of the content of message, e.g. gestures for 'broadening out', 'contained within', with a cup-like shape, and so on; (c) gesturing with the 'beat' of the spoken utterance, for emphasis, or marking stress, information structure, and so on.

5

Hominids and Humans

This chapter will review evidence for changes in behaviour and social organisation, and therefore for language, among ancestral humans. Three stages are discussed:

Australopithecines (*c.* 5 million to 1.5 million BP);

Homo habilis and *Homo erectus* (2.5 million to 250,000 BP);

archaic *Homo sapiens* (250,000 BP to *c.* 100,000 BP).

While three apparently separate stages are identified here, it is important to bear in mind the gradual changes going on between the apparent leaps from one stage to another.

The normal criterion for dividing the fossil record is increases in brain size, in two phases of rapid increase between the early Australopithecines and *Homo habilis*/*Homo erectus*, and between *Homo erectus* and archaic *Homo sapiens*, when brains of modern size appear. The other criterion is the record of stone tools, on which basis stages of hominid history are divided according to the tool industries Oldowan, Acheulian and Mousterian (see Table 5.1), the implication being that advances in tool technology are associated with other social and cultural advances.

TABLE 5.1: Prehistoric tool industries.

Tools/cultures	Date	Hominids
Oldowan (single face, choppers)	2.5m BP	Late Australopithecines/*Homo habilis*/*Erectus*
Acheulean (bifaces, hand-axes)	1.5m BP	*Homo erectus*/Archaic *Homo sapiens*
Core-and-flake technology	250,000 BP	Archaic *Homo sapiens*/Neanderthal
Blade technology	100,000 BP	Neanderthal/AMHS

Anatomical advances and cultural, behavioural advances proceed together, though not in step. Stone tools first appear in a human context at the time of *Homo erectus*, after 2 million years BP. Leroi-Gourhan (1993, p. 135) shows over time both an increase in brain size and an increase in variety and efficiency of tools, measured in terms of length of cutting edge of stone per kilogram. Neither tool technology nor brain size should be seen as the single key factor in evolution, but in Wind's phrase, 'virtually the whole process of hominisation has to be taken into account' (Wind 1983, p. 35) Wind identifies almost a hundred interconnected features of the human condition that he considers important to the development of language. Some of the crucial anatomical developments in human evolution are:

1. Bipedality and upright stance: whatever the proposed reasons for bipedality – new feeding techniques, carrying tools or weapons, carrying food, carrying babies, keeping cool,[1] better distant vision – bipedality was a crucial step for the development of tools, and of language.
2. Bipedality created the human foot, different from the ape's. Our upright stance freed the hands and mouth from the function of carrying, which it has in monkeys, dogs, cats, and so on.
3. If bipedality was a means of cooling the body, it is no doubt linked to hairlessness and sweating, which enabled us to work and travel in the heat. Humans have more sweat glands than any other species.[2] Lack of body hair also made the arms more important for carrying babies, once they could no longer cling on to their mother's hair.
4. The hands, no longer being used primarily for clinging to branches or for walking, were able to develop finer muscular control. The opposable thumb was important in developing first the power grip and then the precision grip, so improving the manual skills required for manipulating and processing materials, for tool-making, for gesturing, and so on.
5. The increased ability of the hands to obtain and to process food (e.g. by using tools) meant reduced reliance on teeth, jaws and tongue to obtain food directly. Jaws and teeth could grow smaller, resulting in changes in dentition, in the shape of the jaw, palate and nose, all significant aspects of the modern capacity for speech. The many functions carried out by hands and arms made it more likely that we would eventually prefer our mouths for communication.
6. The growth of the brain is linked, above all, to the increased number of neural connections governing movements of hands and vocal organs. The increased size of the brain and hence the skull may have influenced the development of the vocal tract, pushing the larynx downward in the throat, and bending the airway (pharynx). Brain asymmetry is linked to two-handed control. Whereas tree-dwelling apes tend to manipulate objects with one hand, while the other holds on to the tree, ground-based hominids developed the ability to hold an object in one hand while working on it with the other, leading to the development of a preferred hand, and accentuating brain hemispheric lateralisation (Marshack 1989, p. 27).
7. It has been argued that the lowering of the larynx and lengthening of the pharynx were essential for the development of speech (e.g. Lieber-

man 1991). These anatomical changes may have been linked to upright stance and the growth of the brain, but could also have been adaptations to the requirements of long-distance running – the ability to breathe rapidly through the mouth.

8. The reduction of sexual dimorphism (size differences between sexes) in human evolution suggests increased co-operation in hominid groups, and therefore sharing of tasks and division of labour.

9. Female anatomy, a clever compromise between the requirements of bipedality and the requirements of carrying large-brained babies, is also relevant to language. Because of our upright stance, the birth canal is relatively narrow, so babies have to be born at a relatively earlier stage of development, and need increased maternal protection. Earlier birth is linked to the size of the brain and to the need for a longer period of infant learning, and thus of brain plasticity. There is no advantage in a longer period of infant helplessness, but it must have placed a premium on social co-operation in caring for children, providing food for nursing mothers, and so on. Our relatively long period of childhood dependency maximises mother–child contact, enhancing transmission of information.

10. The change of diet from apes' vegetarianism to human omnivory, the result of a diversity of gathering and foraging techniques, may explain some of the changes in the tongue and other parts of the mouth.

Most of our anatomy can thus be shown to be relevant to the evolution of speech. Our bodies, and our very existence are in every way 'biological', but by the time we have considered all the above factors we can see that biology alone is not enough. As we piece together human anatomical evolution, we simultaneously have to piece together the history of society – how food was obtained; how children were fed and cared for, grew up and were integrated into adult society; how sexual alliances were formed; how skills were passed on; the forms of social organisation and the form that communication took at each stage – all of these, aspects of the labour process.

[handwritten margin note: only ?]

AUSTRALOPITHECINES

Discussion of the course of human evolution should start from the observation that modern human beings are co-operative creatures. Historical accounts of our evolution usually start with the Australopithecines, close relatives of tree-living apes not dissimilar from modern-day bonobo. However, apes, while gregarious and not specially aggressive, are not particularly co-operative. Their behaviour can accurately be described as 'egocentric'; while two individuals may be observed to do the same things simultaneously, it is more a case of acting in parallel than in co-operation. So at some point, Australopithecines must have made the transition from ape-like behaviour to the co-operative behaviour that set them on the path to humanity and to language. This has to be borne in mind in examining the record of their existence.

The split between the common ancestor of apes and humans probably took place between five and ten million years BP, during a period of global cooling, when areas of forest were replaced by grassland. One group of primate species, the Australopithecines adapted to change by spending more time on the ground, and were thus able to take advantage of opportunities of terrestrial foraging at the edges of woodland (Klein 1989, p. 181).

The Australopithecine adaptation was a complex of features – both anatomical and social, involving not only changes in the skeleton, but also in female reproductive anatomy and thus, presumably, behaviour, diet, use of hands and feet, brain size and social behaviour – an extremely complex adaptation, associated with a new habitat and a new behavioural strategy, related to ways of obtaining food, reproducing, survival, self-defence, and so on.

Australopithecines occupied a mosaic habitat, unlike great apes, and were omnivorous. Their survival in this habitat indicates behavioural flexibility, including probably an ability to find hidden foods. Since their greatest danger would undoubtedly have been from predators, they were slow to abandon trees entirely, until they developed the ability to run and to drive away predators (Campbell 1988, p. 227).

It is most helpful to regard Australopithecines as apes, whose bipedality and social organisation had consequences that led towards humanity. Their anatomy may have been simply a specialised feeding adaptation – upright posture for feeding from trees in mixed grassland and forest habitat, that served as a pre-adaptation for walking among *Homo erectus* (Hunt 1994). While they were skilful climbers, they may have been less adept bipeds, who did not walk long distances (Susman, Stern and Jungers 1985, p. 190). Senut and Tardieu suggest that while humans are endowed with lax elbow joints and solid knee joints, making us good at walking but not so good at climbing, Australopithecines have lax knee joints and solid elbow joints – good for climbing but not so good for walking (1985, p. 199).

The Australopithecine foot changed fairly dramatically with bipedality, losing much of its movement and sensitivity. The toes were short compared with apes', though long compared with humans' (Susman, Stern and Jungers 1985, p. 185). The hand changed little in form, but probably gained in neurological control, hence in skill, two-handedness, and so on (Marshack 1989, p. 27). They had shorter fingers than apes, with fully opposable thumb. Their skulls and dentition were ape-like, males having a pointed canine (Campbell 1988, p. 211).

Australopithecine brains

Reconstructions or 'endocasts' of Australopithecine brains show them to be shaped differently from apes, though much of this difference is the result of bipedality. In the course of evolution the brain turned round the ear, which had to preserve its horizontal orientation in order to maintain balance (Wind 1983, p. 32). The Australopithecine brain was slightly larger than today's chimpanzee brain, though most of the extra brain may have been dedicated to maintaining balance for walking upright. The ratio of neocortex (new brain) to the overall brain was very similar in *Australopithecus afarensis* (3.29) to chimpanzee (3.15) (Aiello and Dunbar 1993, p. 18). There is very little evidence in endocasts of Australopithecine skulls of any of the claimed speech areas.

Tools

With hominids after Australopithecines there is abundant evidence of tool use, and it is possible that later Australopithecines, the so-called robust varieties that lived contemporaneously with early *Homo,* were tool-users. Among the early Australopithecines the absence of evidence of tool use suggests that co-operative labour had not fully developed, though it is of course possible that they used sticks or bones as tools – materials that leave no trace.

Males and females

Australopithecines were quite small and ape-like. Females were about 3 ft 6 in. (1.06 m.) tall; males 5 ft (1.52 m.). There was a high level of sexual dimorphism – females are between 64 per cent and 79 per cent of the size of males, roughly the same proportion as among modern chimpanzees.[3] Female Australopithecines were small and matured early. The fossil evidence suggests a poor, low-protein diet, and seasonally unreliable food sources.

As a response to these circumstances, with the increased risk of infant mortality, it appears that females grew rapidly and matured early, with frequent births relative to other apes (Ragir 1994). A less stable environment gives rise to a need to replace infants quickly if they die. This feature persists in humans today in that female fertility resumes within three to six months of giving birth, compared to two to three years for apes (Ragir 1985, p. 454). In this respect humans are similar to baboons, which, like early human ancestors, live on the edge of forests and in the savannah.

It is even more remarkable, then, that in this period started the progressive prolonging of intra-uterine and post-natal phases of development – the birth of large yet skeletally immature babies (Ragir 1994, p. 2). These early hominids display retarded development in foetus and neonate without proportionate increases in adult size (Ragir 1985, p. 455). In other words, adults did not get bigger, but babies got smaller – they were born at a less mature stage, with more growing to do.[4] This retardation starts in the *Australopithecus* stage as an effect of bipedality, influencing the width of the birth canal. The consequence of this is a longer period of learning for young Australopithecines than for young chimps. Since slow maturation is in many ways a disadvantage for the survival of a species, it must have been compensated by the advantages that slow maturation gives in terms of length of learning period. This implies that the Australopithecine way of life required the learning of a greater number of survival techniques than any previous apes, and that the young had to learn these skills in order to survive.

Sexual behaviour

Bipedality has an effect on sexual signalling. The sexual swellings of the female ape would no longer be so obvious if they walked upright, so females may have had to develop other ways of showing sexual interest in males – gestures, facial expression, vocalisation (Tanner and Zihlman 1976b, p. 606). C. Power (1994) points out that concealed ovulation, in a close-knit group, means that no dominant male can monopolise fertile females, and it then becomes possible for females to select as mates those who will provide food and help with child-rearing. Among chimpanzees it is in any case females who tend to choose mates.

Tanner and Zihlman (1976b) emphasise the important part played by female choice in the development of social life. If females were burdened with both child care and half of the group's food production, they would need at an early stage to choose as mates males who would be supportive, and not disruptive of social life by noisy displays, aggression and competition. This selection of non-aggressive, co-operative males may have started among the Australopithecines.

One piece of evidence to support this contention would be a reduction in sexual dimorphism. Although there is as we have seen little difference in body-size dimorphism between chimpanzees and Australopithecines, there is a marked reduction in male canine-teeth size among the latter. This is partly a necessary consequence of chewing tough vegetation (Campbell 1988, pp. 231–3; Wind 1983, p. 26), for which molars become more important and canines less so. The reduction of canines also suggests that males have less use of them for fighting or for threat display. Large canines are an exclusively male feature among chimpanzees, and thus not a reflection of their diet. Their reduction among Australopithecines (Klein 1989, p. 401) may be an indication that social relations within groups and between the sexes had started to become more co-operative.

Social organisation

We find differing accounts of what social organisation was like among Australopithecines. At one time it was assumed that they lived in male-dominated 'harems', rather like baboons living on the savannah. A more common view today is that Australopithecines lived in a close-knit, but undifferentiated family or herd.

We have seen that Australopithecine life appears to have been quite hard, compared with today's chimpanzees'. For apes in the tropical rain-forest, fruit is available thoughout the year, there are few predators in the trees. Even leopards can only get to baby apes if there are no adults around to defend them. So apes' social organisation is very loose, and may take a variety of forms.

When our ancestors moved out of the trees, their habitat was much more dangerous and exposed to predators and new competitors. Two choices faced our ancestors then: the competitive and the co-operative.

The competitive response to danger is that males grow larger, and start to behave jealously, keeping their females and young close to them all the time, as do certain types of baboons. This has advantages, because it means the male is constantly on hand to defend against predators. The disadvantage is that when one male denies other males access to females, fighting is encouraged among males, and the biggest, most aggressive male will end up taking over.

The alternative, co-operative, possibility, is to form a large herd of both male and female adults. For this to work, behaviour, and with it anatomy, have to change to minimise in-fighting and maximise co-operation. As we have seen, there is at least as much evidence pointing to the co-operative solution as to the competitive one.

The size dimorphism between male and female Australopithecines might indicate that males were dominant in Australopithecine society, and ate all the best food, while the females struggled along carrying the babies and feeding themselves as best they could. On the other hand, females could have been small simply because there was no need for them to be larger, since males defended them, and their small size meant that the energy they gained from food could be used for reproduction, where it was needed to ensure the survival of the species.

Concealed ovulation, a characteristic of hominids, is not usually associated with females living in groups dominated by one large male. In such circumstances the norm (as among baboons) would be for the female to signal when she is in oestrus – as there is only one male around, she has to make it very clear when she's available for fertilisation. But when there are a lot of males around, concealed ovulation has a number of advantages: the woman has the choice of which male to mate with, or indeed whether to mate or not; and since males cannot tell whether she is fertile, they are more likely to stay around and provide food, help to feed her babies, and be less likely to fight over her (Tanner and Zihlman 1976b; Campbell 1988, p. 244).

The evidence is not yet truly conclusive either way – but a number of anthropologists have concluded that the form of social organisation among Australopithecines was the herd, rather than the harem (Donald 1991, p. 45; Livingstone 1973, p. 26; Woolfson 1982, p. 33). Woolfson supports Engels' point that early humans living in the primitive herd would have been unable to build more enduring human collectives unless 'zoological egoism' began to be subordinated to the social co-operation required for collective labour (1982, p. 33). Foley and Lee stress the importance to females of stable alliances with males, either with individuals or 'with the entire alliance of males' (1989, p. 904).

Eventually membership of the herd, or troop, or tribe, must have become indispensable for survival. Learning started to be a selective factor, so that those who spend a long time with the herd, learning skills from others, are fitter to survive than those independent spirits who, however strong or fit, become more vulnerable to predators or to starvation in lean times because of their isolation. Here is a real material basis for co-operative behaviour. The principles of this first step of social organisation along the road to humanity seem to have been female choice rather than male domination; co-operation rather than competition.

Australopithecines language?

As to the question of whether Australopithecines spoke, or gestured, we can find little evidence from fossils, or from what we know about their lives. Herd life in the open savannah may have fostered the ability to produce sounds at will, to drive away predators, or drive rival scavengers from carcasses. However, the upper respiratory system of the *Australopith-ecus* fossil at Sterkfontein 5 is found to be similar to great apes (Laitman, Heimbuch and Crelin 1979), suggesting that Australopithecines would be making ape-noises, rather than human sounds. Nor is there any evidence of the division of labour that has been suggested as the necessary prerequis-ite for making and exchanging meanings. In the herd, individuals behave the same way, except for the sexual behaviour that is driven by instinct.

Probably the most significant piece of evidence is the fossil record of the transitional period that saw the disappearance of some Australopithec-ine species and the appearance of *Homo habilis* (Milo and Quiatt 1993, p. 573). There may have been two, three or more varieties of upright ape before 2.5 million BP. Then the African climate changed dramatically, growing suddenly cooler and drier. In the fossil record we no longer find evidence of the small-brained *Australopithecus afarensis* and cousins, but instead at least two larger upright creatures: one (or two) robust varieties with huge teeth and jaws, apparently adapted to eating coarse vegetation

– *Australopithecus boisei/robustus*; the other smaller in frame ('gracile') and smaller-teethed, but with a larger brain, known to us as *Homo habilis*. There was, in evolutionary terms, a 'speciation' – the emergence of two (possibly three) separate species, distinct in morphology and apparently in behaviour. Archaeologists speculate that the two existed side by side, specialising in procuring food from different parts of the habitat, for as long as a million years.[5] The fact that the two species remained separate for all this time, without interbreeding, suggests strongly that they, and by implication their common ancestors, had no way of communicating with each other.[6] In our present state of knowledge, it would be justifiable to conclude that Australopithecines had a system of communication little developed beyond that of apes.

HOMO HABILIS AND HOMO ERECTUS

The global reduction in temperature and associated alterations in rainfall around 2.5 million to 2 million BP led to environmental changes in east and south Africa. It is about this time that *Homo habilis* fossils appear in the record (Vrba 1985, p. 66), and some time after that, about 1.7 million BP, fossils of *Homo erectus*. *Homo habilis* may be a transitional form between the Australopithecines and *Homo erectus*. Its brain size is variable, though larger than that of the early Australopithecines (see Leakey and Lewin 1992, pp. 110–12). The Oldowan tool culture associated with *Homo habilis* finds is very primitive, and it may even be that some Oldowan tools could have been made by Australopithecines. At the same time as *Homo habilis* appears, finds are made of large robust Australopithecines (Leakey and Lewin 1992, pp. 101–2), and smaller gracile Australopithecines disappear.

Homo erectus signals what is clearly a different species, more human in appearance, size, stature and culture. *Homo erectus* anatomy remains stable for a long time until about 250,000 BP (Rightmire 1985). It is on this species, the first unmistakable humans, that we shall focus.

Anatomy of Homo

Comparing *Homo erectus* to Australopithecines there is a number of key differences. There is less bulk for height, therefore greater relative surface area to lose heat. Long lower limbs give increased stride length, and a lower position of centre of gravity reducing inertia or drag when running. (Aiello, reported in Leakey and Lewin 1992, p. 196). *Homo* is bigger than the Australopithecines and the brain is noticeably larger, the hands more human and capable of the power grip (Clarke 1969, p. 9). The jaw and mandible are shorter than the Australopithecines', because hands are used more to obtain food and to manipulate objects.

Jaw and teeth reduction result in changes in dentition, and in the shapes of jaw, palate and nose. The hard palate (roof of the mouth), that is flat in apes started to arch. This may have been a consequence of a more varied diet, which would also further reduce the canines in males.

Sexual dimorphism reduced

Between *Homo habilis* and *Homo erectus* and throughout the *Homo erectus* period there is evidence of an increase in the relative size of females. Some explain this increase as due to environmental factors, such as adjustment to heat (Wheeler 1992) or as a response to the stress of parturition (Aiello forthcoming, p. 11). Reduced sexual dimorphism may be a direct consequence of the transition in habitat – from woodland to savannah – and no more than that (Aiello forthcoming, p. 11). However the increase in female size indicates that they must have been obtaining more high-quality food than previously. *Homo erectus* ate more meat than any modern primate. And this change in diet could well be explained as the result of increasing levels of social co-operation, of food-sharing (Aiello forthcoming; Ragir 1994).

Brain size

Homo erectus' brain is larger than the Australopithecine brain (900 cc, going up to 1100 cc). Its skull is human in appearance, with a relatively flat face and high-domed cranium, but prominent brow ridges, sloping forehead and heavy jaws. Over a million years the brain size stays relatively steady, though there is an illusion of average brain growth, due to the increase in female body size mentioned above, while male brains probably remained about the same (Aiello forthcoming).

The brain cooling system changed markedly between the early Australopithecines and *Homo habilis*. Endocasts show traces of blood vessels on the inner skull, which suggests that *Homo* species were more efficient than Australopithecines when it came to physical exertion, or long-distance running (Falk 1980b).

Tools and technology

Homo habilis and *Homo erectus* are associated at first with Oldowan tools – tools with a single face – and later with Acheulean, bifaced tools. It is presumed that other simple forms of technology were part of the Acheulean culture. Evidence suggests that *Homo erectus* made containers, shelters, clothing, traps; and started to use fire; in other words a level of cultural achievement well beyond anything that apes are capable of (Campbell 1988, p. 318; Wynn 1988, p. 280). *Homo erectus* tool-manufacturing is often done at a time and place remote from those where the tool is finally used. There are clearly identified sites where tool-making goes on.[7]

The Acheulean biface (or 'hand-axe') is found from about 1.5 million BP. A tool made by chipping stone from two sides to produce a sharp edge, it is symmetrical, regular in form; it fits neatly into the hand; it is found in Africa and the Levant, but not in Europe and south-east Asia until some considerable time later – between 0.7 and 0.5 million BP, possibly in association with archaic *Homo sapiens*. In the areas where it was used, it hardly changed over a period of a million years What it was used for is not quite clear. Suggestions include a cutter of flesh, a sharp discus for knocking out prey, a kind of all-purpose chopper, or even a digging tool (Gibson and Ingold 1993, pp. 33–4). It is not easy to make – as Toth and Schick (1993) have shown in their own attempts to reproduce the technique.

Homo erectus spread from Africa into Europe and Asia. This geographical spread in itself is evidence for their capacity to adapt limited technology to a variety of uses (Marshack 1989, p. 30).

Homo erectus as hunters

Homo erectus were probably not great hunters – the early hunting hypothesis is now discounted. They are more likely to have been scavengers or foragers, and one of the purposes of their first stone tools may well have been for cutting the flesh of thick-skinned carcasses. However, there may not be a hard and fast line between hunting and scavenging. It is not so romantic to discover that our ancestors had a lot in common with hyenas, but they were probably in direct competition with them, as suggested by the fact that many carnivore species such as wild dogs decreased in numbers after 2 million BP (Klein 1989, p. 182).

Children

Homo habilis and *Homo erectus* females have a larger pelvis than apes. Tooth-eruption patterns appear to be delayed among young *Homo habilis* and *Homo erectus*. These two factors suggest a continuation of the trend to infant helplessness, and prolongation of childhood, that started among Australopithecines. The *Homo erectus* birth canal was probably smaller than the modern human, suggesting that *Homo erectus* babies were born helpless like modern humans. Leakey and Lewin show that babies tripled their brain size between birth and maturity – the modern human ratio (Leakey and Lewin 1992, p. 161; see also Milo and Quiatt 1993, p. 571) – and that while the brain grew quickly, the body (including face and jaws, therefore teeth) grew relatively slowly until adolescence. The Turkana boy, an early *Homo erectus*, was reckoned by Leakey to have been weaned at less than 4 years and to be sexually mature at 14–15 years (Leakey and Lewin 1992, p. 143). He concludes that the length of childhood was extended over the *Homo erectus* period – because of culture; more had to be learned.

The human factor

To Leakey, *Homo erectus* is a landmark, standing at the dawn of humanity. All before *Homo erectus* is ape-like (except maybe *Homo habilis*), all after is more and more human.

Clearly something quite dramatic happened in the period around 2.5 million BP, as a result of which some Australopithecines became extinct, some evolved into large, more robust species, and from somewhere, either from Australopithecines or from an earlier ancestor, emerged the first representatives of the genus *Homo*.[8] What could have been the factor that enabled early forms of *Homo* to survive a natural catastrophe and to set out along the path of humanity? By now it is not only bipedality, since we have both *Homo* and upright Australopithecines. Some Australopithecine species survived by adapting physically, becoming more robust, and specialising apparently in chewing tough vegetation. The gracile *Homo habilis* had no such physical adaptation. If anything they grew less robust, but their brain size increased. To what use was this increased brain capacity put?

The best suggestion we can find is a new form of social behaviour organised round the practice of sharing food – meaning, specifically, males sharing food with females, and with children. Bearing in mind that babies are born smaller and more vulnerable among hominids than among apes and that they have a longer period of dependency, greater need of care from adults, and more social skills to learn, this would be a critical development that would enable hominids to survive what appears to have been a catastrophe between two and three million years ago (Foley 1994). Burke Leacock makes the point:

> Institutionalized specialization by sex must have been critical somewhere along the line of human emergence. A lengthening period of childhood dependency accompanied growing reliance upon tool manufacture, increasing learning capacity and expanding co-operation, and this prolongation of childhood had important implications for group composition and optimum size. My point is that to meet the problems this posed – or to take advantage of the potentials it offered – the institutionalization of exchange between women and men . . . was the revolutionary solution. (Burke Leacock 1981, p. 229)

The helplessness of babies, combined with the ability of adult *Homo erectus* to travel long distances, implies that the needs of nursing mothers and therefore the survival of the species required a different form of organisation than a large herd chasing around searching for food.

Foley and Lee note that by 1.6 million BP, hominids – both men and women –. are eating more meat than any extant primate. This implies male co-operation in food acquisition. They deduce that social organisation must have been marked either by alliances of males to prevent fighting over females, or by specific male–female links, perhaps polygamous (Foley and Lee 1989, p. 905). In other words, either the herd changed in composition to produce increased co-operation or some form of family organisation started to emerge from the herd.

The home base and the generation taboo

From the herd life of the Australopithecines, a new form of social organisation must have evolved. We can only guess how it came about; but a number of archaeologists have suggested that a feature of *Homo erectus* life was the establishment of temporary camps or 'home-bases'.[9] At some sites evidence has been found of rudimentary shelters, circles of stones, and so on.[10] It is suggested that at these sites nursing mothers and children, possibly accompanied by the old and the sick, would feed on locally available sources of food, while other adults would forage farther afield for plant food and, increasingly, for meat. The result would be the division of the herd into two groups, one staying at the base, foraging for nearby foods, the other travelling out to forage at a further distance. The exchange of food gathered by the two groups would thereby become a central feature of social life.

This elementary division of labour (or it might better be termed 'separation of labour' – different groups doing basically the same thing but in different places), solves a number of problems, such as the long period of child care, care of the sick, increased productivity of food. The increased dependency of the young on their mothers makes the choice of a mate more important for women, and this may have led to the gradual emergence of a taboo against cross-generation mating. It would simply make more economic sense for a woman to choose as a mate (or mates) a fit young man (or men) who could cover long distances in search of food, particularly in view of short life expectancy. From the point of view of the men, any potential jealousy over who has access to females while they are away is overcome by the taboo on older men mating with the women at the home-base. This would be a first step to some form of social organisation, language, rules of social behaviour, awareness of 'right' and 'wrong'. Many archaeologists and anthropologists see such a level of sophistication as emerging much later in human history – only with modern-type humans in fact (Binford 1985; 1989; Davidson and Noble 1989; Mellars 1991; Milo and Quiatt 1993). But they then have great difficulty both in explaining what humans were doing for millions of years, and in explaining how the change from ape to human happened when it did.

How taboos are relevant to language

Home-base organisation would provide the economic basis for the first form of family that Engels and Morgan identified[11] – the generation marriage, the product of a kinship division by generations.

It has to be acknowledged that there is no indisputable evidence for such a development and that the suggestions of Morgan and Engels have been strongly criticised in the past. The subject is, however, closely connected to that of the development of language as a product of social life (Armstrong, Stokoe and Wilcox 1995, p. 223), for the following reasons.

1. Chimpanzees have no institutional taboos, modern humans have; therefore some explanation is called for. Chimpanzees may have ways of avoiding incest, for example, adolescents may change groups. It would probably have been harder for hominids to do so in close-knit groups out on the savannah. Human populations were very small in the past, and therefore there must have been strong pressure on humans for incestuous mating.[12] For society, and for co-operation to develop, some way had to be found of overcoming the twin problems of jealousy and genetics.

2. No better or more logical proposal has been put forward than that of Morgan/Engels. The mechanism for this form of marriage is simple – one rule explains it: the generation taboo, a rule with a sound socio-economic basis. With the first form of family would come the institution-alisation of practices associated with sharing food and raising the young.

3. The relevance of this development to language is clear. Kinship leads to naming of individuals in respect of their social roles. The first such names would be *mother*; *father*; *parent* – *daughter*; *son*; *child*. These ideal forms, symbolising the rules and relationships of the emerging system of kinship, would be much more than simple labels; they would provide a new organising principle for social life.

4. As we shall see in Chapter Seven, the second step is as simple as the first, and brings us easily to the stage of humanity.

Language in this period

There are still many widely differing views as to whether *Homo erectus* had language or not, ranging from those who believe that *Homo erectus* could speak, to those who hold that language and cognitive planning hardly existed until anatomically modern humans. A number of points suggest that *Homo erectus* were at a particular transitional stage of language development.

There is evidence for social organisation around activities requiring tools and for social institutions presupposing language. There can be no doubt that the needs of child-rearing presuppose some kind of social organisation related to the sharing of food, such as organisation around temporary home-bases. This division of labour would inevitably lead to the development of forms of communication.

Homo erectus spread through much of the Old World, with recognisably similar anatomical features and, in some places, Acheulean tools. If there had been no communication between hominid groups, we should expect evidence of speciation. Few archaeologists claim to find such speciation.

At the end of this period, when brain size started to increase, there was no division among the various *Homo erectus* groups into distinct species. Instead archaeologists recognise a variety of anatomical specimens in different parts of the world, combining features of *Homo erectus* and modern humans. This is indirect evidence for inter-group contacts, without which speciation would have been likely.

Such contacts were not apparently happening among Australopithecines. When life got hard, they were not able to share their experiences. Survival was down to those whose bodies changed, rather than those who passed on lessons of survival from their ancestors. At the transition between *Homo erectus* and *Homo sapiens*, evidence points to a variety of transitional forms that archaeologists have grouped together under the catch-all phrase 'archaic *Homo sapiens*', all with one thing in common – increasingly large brains. After a certain period no fossils are found with brains as small as *Homo erectus* anywhere in the world. If a geographical or linguistic separation had caused *Homo erectus* in one part of the world to become cut off from other hominids, we would expect to find fossils of different species, with different brain sizes – but this does not appear to have happened.

The conclusion that has to be drawn is that by the end of *Homo erectus* period there were systematic contacts between human groups in all parts of the world. There was one species, with geographical variations.[13] As among modern foraging groups, they must have had agreements over access to land, exchanged gifts, exchanged information, even personnel, and so on. However, communication was clearly not as effective as modern human languages, as we see in the case of the Acheulean hand-axe.

Tools and language

It has proved difficult to make any general deductions about intelligence and language from tools, though a number of studies have suggested a common neural substrate for tool use, and language,[14] but in the case of the distribution of Acheulean tool technology we have quite specific evidence of the relation between technology and language.

The lack of apparent innovation over a period of approximately a million years has been put forward as an argument against language among *Homo erectus*. It is argued that skills may have been passed on by imitation alone (Davidson and Noble 1989; 1993). Instruction by imitation, it is said, reinforces conservatism, whereas talking about a technique may lead to innovation.

The interesting fact about Acheulean bifaces is that they are found in some parts of the world in association with *Homo erectus* fossils but not in others (for example, Europe), until a great deal later. The key factor determining the presence or otherwise of Acheulean tools seems to be the presence of suitable materials for their manufacture. Toth and Schick argue:

> The different patterns of cultural diffusion during population migrations in the case of *Homo erectus* and the Acheulean, and in the case of the late Pleistocene spread of modern peoples into Australia and North America, may show something very important not only about the culture of these two hominid forms but also about their communication systems. Even if biface technology was learned primarily through demonstration and non-verbal communication it may well have depended for its long-term survival on verbalized knowledge and traditions to carry it through times and places in which the necessary raw material was unavailable or its location undiscovered. *Homo erectus* may well have been deficient in the ability to verbalize the traditions of Acheulean technology sufficiently to pass such accumulated knowledge on to succeeding generations in a verbal rather than a demonstrative way. (1993, p. 35)

The implication is that the importance of language for the technique of tool-making is not in the matter of teaching the skill, which can still today be done by showing how rather than by explaining. Where language makes a difference is in an oral (or gestural-sign) tradition, capable of conserving and transmitting the lessons of past generations, beyond the point where tool-making materials are temporarily unavailable. It seems from the evidence that such a tradition was not established among early *Homo erectus* cultures, and on the basis of the spread of Acheulean technology, not until between 700,000 and 500,000 BP.

Homo erectus and language

The possibility of a gestural language among *Homo erectus* has been proposed by a number of writers from various fields (Lock 1983; Donald 1991; Jaynes 1976; Hewes *passim*; Milo and Quiatt 1993). Donald's is the best worked-out proposal of these. He suggests a language based on what he calls 'mimesis', something that is different from imitation and mimicry in that it involves the invention of intentional representations, as in, for example, pantomime (Donald 1991, p. 171). 'Language is not necessary for the development of complex social rules, but mimesis is essential' (1991, p. 175). Mimesis is the basis of group co-ordination. In the absence of words and symbols, thought is pretty well limited to the act of event-modelling and representation; no further analysis is possible' (1991, p. 176).

However, Donald's proposal of a 'mimetic controller' in the brain, which he considers necessary to account for the break with egocentricity that underlies the initial development of communication, is both unlikely and superfluous. There is no need to propose an unmotivated biological mutation to explain what is entirely explicable in terms of the development of activity to the point where humans focus jointly on events and objects that are of social value to them. The requirement to co-operate in activity not only makes possible an increase in the ability to control the environment. It also leads to the basis of mimesis – the recognition of the importance of other members of the group, of their actions, and of the objects of their action, to one's own individual survival.

ARCHAIC *HOMO SAPIENS*

After a million years or more of *Homo erectus*, a further change in climate between 0.9 and 0.5 million BP led to a series of changes in the hominid populations. The remaining Australopithecines became extinct,[15] and among *Homo erectus* a phase of brain-size increase, and other anatomical changes, led into the transitional types generally labelled archaic *Homo sapiens*.

This period was once perceived as two leaps, from *Homo erectus* to archaic *Homo sapiens*, including the Neanderthals, and then a subsequent leap to anatomically modern humans at about 50,000 BP, but that picture is changing as the origin of moderns is progressively being pushed back to round 200,000 BP. It now seems more accurate to say that modern humans were one variety emerging from a long transitional period (Donald 1991, p. 201).

During the transition, from perhaps 400,000 BP, brain size started to grow, and smaller-brained hominids disappear from the record. Transitional types appear in Africa, Asia and Europe, showing modern features mixed with archaic ones, like brow ridges. Specimens found in Java, Beijing, Heidelberg in Germany, Broken Hill in southern Africa, Petralona in Greece, are all examples of intermediate types. Leakey's description of the Petralona find illustrates this mixture of features:

> Petralona . . . is older than any Neanderthal, possibly dating to about 300,000 years ago. It has a big brain, about 1250 cc, which is a hundred less than that of the average living human; its face is thrust forward less than in *Homo erectus* but more than in modern humans; its brow ridges are less prominent than *Homo erectus* but more than in modern humans; the cranial bone is thick. A good mix of old and new, an apparent mosaic of features. (Leakey and Lewin 1992, pp. 209–210)

The question is whether these transitional types should be considered as separate species. The case for 'speciation' is weak.[16] Whereas the transition from Australopithecus to *Homo habilis/Homo erectus* conforms to Gould's picture of bush-like growth – both speciation and extinction of species, the transition to archaic *Homo sapiens* takes on quite a different appearance – of a whole species undergoing a tortuous change in anatomy, as a variety of routes are followed of adaptation to the need to accommodate a larger brain.

The fact that clearly separated species cannot be identified throughout this period, and that transitional types are found in all three continents of the Old World, suggests strongly that hominid groups are in contact, and genetic features are being exchanged between the groups, so that speciation cannot easily take place.

The number of humans in the world at this time was extremely small – maybe a million individuals in all (Rouhani 1989, 49). Therefore contacts between groups would have been a matter of some importance.

During this transition, one group of *Homo* – the Neanderthals – got cut off from the rest of the world in western Europe by ice-sheets, surviving for 100,000 years or more. The apparent specialisation of the Neanderthals and the subsequent disappearance of Neanderthal features around 30,000 BP are evidence of what might have happened at the earlier period, had inter-group communication not already been established.

Technology

Around 250,000 BP the improvements marking the Mousterian tradition in stone tools – the 'core and flake' technique – start to appear. This technique involves preparing a core, then knocking flakes off the core, either by precise punching or applying pressure. Archaeologists who have attempted to replicate these tools find that it takes a lot of learning:

> Experiments with graduate students show that whereas one day and simple imitation and observation are enough to learn how to make the earlier type of simple tools, it takes more than one semester and specific instruction to master the core-and-flake technique. (Lieberman 1991, pp. 159–60)

Complexity of tools and technology does not ultimately provide conclusive evidence for either social complexity or cultural development, but it gives an idea of the level of manual and therefore mental skill attained by archaic *Homo sapiens* in the Mousterian. Other evidence of cultural achievements – control of fire, construction of shelters, preparation of animal hides for clothing – are strongly suggestive of well developed social organisation and culture, based on co-operative labour and hence some form of language.

Marshack has assessed the level of skill involved in such achievements as the construction of a shelter based on posts in holes by archaic *Homo sapiens* at Terra Amata, around 300,000 to 400,000 BP:

> The pre-Mousterian structure at Terra Amata, therefore, suggests planned activity, practical and symbolic, the presence of some sort of cognitive map and model of the functional, cultural territory that was structured in time and space, the use of diverse materials and technolo-

gies, and use of the 'hole' and perhaps the container. (Marshack 1989, p. 12)

Fire, diet and anatomy

While there is some evidence of use of fire among *Homo erectus*, the consistent control of fire appears during the transitional period (Ragir 1985; 1994; Strauss 1989, p. 490; de Grolier 1989, p. 90). Second to stone tools, the control of fire is probably the most significant human technology. Fire externalises part of the digestive process; not only making meat easier to digest, but also vastly increasing the range of vegetable foods that can be eaten. Brain-size increase at this transition could be related to increases in animal protein in the diet and more energy-efficient food preparation. Long-chain fatty amino acids are essential for brain development (Ragir 1994), and there is no doubt that fire makes such vital food elements more easily available.

So growth of the human brain is a result of human technique – a wonderful illustration of the truth that 'Humans made themselves.' The human brain seems to have stabilised at the modern size by about 300,000 BP in late *Homo erectus*/early *Homo sapiens*, though some Neanderthal fossils have slightly larger brains even than modern humans.

Social effects of fire

Fire solves the so-called 'problem' of male selfishness, which often vexes those who see humans as intrinsically competitive. Their problem is to explain how, once the techniques of hunting are acquired by humans, women can ensure that male hunters bring back their meat to be shared. This problem has led to a number of fanciful accounts (such as the sex-strike theory (Knight 1991)), which become redundant when you realise that once the human body becomes accustomed to eating cooked meat, it is not possible for it to digest raw meat any more. Hunters, having been reared to eat cooked meat, could not keep meat to themselves, even if they wanted to, as long as fire-tending was the province of the women at the home-base. Aiello points out:

> With the use of fire for cooking, females acquired, perhaps for the first time, through control of food preparation, systematic access to meat. Easy-to-digest higher-protein diets for females not only reduced the size dimorphism between adult males and females but also maximised foetal growth, resulting in increased cranial volume and body size in both sexes. (Aiello 1993, quoted by Ragir 1994, p. 589)

And Ragir argues:

> Controlling fire for cooking marks the first undeniable evidence for modern human social organization – the accumulation of food,

sexual-based division of labor and redistribution of produce. (Ragir 1994, p. 13)

Fire is also, of course, an indirect form of evidence of the use of language as a psychological tool. Bickerton (1990, p. 141) makes the point that it is hard to imagine fire being handled by a species with no system of signs, to overcome fear and panic. Language would 'uncouple stimulus and response'. We use language to overcome our own nature as well as our environment. To overcome fire we also had to overcome our instinctive fear. The reaction of the chimpanzee, Sherman, to an indoor sparkler, signing 'straw give scare', suggests the instinctive reaction that had to be overcome (see p. 49). It is probable that forms of language would have arisen arose around fire-keeping and fire-making, to conserve and transmit details of this crucial technology.

Thus archaic *Homo sapiens*, between 400,000 and 200,000 BP, developed a technology to help survival in glacial conditions, and make possible survival in Ice Age Europe.

Archaic Homo sapiens *and cooking*

Fire and cooking contributed to further anatomical changes. At the beginning of this period, the rib cage appears to change from tent-like to barrel-shaped, a change that has been associated with the advent of cooking and the reduction of demands on the digestive system (Aiello 1993, quoted by Ragir 1994, p. 11). Fire may also have had an influence on the evolution of speech. The mouth, teeth and jaws have less work to do once food is cooked, so the jaw reduces further, reshaping the face. A more generalised diet also means the mouth is less specialised, leading probably to increased flexibility of the tongue (Brace 1979; Wind 1976; 1989). Laitman (1983), considers that archaic *Homo sapiens* around 300,000 BP had the vocal apparatus requisite for human speech.

Archaic Homo sapiens *and language*

We have seen that at the end of the long *Homo erectus* a period of brain-size increase led to humans with modern-size brains. We know that brain tissue is expensive to maintain – it requires, above all, protein. Therefore the species must have needed that extra brain capacity, and we have to ask what were they using it for? Clearly a whole range of new social activities must characterise archaic *Homo sapiens* life – the building of shelters, making of fires, and other skills become a regular part of life.

Are these activities evidence for language? There seems little doubt about it. Perhaps the most revealing activity is tool-making, where we can compare the distribution of the Acheulean hand-axe and the Mousterian core-and-flake technique associated with the later stages of the archaic transition. The fact that the Mousterian core-and-flake technology spreads across large parts of the world, whereas Acheulean hand-axe technology seems to stop short where materials to demonstrate techniques on are missing, is suggestive of the kind of advance that must have taken place in communication in this period.

A true transition

We have seen that at the end of the long and stable period of *Homo erectus* a number of changes were taking place among human populations across the Old World, changes that foreshadow modern human existence: a sophisticated tool-making technique, the control of fire, the development of technologies of construction, clothes-making, and so on – the development of inter-group contacts and clear evidence of a sexual division of labour. Diet improved, brain size and bodily proportions approached modern human form, while the picture of child growth approached the modern pattern.

These were unmistakably human people. We do not know whether they were speaking languages like ours, but there are strong suggestions that they had the capability to do so, and certainly that they had some form of oral/manual sign tradition of conserving and transmitting information across generations.

NOTES

1. Wheeler (1990; 1992) estimates that there was a 60 per cent reduction in heat absorbed when primates adopted upright gait.
2. Campbell (1988, p. 324) estimates that the modern human body has between two and five million sweat glands.
3. Among *Homo erectus* the figure is 83% (Aiello 1994, p. 11); among humans 85% (Campbell 1998, p. 147).
4. For example, Macaca mulata monkeys have achieved 65% of adult cranial capacity at birth; chimpanzees 40%; humans only 23% (Gould 1977, pp. 371–2), whereas Australopithecines are estimated to have a capacity of between 25% and 37% (Leutenegger 1972, quoted in Ragir 1985, p. 456).
5. See, e.g. Leakey and Lewin (1992), who even suggests that the robust Australopithecine may have been hunted and eaten by *Homo* (1992, p. 171).
6. Tanner (1981) believes that there was some reduced sexual contact between gracile and robust Australopithecines (1981, pp. 257–8).
7. Woolfson mentions the site of Koobi Fora where tools have apparently been carried from elsewhere (1982, p. 13).
8. Foley (1994) shows that extinctions are often linked to catastrophic climatic changes, but speciations less frequently so.
9. Isaac (1979, pp. 112–13) argues that an important feature separating humans from primates is that they share food, at agreed locations or home bases, and that when they obtain food they postpone consumption in order to share it. Though Binford has disputed some of the evidence claimed to show the existence of 'homebases' (1989, p. 25), Isaac's principles still stand as defining characteristics of human society.
10. See Klein 1989, p. 403; Campbell 1988, pp. 238–42; Isaac 1979; Donald 1991,

p. 114; Hewes 1973, p. 67; and Milo and Quiatt 1993, p. 571. Leakey and Lewin's account of the debate over Site 50 at Karari ends with the conclusion that this was not just the accidental site of a kill but a temporary foragers' camp. However, Binford (1985; 1989) has contested the interpretation of these sites, suggesting that tool finds coincide only with places where tool use is required, such as vegetation that requires bashing, and not with early human residence (1989 p. 27).

11. Engels (1942), much of whose argument is based on Morgan (1877). The suggestion is dismissed by many, not for its implausibility but for lack of convincing evidence.

12. Rouhani (1989, p. 49) estimates population density in the archaic *Homo sapiens* period as 50 people per 500 square miles – one person per 10 square miles.

13. This 'multi-regional hypothesis' is argued by Wolpoff (1989a; 1992), but currently opposed to Wolpoff in the debate about single or multi-regional origins are, e.g. Bräuer (1989), Stringer (1989) and Binford (1989).

14. As suggested in Wynn (1993); Gibson and Ingold (1993); and Greenfield (1991).

15. Disagreements over the timing of Australopithecine extinction range from less than a million BP (Vrba 1985, p. 68) to 1.5 to 2 million BP (Milo and Quiatt 1993).

16. Cf. Rightmire (1985): 'It is not clear that any split giving rise to distinct contemporary species actually occurred' in the middle Pleistocene (1985, p. 261).

6

Origins of Speech

The question of speech origins is the one that has led to some of the most fanciful and bizarre theories. Yet this is a vital question for any theory of language origins.

Chapter 4 presented the case for gesture preceding speech. In fact the questions surrounding the origins of speech are the same whether we accept a gestural origin or not. If gesture came first, the question is why did speech replace it (Kendon 1991, p. 215)? If speech was the predominant form of language from the start, what were early forms of speech like?

Advantages of speech

Of course it is not difficult to demonstrate that spoken communication has certain advantages over gestural signing. Some immediate advantages are, for example:

1. speech is effective when your audience is looking away, or inattentive
2. speech is effective when your hands are occupied
3. speech is effective in the dark[1] and when the audience is out of sight
4. there is a limit on the number of gestural signs that can be created, but no practical limit on the number of spoken words that can be invented
5. the converse of the universality of natural gestures is their ambiguity
6. speech may require less energy than gesturing.

However, spelling out these differences does nothing to explain the origins of speech, or the transition proposed between gestural and spoken language, any more than spelling out the advantages of upright gait explains how we came to be walkers.

FOSSIL EVIDENCE FOR SPEECH

Could examination of fossils answer the question of how and when speech developed? Some have looked to evidence from fossil brains, for the development of the so-called speech areas in brain endocasts. These areas are not found in Australopithecine fossils (Falk 1980b), are rudimentary at the *Homo habilis* stage (Tobias 1987, p. 756), but are developed in *Homo erectus* and *Homo sapiens* (Falk 1980a; 1980b; Laitman, Reidenberg and Gannon 1992). However, while the development of these brain areas might show that language is starting to appear, it cannot of course differentiate between gesture and speech.

It was shown on p. 17 above that Broca's area in the brain is associated not only with the musculature of the mouth and throat, but also with generalised motor skills governing the arm, hand and fingers, rather than specifically speech organs. Lieberman argues that there are special brain mechanisms for the lips, tongue, vocal cords, larynx and lungs – specifically to do with speech (1991, pp. 82–3). But it is impossible to separate, for example, the use of the muscles of the mouth in speech from their use in facial expressions. The former might be said to be speech-related, the latter gesture-related. Given that we can be fairly sure that the growth of the brain was accompanied by a growth in neural connections between the parts of the brain active in language-processing, we have to conclude there is no evidence from the brain of when, where and how speech, as opposed to gesture, originated.

We come back to the question raised earlier: what does the brain do? It is part of the central nervous system, a massive storehouse for receiving and sending out signals – a processor of information. What the steady increase of brain size in evolution tells us is that individual hominids came to handle increasing amounts of information. At a certain point, however, the brain stopped expanding. The fossil record shows that the period when the brain stabilises is not at the stage of anatomically modern humans, but earlier, among the transitional archaic *Homo sapiens*.

Clearly we did not suddenly reach a point where the amount of information required for continued human survival stopped increasing; Humans today handle far more information than the archaic *Homo sapiens* forager, but with roughly the same size brain. So what happened at that historical point? If the individual brain ceased to expand, another form of memory must have appeared – an 'external memory store' – in other words, language. The point where human brains stop increasing, must be the point at which language is firmly established as a social practice.

The importance of a linguistic tradition

The collective knowledge of a group of humans is as effective a memory store as the individual brain, and much more long-lasting. The oral tradition – stories, myths, songs, rituals, spells, mnemonic forms, proverbs, and so on – stores and passes on information using all the brains of the group rather than placing the burden on the individual brain. Specialisation and division of labour in memorising make the process more efficient. Old people become good story-tellers – acting as the memory of the whole group, and contributing to collective activity beyond the age when they cease to be physically active themselves.

So was this the historical point when speech originated? We have to consider whether gestural signing could fulfil the functions that vocal, oral traditions fulfil among present-day foraging people. Think again about deaf signing. Deaf signers can tell stories, recite poetry, create names, tell jokes, trade insults, and so on. So while we can be sure that some kind of communicative tradition must have become an established part of behaviour, we still cannot be sure that it was based on speech. We have seen the strong support for the idea that *Homo erectus* communicated with gesture; among archaic *Homo sapiens* there are three possibilities – either a more developed form of gestural signing; or a language using signing and speaking together; or a form of spoken language.

Anatomical changes in the vocal tract

If we cannot infer speech from the brain, what about evidence of changes in the airways – the lungs, throat and mouth – found in fossils? We can trace a number of evolutionary changes in the mouth and the throat, some of them associated with the enlargement of the skull.

The lowering of the larynx in the throat

In the chimpanzee, the larynx or voice-box is high in the throat, so high that it can be drawn up to touch the roof of the mouth during swallowing. This enables the chimpanzee to breathe while swallowing food. Air passes from the nose through the larynx into the wind-pipe, while food passes down two channels at the side of the larynx into the gut. Pulleyblank puts it nicely – apes 'have no throat' (1983, p. 375).

Human babies are similar to apes in being able to breathe and swallow simultaneously, but after a few years our larynx starts to descend into our throat, and for ever after if we try to eat and breathe at the same time we are in danger of choking. The larynx is roughly level with the fifth vertebra in the adult male human, slightly higher in the female. The unusually long human throat is said to be important in producing the *quantal vowels* [i], [u] and [a][2] though it has to be said that the larynx is still fairly high in 5– and 6–year-old children, who seem to be able to produce these quantal vowels perfectly well.

The larynx is made of cartilage, not bone, and does not survive in fossils. Rather than observe laryngeal descent directly, its position is generally reconstructed (a scientific way of saying 'guessed') from measurements of the angle of basicranial flexion, derived from various points on the base of a fossil skull.[3] The conclusion of these measurements is that basicranial flexion, hence larynx position, among Australopithecines is no different from that of apes. Among *Homo habilis* and *Homo erectus* it starts to develop in the human direction, and human proportions are found among archaic *Homo sapiens* (Laitman, Reidenberg and Gannon 1992, p. 359) Correlation of basicranial flexion with lower larynx position, while not proof that archaic *Homo sapiens* spoke, certainly indicates that they could have done.

The course of basicranium development is not a smooth progression, unlike brain-size growth. Neanderthal basicranial flexion is apparently no more advanced than some *Homo erectus* specimens, representing a regression in respect of the angle of basicranial flexion,[4] oddly, since Neanderthals are assumed to have evolved from archaic *Homo sapiens*

But why did the larynx lower? We cannot be sure it was a result of speech – the first changes in basicranial flexion are observed among species for which there is no evidence of speaking. More likely explanations are: (a) the skull, growing in size to accommodate the increasing brain, pushed the larynx downwards; (b) standing upright, gravity caused the larynx to move downward, once the necessity for a high larynx was removed (i.e. no need for smell, so separated from epiglottis; no need to breathe and eat simultaneously – especially as food became easier to chew and masticate); (c) Negus argues that the backward passage of the tongue pushes the larynx down in the throat (quoted by Schepartz 1993, p. 99); (d) Krantz argues that laryngeal descent took place in two stages, the first noticed in archaic *Homo sapiens* (1988, p. 175). The result of this first stage of lowering was to enable 'easy and controlled exhalation though the mouth' (1988, p. 179). This change may well have had nothing to do with speech, being an adaptation to long-distance running, associated with pursuing game.[5] Taking in oxygen efficiently through the mouth would certainly have been a big enough advantage to outweigh the disadvantages of food passing over the opening to the windpipe. Our larynx still lowers in the throat, and our tongue retracts, when we inhale deeply.

Changes in the glottis

The glottis is the narrowing of the air-passage inside the larynx, the point at which voice is produced. The internal shape of the glottis is shown in Figure 6.1.

There are two points where the airway can be blocked – the upper and the lower thyroarytenoid folds. The glottis can function both as an inlet valve and an outlet valve. Air from the lungs can be stopped at the lower folds, but because of the shape of the walls of the airway at this point, and their soft flexible tissue, the folds are more likely to vibrate and produce the sound we know as voice. Lung air is stopped more effectively at the upper folds, which close together sharply, while air drawn inward from the mouth is more effectively stopped at the lower than the upper folds.

In climbing species, such as lemurs, monkeys, gibbons and chimpanzees, the inlet valve function of the lower folds is very important. The action of

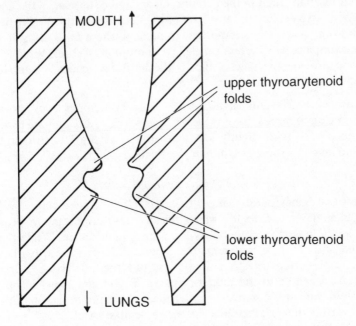

FIGURE 6.1: Cross-section of the glottis.

jumping from branch to branch and grasping with the forelimbs throws a strain on the chest muscles. If the lungs can be immobilised, to stop them either emptying or filling with air, the chest is strengthened. At the moment of grasping the branch, the glottis is closed, the lungs cannot fill and expand, and:

> there is reduction of pressure in the pleural spaces and the thorax . . . the result is immobilisation of points of origin in the pectoral muscles – i.e. a mechanical process to conserve energy, by increasing efficiency of forelimbs and relieving the abdominal muscles of strain. (Negus 1949, p. 106)

In the more terrestrial species – baboon, gorilla and human – this function of the larynx is less important, and therefore less effective (Negus 1949, p. 107).

The lower folds can also close and stop outgoing air, for mildly strenuous activities, such as lifting and for manual operations. Even for quite delicate operations we use these folds to hold our breath. Effort with the forelimbs is most efficient when the chest is half-full of air, but for greater exertions it is sometimes necessary to fill the chest and hold in the air, using the upper thyroarytenoid folds. The most important of such exertions is probably the pushing down that is necessary at childbirth. Other cases include the straining of constipation and the grunting of athletes (e.g. serving in tennis).

What has happened in the evolution from ape to human, is the development of a larynx suited to terrestrial tasks. Because the inlet-valve function of the lower folds is less important to us now, these folds are softer than in the chimpanzee, with less cartilage and more muscle (cf. Wind 1983, p. 22), and provide the voicing that is the basis for speech. Negus tells us that species:

> with very efficient valvular folds, such as Lemurs, most Monkeys, and Chimpanzees, have voices of a piercing quality and great volume, but others, with slightly less sharp folds, have a less strident voice, and amongst these [are humans]. (Negus 1949, p. 137)

Shape of jaw, teeth and tongue

Dietary and behavioural changes from the *Homo erectus* stage on, led to changes in jaws and teeth, which became less important in procuring food, as the hands (and tools) took on more importance. While the jaws reduced and the face flattened, the tongue did not reduce to the same extent, and started to take a shape less like the chimpanzee's long flat tongue and nearer to the modern human, round and bunched up when seen from the side. Omnivorous diet meant that the tongue had to cope with a variety of foods, and became more flexible (Aiello 1994, p. 13). As a result of the reduction of the jaws, the position of the tongue in the oral-pharyngeal cavity has altered such that it can be retracted towards the pharyngeal wall.

Changes in breathing

An interesting feature of the anatomy of *Homo erectus* from the point of view of speech is that its spinal column in the region of the lungs is relatively thin. In anatomically modern humans the neural canal that carries nerves along the spinal column is relatively thick, and it is suggested that this is because it has to carry a large number of nerves controlling the sophisticated movements of the lungs during speech.[6] The absence of this thickening of the spinal column suggests that the control of breathing required for speech would be difficult for *Homo erectus*.

Summing up, fossil evidence cannot tell us when speech appeared, but it suggests that it was probably not a feature of human communication before the archaic *Homo sapiens* period.[7]

THEORIES OF SPEECH ORIGINS

The following sections examine some theories of how speech might have become established as human behaviour. Notice that if gestural signing developed to a stage where humans had systems of communication based on a mixture of iconic and arbitrary signs, with some embryonic forms of grammar, the problem is not great – we do not have to account for syntax, semantics, brain areas specific to language, and so on – but a relatively simple task – explaining why communication came to be based predominantly on sound rather than gestural sign.

From animal call or birdsong

Some who see no clear dividing line between animals and humans suggest that speech may have developed from animal calls – in other words, that such calls persisted through millions of years, to be incorporated into human behaviour when meanings started to be exchanged.[8]. The implica‑ tion is that human vocal activity evolved from animals' instinctive cries (Pulleyblank 1983, p. 375). However, animal calls have a quite different function than human speech. They provide emotional release and social contact, as opposed to the linguistic function of representation (see Kozulin 1990, p. 153). These primitive functions can still be seen in human behavi‑ our, when we laugh, cry, scream with fear, gasp in response to pain, and so on. But these emotional, instinct-based vocalisations are not the roots of speech. Babies' crying does not develop into children's speech; it remains quite separate, and most humans have learnt to speak through sobbing or laughter. The only area of language that has come to be linked with our 'limbic' or emotional system is swearing. It is still very hard to swear silently. It may be that swearing is functionally associated with the suppres‑ sion of instinctive reactions such as crying aloud in response to pain.[9]

It is hardly to the point that monkeys and primates can produce very human-like sounds (Wind 92, p. 26), or that geladas can make human sounds or 'distinctive features' (Richman 1976). They cannot usually pro‑ duce them at will, but only in response to external stimuli; they cannot exchange messages – there is an unequal relationship between the monkey that produces a call and the rest of the group that responds; their calls are not structured into consonants and vowels the way that human speech is; and ironically the apes that are genetically closest to us, chimpanzees, are also those with the least human-sounding cries (cf. Kelemen 1948).

Speech from music, song and dance?

A related suggestion is that human speech derives from animal social behaviour, evolving into singing, music and activities such as the chanting and dancing that accompany ritual (Donald 1991, p. 38; Richman 1993).

The idea that human ritual (as practised among foraging people at significant moments, among religious groups, and so on) is a continuation of instinctive behaviour from animals has to be rejected. Animal collective singing has no meaning and no such individual psychological functions – 'vocal grooming' expresses it well![10] Human ritual, as we have already seen, is essentially re-enactment of significant activity – in other words, it is based on prior human activity, not instinctive behaviour.

Mimicry as source of speech?

Mimicry of animals, or natural phenomena (wind, thunder, water) is often suggested as a possible source of spoken language. The argument is based on chimpanzees' ability to imitate the behaviour of other creatures (though they cannot imitate sound well), and on the presence of some words in our language that are obviously imitations – *cuckoo, cock-a-doodle-doo* (Jespersen (1922, p. 413) terms this the *bow-wow* theory). The human respiratory/vocal tract is very good at imitating – we are probably the best animal mimics there are (better than parrots, because more versatile).

There is no doubt that imitation is a factor in the formation of words, both historically and today. But it is not sufficient cause in itself. For an imitation (gesture or sound) to become a sign, functioning in communication, would require joint attention of speaker and audience on the phenomenon to be imitated. Attention depends on two communicators sharing an interest in the phenomenon in question. So imitation of animals, for example, would only happen once we started depending on certain animals for food, whether scavenging, hunting, or competing with them – only when the animal or bird in question has become a solution to a joint problem. Such a focus of interest on the imitated phenomenon presupposes the development of collective activity, and therefore society to a certain level.

Motor (mouth-gesture) theory?

A more developed theory of imitation is the motor theory, or mouth-gesture theory of speech.[11] This proposes that there are basic elementary motor programmes from which all bodily movements are constructed, controlling the precise movements of the hand and arm. These programmes when redirected to the articulatory organs produce an equivalent set of elementary speech sounds.

Gestures of the hand and arm represent the contours of perceived objects or of larger bodily actions, and every gesture structured by a perceived or recalled object or action can be redirected to produce an equivalent articulatory action. So specific articulatory gestures generate specific phonetic utterances.

This is a well-worked out theory with a number of eminent protagonists. However, like the theory of imitation, the mouth-gesture explanation still requires the prior development of a joint focus of attention on the object. The object to be traced in the air by a manual gesture, or imitated in sound, or echoed in a mouth-gesture, has to first become the object of attention of a social group in order for it to enter their consciousness and their communication. Collective activity again has to develop to a certain level before individuals can develop gestural representations of the objects of their interest with the hand or the mouth.

Sound symbolism?

The motor theory of speech is a version of the more general theory of sound symbolism.[12] This theory suggests that speech originated in iconic forms, where the sound of the word is related to its meaning in some way, including not only imitation and onomatopoeia, but also relations between size, shape, location and sound. So, for example, a sequence of sounds like [pipi], in many languages of the world is associated with meanings like small, high-pitched. [kaka] would have connotations of large, lumpy. World-wide coincidences of sound and meaning are too frequent to be accounted for by chance, and Sapir (1929) showed in a series of experiments that speakers of different languages reacted to unfamiliar words in very similar ways that could be predicted on the basis of the relation of sound to meaning. Given a pair like [takete] and [maluma], the majority of people associate the former with a thin or spiky figure, and the latter with a round dumpy figure.

Nevertheless, this is no reason to suppose that spoken words were all formed on these principles. Iconic signs probably remain in the language because they are easy to remember (Englefield 1977, p. 51), or are felt to be appropriate in certain situations. In other situations, iconic forms are avoided. So in English we have the words *little*, which is iconic, and *small*, which is not. Sound symbolism reaches far into every language, and is probably responsible for many associations between what might appear remotely related terms. For example in the English final *-le*, with a linking meaning that is hard to define but is clearly there – the 'iterative' or 'repeating' meaning in *tickle, juggle, giggle, chuckle, wiggle, muddle*.

While the subject is one of great interest, it seems to apply very particularly to certain registers – nursery talk, expressive language – and not to be a central organising principle of language. The estimate that no more than 10 per cent of the vocabulary of any language is iconic in this sense (de Grolier's survey 1990, p. 145) seems about right, the proportion being roughly the same in spoken and gestural languages. Hewes comments: 'To be sure, mouth-gesture theory and sound-symbolism research still leave most of the postulated transformation from gestural to a vocal language unexplained' (Hewes 1973, p. 70).

Like imitation generally, sound symbolism would only affect an individual's choice of sounds when other aspects of social behaviour had progressed to a certain level – the level of a sufficient social awareness to be able to name objects of joint attention, to be able to imitate phenomena of joint interest, and to be able to distinguish individuals within the group on the basis of different social roles.

While there is no doubt that imitation and sound symbolism does play some role in languages, influencing word formation and word retention, these theories do not have sufficient explanatory power to account for the origin of speech as a medium, and certainly not for the origin of language as a system.

Secret languages?

A number of accounts of gestural origins, explain the transition to speech as the result of secrecy or conspiracy on the part of a small group. Englefield maintains that speech must have been the invention of a small group of people, as a secret, inaccessible code, based on the fact that whereas gesture is an iconic, public medium, speech is arbitrary in form, and would therefore lend itself to secrecy and mystery. For Marr, the original spoken language consisted of a small number of words, derived from tribal names,[13] and more recently Knight (1994) has proposed that speech was created secretly by women in devising ritual dances.

Englefield's account is worth examining in some detail, since it highlights the difficulty of explaining the transition from gesture to speech:

1. An exclusively vocal language cannot function in daily life until vocabulary has reached a critical size. So there is no question of a gradual replacement of gestural signs by spoken words.
2. Natural gesture signs are relatively easily understood, but the number of natural vocal signs (onomatopoeia, animal imitations, sound symbolism) and their restricted range of reference are insufficient to create a working vocabulary.
3. The bulk of spoken words are conventional, and have to be learnt. This implies a heavy memory load for both vocabulary and syntax.
4. If a spoken language is to be established it must be within a living generation. People who have not learnt to speak in childhood must agree within a short time to use signs with the same meaning, and use them frequently enough for them to stay in the memory, and be transmitted to the next generation.
5. Therefore, spoken language could not emerge gradually from gestural communication. It must in the first instance have been the work of a small group of people, who had time to spend together, and who had a common purpose, restricted enough for them to be able to develop a relatively small vocabulary of names and actions, and who wanted to keep their communications secret (Englefield 1977, p. 89).
6. Later this spoken language would be adopted by the whole group, replacing gestural signs.

Objections

The model of speech as an invention raises a number of difficulties.

1. Who exactly were the inventors? On this the proponents cannot agree. For Marr. it was druid-priests. For Knight it is the coalition of women, organising a 'collective deception' of men. For Englefield it is unspecified,

but the motivation is not magic. Marr's description depends on the interests of druid-priests differing from those of the rest of society – in other words, a class society before people could even speak. But if foraging society is accurately described as egalitarian, there will be no fundamental difference of interests between one group of people and another – and therefore no motivation for a secret language. Knight's model is based on a fundamental difference of interests between males and females – again, there is no evidence that this was the case in early human societies, or that it is the case in modern foraging societies.

2. The theory requires the inventors of speech to translate gestures into spoken words. Englefield rightly points out that the invention of new terms is not a normal feature of language. In so doing he puts forward the strongest objection to his own theory. In the history of natural human languages, neologisms are rare, and the majority of words are learnt from an older generation. Natural languages avoid synonymy, and do not duplicate words needlessly.

3. The model also requires the abandoning of previously established gestural signs. This too is hard to explain: why should people give up forms of language that are perfectly adequate for communication?

4. It is true that there are many attested cases of secret languages among both adults and children, where invention of words occurs and develops rapidly.[14] In Britain, Cockney 'rhyming slang' is still actively producing new forms today – indeed, for a secret language to remain secret it is forced continually to innovate. However, the problem here is that because it is secret its form is bound to be inaccessible and difficult, and therefore not suitable as a general medium of communication. Malinowski's description of magic language, with its 'coefficient of weirdness', makes this point. Halliday's study of anti-languages – the languages of outgroups, of the underworld, languages of beggars, thieves, and so on, interprets them as reflections, distortions of existing language (Halliday 1978, pp. 164–82). It follows that they cannot therefore be the origins of anything.

5. When we look for other areas of activity that lead to the invention of terms, we find that invention can and does occur, in any society, at any time, when a new form of social activity arises, leading to new forms of communication. This fact provides the solution to our problem. If spoken communication developed in connection with certain activities, at first restricted, while gesture continued to be used for traditional purposes and for a lingua franca, then the problem of wholesale replacement of gestured with spoken signs does not arise. Speech could have spread from specific communicative contexts, only slowly diffusing to other forms of communication. The next section considers which forms of activity may have led to the development of spoken forms of communication.

SPEECH AS ACTIVITY

We have seen that a number of theories that seek to explain the origin of language have had to be rejected as partial explanations. Many of them could provide possible explanations for processes of word formation, but they do not seem adequate as explanations of the origins of speech. All seem to take the position that speech, language and meaning, all emerged at once. But this is not necessarily so, and speech is much more likely to have evolved in a long slow process, with many of the key developments happening long before spoken language emerged. Englefield recognises that 'we cannot explain how humans could "adapt" a form of behaviour which did not exist' (1977, p. 86), so must assume that the sounds of speech were at least in part available before the time came for them to appropriate to the needs of the community.

The first consideration then, before the question of the association of sound with sense, is the simple emergence of the human capacity ot produce sounds that would be recognised as speech. An evolutionary account, taking as its starting point the capabilities of apes, has to explain:

1. how vocalisation came to be freed from instinct and brought under the voluntary control of individuals. This is in part a question of anatomy, but we also have to account for things like the control of muscular movements governing breathing and the pitch, volume and rhythm of vocalisations;

2. how the structure of human vocalisations, with their characteristic cv form developed. Note that chimpanzee vocalisation may have a rhythmic structure, but it is not cv organised. Rhythm in chimps' cries, for example their pant-hoots, is often a product of alternate inward and outward breathing,[15] whereas human speech is based on the rhythmic alternation of vowels (unrestricted flow of voiced sounds through the mouth) and consonants (obstruction of air-flow at some point in the airway);

3. how structured phonetic syllables came to be used to convey contrastive meanings.

In all three of these developments, the most instructive path to take is to focus on the development of social activities.

Vocalisation freed from instinct

Looking first at three possible activities that might lead to early hominids gaining control over their vocalisations: intimidation; calling; and co-ordination.

Self-defence and intimidation

The ability of chimpanzees to turn on a display of noise to drive away predators has already been noted on p. 57. A chimpanzee display is not totally under control, since the individual first needs to be 'hyped up'. However it is quite easy to appreciate the way that the circumstances of a foraging life would encourage control of vocalisation to drive away predators or rival scavengers from a carcass, gradually bringing it under individual control.

It is suggested that archaic *Homo sapiens* may have organised mass hunts, using the technique of 'driving' animals into places where they could be immobilised and killed. Hunting by driving is an adaptation of the intimidatory effect of sound on other creatures. It is still debatable whether such hunts took place or not. If they could be established beyond doubt, we would have clear proof of control of intentional vocalisation – without which such a hunting technique would not be possible.

Ohala has suggested that the enlargement of the human male larynx and consequent deepening of the male voice – a feature not observed among apes – may have had the evolutionary function of creating the impression of a large powerful creature, related to the need to drive off other species. (Ohala 1983; 1984).

Calling

Calling at a distance is observed among groups of chimpanzees, and it would certainly have continued among early hominids, especially in the dangerous habitat of the savannah. Calling would grow in importance when, among *Homo erectus,* foraging groups started to travel out from a home-base.

Co-ordinating activities

The co-ordination of work is another area of human activity which would encourage speech, since gesture is more or less ruled out when the hands are engaged in work and attention is on the immediate task. In such circumstances noise both as a way of attracting attention and as a way of co-ordinating activities would be favoured. Here, clearly the more advanced co-operative techniques and social organisation become, the greater the predisposition to co-ordinate with sound.

Though these three activities would lead to control by individuals of sound-making ability, they do not imply structured speech. Nor do they suggest how the organisation of the syllable in terms of cv structure might have originated.

The structure of human vocalisations
cv structure: why is it important?

Speculating on the possible nature of the first meaningful sounds, there are two forms these words might take. On the one hand, there is a great variety of distinct sounds that our anatomy can make, sounds that are a part of our conscious repertoire of sounds, but are not structured in consonants and vowels in the same way as words. We can and do make a variety of non-linguistic interjections, expressed in print as 'tut', 'phew', 'ouch' (a sharp intake of breath), and so on. It is quite easy to think up fifty or more such interjections, not including imitations of animals, machines, and so on. Any individual might have at their disposal around a hundred or so such *quasi-signs*.

By contrast, true words are structured in terms of a few simple consonants and vowels, the number varying from one language to the next, but averaging between thirty and forty. From this limited number of sounds vast numbers of words can be constructed. Even languages with simple phonological structure have vocabularies of thousands of words.

Quasi-signs are generally expressive of emotional reactions to a situation – annoyance, amusement, pleasure – though they are more under control than the clearly emotional reactions of laughing, crying, and so on. Now the question is whether speech might have emerged from these quasi-signs, or whether, from the start, it consisted of structured sound. Jespersen suggested that early utterances were totalities – sentences rather than words – and that therefore the first vocal forms would also be totalities, articulatory gestures such as quasi-signs (Jespersen 1922, p. 421).

But if we consider that human activity has the function of establishing order in the world, we should expect communication based on such activity to seek to create order out of the complex of sound types available to the human anatomy.

It is observed that the babbling that precedes the infant's first words, appears to grow out of a period of relatively unstructured sound production (cooing), resolving eventually into the form of repeated syllables of cv form – syllables like [dadada], [gugugu], [wowowo]. Whereas cooing is simple vocal activity, analogous to babies' kicking of legs and waving of arms, babbling is directed, conscious activity of the articulators.

Babbling is not language, any more than play is real activity, or singing is speech, but it is arguable that it provides a necessary preliminary stage of ordering and structuring sound production. Infants' babbling suddenly ceases when the child starts to attempt consciously to make words and meanings.

We therefore suggest that early humans would learn to produce structured cv syllables before they started using them for meaningful communication, and that once speech began, words would be structured in consonants, vowels and semivowels, as modern languages are. But we have now to explain the prior stage where hominids learnt to control their sound output – to play around with sounds until they learnt to alternate vowel and consonant.

Where do vowels come from?

There is little problem in explaining the origin of the vowels we use in speech. Many, though not all, are present in a primitive form in chimpanzee vocalisations. In de Waal's study of bonobo vocalisations we find the following functional descriptions: low hooting, both ingressive and egressive; high hooting: pant-hoot; high-pitched whooping; wiew-bark: contest hooting: greeting grunts; panting laugh; pout moan 'hoo hoo'; whistle-bark; food peep associated with foraging and feeding; alarm peep; peep yelp; scream (de Waal 1988). All these are vocalic type sounds – no hint of a consonant here. The vowels appear from de Waal's description to be formed in a way similar to human [o], [a], [e].[16]

The activities we have considered above – calling, intimidation and co-ordinating – all require considerable volume. Vowel-like sounds therefore appear as carriers of sound, possibly with pitch and rhythmic variation.[17] The use of noise for intimidation would require the loudest possible noise – opening the mouth wide, to produce a sound like [aa], or, if the vocalisation started while the mouth was not fully open, [wa].

A sound that is often associated with distal calling is a long rounded back vowel [o]. This may be associated with an extension of the lips (protrusion and rounding) in the direction of those being called – pointing with the lips, as it were.

Sounds that accompany work may take a different form. We have seen that one anatomical feature that may distinguish chimpanzee and human is the human ability completely to close the glottis (Aiello and Dean 1990, p. 240–1), the action we perform when we hold our breath to carry out a conscious, delicate movement. One vocalisation which may have developed from this is the syllable that we associate with strenuous effort [hə], produced by initially closing the glottis, then releasing the air from our lungs, to produce the consonant [h]. As the flow of air slows slightly the vocal cords in the glottis start to vibrate together, producing a vowel, something like the central, neutral quality vowel [ə].

We see then that it is not a great problem to suggest routes by which at least three distinctive vowels might find their way into the vocal activities of our ancestors.

Where do consonants come from?

It is a somewhat harder problem to suggest how consonants might emerge from the vowel-dominated sound activity of hominids at the Australopithec-ine or *Homo erectus* stages. We cannot suppose that consonants came out of nowhere to start signifying meanings. We need to look for an activity that will lead to the emergence of consonants.

Children's babbling and its rhythmic basis may provide the clue. In babbling, vowels follow one another in succession, and the function of the consonant is at first merely a divider, a trough between two crests, breaking the vowels up into rhythmic units. From what are at first rather variable articulatory movements in the mouth, the infant gradually establishes sufficient articulatory control to be able to produce consistent consonants between the vowels, and simple syllable structure is established.

The route to control of consonants must then have emerged from some kind of rhythmic sound-based activity, in other words singing or chanting (As Richman (1993) suggests). Music among humans is a controlled, and therefore learned, activity; not a development of the ape's instinctive reaction to excitement, but based on conscious, intentional activity. While there is not scope here to consider the complex question of the function of music in human society, it is clear that rhythmic forms of activity have always tended in human history to be accompanied by patterned forms of sound.

Regulating social and individual activity

The suggestion that work-based chants and songs may be the origin of speech was made originally by Noiré (1917; see also Thomson 1975), and characterised by Jespersen as the *yo-he-ho* theory (1922, p. 415). While we do not suggest that such activity could lead immediately to meaningful use of sounds – spoken words – it is possible that it might have played a vital role in the development of a repertoire of sounds that would later be available for sound contrasts.

Prosodic control of the voice – pitch, tone, loudness, and so on – is logically prior to phonetic control. Darwin supposed the origin of speech to have been song. Thomson (1975) suggests it is strongly tied to the co-ordination of work, either group work – though at what stage humans started to undertake large-scale works we cannot say – or the work of the individual. Looking at the Ju/'hoansi,[18] the Iñupiat, and other foraging peoples, we see that skills tend to be passed on from adult to child, and that individual craft work is frequently accompanied by song or chant. In other words, learning the craft implies learning the song or chant. Work-related song or chant has two functions – recording in words the technical content of how to do it, and also the psychological tool function – the chant helping the timing, the rhythm of the work. The tongue co-ordinates with the hands in manual work.

This latter function may have been important before the transfer of meaning from gesture to sound. So, it may be that the making of artefacts, or the preparation of food (for example, rhythmically pounding roots and tubers with stone tools till they are soft enough to eat), came to be accompanied by song or chant, in the form of rhythmic successions of initially meaningless syllables.

Vygotsky's concept of linguistic forms as psychological tools may help us understand how sound could be used to accompany complex manual activities (Luria and Vygotsky 1992, p. 56). The process of making core-and-flake tools, for example, is extremely complex. It is not inconceivable that the tool-makers had a series of vocalisations which served to accompany their work. These vocalisations may or may not have had meaningful content, but would have helped the tool-maker to (a) memorise the sequence of actions; (b) help concentration and timing; and (c) help pass on the skills to the next generation. While a gestural sign language may well have been in use at this period, gestures would of course be unavailable in the function of guiding the actions of the tool-maker, whose hands would be fully occupied.

Rhythmic chanting on a vowel base leads to the control of mouth and tongue movements, to separate vowels from each other. The first and most basic movement is the opening and closing of the lips, which an ape can in theory do, but in practice does not: [mamama]; [bababa]; [wawawa]. Opening and closing of the glottis is also in principle possible for apes, and would become easier over time, with the development of the human glottis, to produce [hahaha]; [ʔaʔaʔa].[19] As the tongue grew more flexible other consonants would appear – [d], [t], [n]. These sounds are produced with the tongue tip, and could be made by ape vocal tracts, if only they had sufficient muscular control of their tongue muscles. At a later stage sounds like the velars [k], [g], uvulars, and other sounds of the modern human repertoire would appear, but not until the jaw and face had altered sufficiently to produce the characteristic round human tongue (Lieberman 1991, pp. 58–9, reporting studies by K. Stevens).

The beginnings of contrastive sound

Thus it seems plausible to trace the origins of speech sounds back to socially-based activities. These activities are by no means totally primitive. They all presuppose a certain level of technical and social development, reinforcing the case for gestural communication as an initial organiser of social life while speech skills were slowly developing. We have shown in the discussion of factors traditionally supposed to give rise to speech – factors such as imitation and sound symbolism – that they presuppose a level of attention and consciousness that can only be associated with the development of a certain level of labour.

The emergence of meaningful sound

Our third task is to explain the final transition to speech – when sounds came to be used in a way that exploited contrastive differences between syllables. The most likely source of spoken language would be some activity that
1. had some economic or social significance
2. could not be carried out or executed with gesture
3. required an exchange of meaning.

As a possible example, we might consider joint foraging on the move, over variable terrain.[20] For a group of foragers in such circumstances, vocal contact and communication would be absolutely imperative, first, to maintain contact between members of the group; second, to warn dangerous animals of the group's approach (a predator hearing approaching noises is more likely to get out of the way than to attack); third, to inform fellow group members of the discovery of things worth attending to – something to eat, something to drink, something to beware of, something to chase, and so on. In this last function, we see the need to use syllables that contrast in sound, perhaps initially by varying the consonant attached to the vowel.

The essence of success in foraging is the more there are of you the greater the chances of success, and if you split up into small groups and spread out, your chances are even greater – but maintaining audible contact between groups becomes more and more important. Gestures are, of course, useless in this activity; sound is indispensable and the need to differentiate messages would lead to the contrastive use of sound.

Since the practice of reference and of naming may already have developed some way using gestural signs, it is not necessary to explain here the development of contrastive meanings. What is being described is simply a particular register of language, one that has the particular form of speech imposed on it by its context, and as a result starts to make use of sounds that are already socially available. Over time, and over many generations, the social value of foraging may lead to the extension of the speaking habit to other areas of activity, eventually reducing the importance of gesture.

If speech developed late, it would not be the result of inherent properties of speech as a vehicle of abstract thought, nor of any inherent deficiency of gestural signing as a way of handling meanings and thoughts. The initial motivation for the development of spoken forms could well have been quite practical, and work-related. However, its long-term effect was that language took one step away from activity, towards a capacity to reflect on and organise that activity.

A variety of factors led to the changes that prepared our anatomy for the eventual arrival of speech. It is possible that once speech was established as a human behaviour it may have influenced anatomy somewhat further.[21] However, the origin of speech appears to be a case of humans using the physical apparatus available, adapting it to communicative purposes, at the historical time when they were ready to speak.

NOTES

1. Though Hewes (1983) argues that the light pigmentation of the palms of human hands, whatever the colour of the individual's skin, is a result of the need to continue communicating in poor light, or at night around fire.

2. Vowels that enable the listener to calibrate the acoustic information coming from a speaker (Lieberman 1991, pp. 57–8).
3. A technique first suggested by Wind, and carried out in some detail by Laitman and colleagues; see Laitman, Heimbuch and Crelin (1979); (1988); Laitman, Reidenberg and Gannon (1992).
4. Lieberman 1992, p. 407 – though criticisms have been made of the method of obtaining the measurements from the La Chappelle fossil on which Lieberman's findings are based. See e.g. Burr (1976); Houghton (1993).
5. Campbell 1988, p. 326, who suggests that the first human hunting was predominantly persistence hunting, relying on endurance and strength more than skill and technology.
6. This is true of the specimen known as *Homo ergaster* at Nariokotome – (MacLarnon 1993).
7. Hewes suggests spoken language is not likely to have been earlier than 300,000 BP (1988, p. 82).
8. Hockett and Ascher (1964, p. 144) call this theory 'vocal blending'.
9. In certain cases of brain dysfunction swearing persists when all other forms of language are disordered – as in coprolalia (Hewes 1976). On swearing and coprolalia, see p. 22, n. 21.)
10. Aiello and Dunbar's phrase (1993, p. 187).
11. An idea with a long history, from Paget (1944); see Allott 1992).
12. The theory that early spoken languages were made up not of arbitrary sounds as today's languages are, but of a number of iconic elements of sound – sounds that had some symbolic and non-arbitrary connection with the world around. See Foster (1983; 1989).
13. Marr variously suggested twelve, then four – and even claimed to be able to identify the four – *ber, ros, sal, yon*, surviving in the names *Iberian, Etruscan, Sarmatian, Ionic*. See Matthews (1950, p. 14); Ellis and Davis (1951, p. 215, fn. 22).
14. For instances of secret languages see Englefield (1977, pp. 87–8); Halliday (1978, pp. 164–82); Kendon (1988, p. 66).
15. The characteristic 'hee-haw' sound produced by donkeys similarly consist of a sequence of ingressive and egressive sounds – sounds produced on an inward and an outward breath.
16. Lieberman (1991, pp. 57–8) suggests that chimpanzees cannot produce the 'quantal vowels' [i] and [u], but it does seem they can make something like an [a].
17. 'Vowel-like sounds' here refers simply to the quality of a sound. The term *vowel* implies some contrastive function, so it is not strictly correct to use the term here – but it is much easier to do this than use an unfamiliar term like *vocoid, vocable, vocalisation*, or whatever.
18. Ju/'hoansi is now the preferred name to !Kung (Alan Barnard, personal communication). The symbol / denotes a dental click – the sound used in English to 'tut'. The apostrophe denotes a glottal stop. For a fuller description of clicks and their symbolisation, see Ladefoged and Traill (1994).
19. [ʔ] represents the glottal stop.
20. This is suggested by Wallace (1994, p. 364).
21. This is argued by Krantz (1988, p. 174); Lieberman (1991, p. 408); and Bickerton (1990, p. 144. However, lacking an adequate explanation for the initial use of speech-sounds, these accounts over-emphasise the individual motivation of speakers, and fail to take account of the importance of activity.

7

Human Languages Appear?

The earliest period for which there is general agreement as to the presence of a developed language is the Upper Palaeolithic period in Europe, around 25,000 BP. This period is associated with an unprecedented upsurge in human technological and cultural achievements – forms of symbolic behaviour, such as cave paintings and decorative body adornment; more elaborate and sophisticated stone tools and living structures; use of different materials such as antler, bone, soft stone; elaborate burials; and so on.

In western Europe the contrast between the artefacts of this period and what went before, in the Mousterian period, appears so sharp that some talk of a 'human revolution' (see, for example, Stringer 1989; 1992), with anatomically modern humans (AMHs) and modern human culture spreading from Africa or south-west Asia, through central Europe to western Europe, seemingly developing as they went. In other parts of the Old World the emergence of modern human culture and behaviour presents the picture of a steadier, more gradual development from the preceding cultures of the Middle Palaeolithic or Middle Stone Age.[1]

A common explanation of the flowering of the European Upper Palaeolithic is that it was the result of the appearance of fully developed forms of spoken language, similar to languages spoken today (see, for example, Noble and Davidson 1991). The implication is that in the preceding period people were not speaking as we do, and that their language was in some way not quite fully developed. The Neanderthals of western Europe are central to the picture, since in both popular opinion and scholarly writing, it is often assumed that Neanderthal culture and behaviour was deficient in comparison with that of the AMHs who appeared to succeed them.

It is, therefore, worth looking first at the Neanderthals, the best documented representatives of archaic *Homo sapiens,* discussing what happened at the point where anatomically modern humans appear in the record, examining the characteristics of human life in the Upper Palaeolithic, and considering the implications for language.

THE NEANDERTHALS

Despite a wealth of archaeological evidence about the Neanderthals and volumes of commentary, it is still very hard to get a clear picture of Neanderthal existence. Many people feel that there was some undefinable difference about them – not apes, certainly, but not quite human. Yet what this difference was, nobody can quite say. The question everyone is interested in – 'Did they speak?' – does not have an easy answer.

Facts about Neanderthals

They lived from around 150,000 BP to 30,000 BP.[2] Like modern humans, they evolved from archaic *Homo sapiens*, but in a different direction, apparently developing an anatomy adapted to life in cold northern conditions, and to a specialised technology and culture. After about 30,000 BP they, or at least their anatomy, seem to have disappeared completely.[3] It is still not certain whether they were displaced, marginalised or integrated into the mainstream of AMH life.

At one time it was thought that Neanderthals were ancestors of modern humans. This theory has been disproved by the discovery that AMHs date back almost as far back as Neanderthals do – certainly to around 120,000 BP, possibly earlier. Dating of artefacts from the Qafzeh site in the Levant places near-modern *Homo sapiens* there *c.* 92,000 BP – long before Neanderthals occupied a near-by site (Milo and Quiatt 1993, p. 574). At many sites in Europe and south-west Asia, over a period of almost 60,000 years Neanderthals and AMHs lived practically side by side, though whether simultaneously, or whether their occupations of sites alternated – Neanderthals in colder weather, AMHs in warmer weather – is still unclear.

Anatomy

Neanderthal anatomy differs from that of contemporary humans in a number of ways. The Neanderthal head had a distinctive shape, dominated by a long, projecting face that seems to be related to the size and strength of the front teeth. Biomechanical studies of their facial morphology, and evidence of accelerated rates of wear on their front teeth, indicate that they habitually put great strain on these teeth, for purposes not associated with eating, possibly using them as a vice. Their heavy brow ridges were probably associated with the size of the teeth and jaws – the brow ridge strengthening the skull at a point where jaw muscles are anchored (Trinkaus 1989c, pp. 52–3), and possibly also protecting against the cold, air chambers behind them acting as insulation. Their skulls were also distinguished by an occipital bun – a projection at the back of the skull, whose function is again obscure, but which may have had the function of balancing the weight of bone in the face and jaws.

Like other archaic humans, they were powerfully muscled, in both upper and lower limbs. Compared to moderns, their arms were not so well adapted to throwing, and their hands shaped to maximise power rather than precision in their grip (Trinkaus 1989a, p. 49). While Neanderthals used spears, it was probably for thrusting rather than throwing (Trinkaus 1989a, p. 51).

Neanderthal locomotor anatomy shows great strength and endurance which 'suggests they spent a significant portion of their waking hours moving continuously and/or vigorously across the landscape, far more than did early modern humans' (Trinkaus 1989a, pp. 54–5). Evidence for a very active lifestyle is also found in the muscle attachments to bones. Their noses were big and capacious, apparently designed to dissipate heat and therefore an adaptation to a vigorous lifestyle. (Trinkaus 1989a, p. 57). Neanderthal brains were as big as those of modern humans, in some cases even slightly bigger (Leakey and Lewin 1992, p. 204).

Between 50,000 and 30,000 BP, AMHs made their way into western Europe, probably from Africa via south-west Asia. After 30,000 BP there is no further record of classic European Neanderthals.

Were they a separate species?

It would be a mistake to think in terms of a simple division of all late archaic *Homo sapiens* into two types, one Neanderthal and one looking like ourselves. There was throughout the archaic *Homo sapiens* transition a great variety of anatomical types, and the development of modern humans was not smooth (Kidder *et al.* 1992, p. 175).

In the fossils found at Kebara in south-west Asia, Arensburg claims to find such a mosaic of characteristics, modern, Neanderthal and archaic traits, that he prefers to talk of the diverse types in the period 90,000–35,000 BP as 'Mousterian' – defining them by culture rather than anatomy (Arensburg *et al.* 1989). Wolpoff and Frayer are reluctant to accept that Neanderthals form a separate species, seeing them as a regional variation of a general human species.

Nevertheless it is clear that there is a distinct physical type associated with the 'classic' Neanderthals of western Europe, central Europe and the Levant, and that this was probably a combination of anatomical and behavioural adaptations to the conditions of the Ice Age, and to a long period of isolation of western Europe behind extensive glaciers.

Some myths about Neanderthals

For over a century, studies of the Neanderthals have been distorted by a tendency to look on them, backwards from our time, as defective human beings, rather than as a successful adaptation to the circumstances of their time.

One school of thought is that once the less robust (more 'gracile') AMHS moved into western Europe from the South and East, the Neanderthals gave way in the face of a superior people, gradually being driven away from their sources of food and becoming more and more marginalised. Whatever the final cause of their downfall – whether it was the result of violence and wholesale slaughter, disease, or simply having to give way to a superior culture – they finally became extinct. Trinkaus' version is fairly representative:

> Western Europe, as a geographical cul-de-sac, stands out relative to the rest of the western Old World, in the lateness of the transition, its rapidity and the essentially fully developed modern human nature of the emerging hunter-gatherer adaptation. It may well be that by the time the transition took place in that region, most of the primary elements of the transition had taken place elsewhere, the different core aspects of a modern human hunter-gatherer adaptation had coalesced, and the contrast between the human population spreading westwards from central Europe and the resident Neanderthals was sufficient to lead primarily to replacement through competition rather than the gradual blending and reorganisation of elements apparent elsewhere. (Trinkaus 1989a, pp. 65–6)

The assumption that they did become extinct has led to a search for reasons for extinction, most of which have focused on supposed deficiencies of the Neanderthals. Some have suggested cognitive deficiencies, proposing that in comparison with AMHS Neanderthals were culturally conservative, their tool-making imitative, rather than innovative; that they were inefficient hunters, not planning their operations, but dashing around after their prey in an *ad hoc* fashion; that they may have been incapable of moving in a straight line over the landscape;[4] that their tool kits reflect an immediate response to immediate problems – on the spot improvisations, lacking planning and forethought, and without 'curation' – that is, preparation of tools in advance;[5] that their shorter time depth of information on environmental variability would probably mean a shallower group memory, and therefore denser population relative to carrying capacity of the environment;[6] that their fires were thermally less efficient (Trinkaus 1989a, p. 63), that their lifestyle was a lot harder, and their children died relatively young.

Comments

Several points have to be made here. One concerns the question of whether they became extinct or whether it was a case of their anatomy evolving, and merging into a general human population over some generations. If Neanderthal anatomy, like archaic *Homo sapiens* anatomy in general, is adapted to tasks that their successors accomplished by cultural and technological means (Milo and Quiatt 1993, p. 574), it follows that once the technology had developed to carry out these tasks, specific physical adaptations would no longer be required, and could be allowed to simply grow out.

The Neanderthals were not particularly unusual for their time, the Middle Palaeolithic or Middle Stone Age. AMHS in Africa, contemporary with the Neanderthals, were no more nor less advanced culturally. Marshack insists:

> the available evidence for complex problem-solving . . . is greater among the Neanderthals during the Mousterian period than it is during the same period in areas outside of Europe, including the Near East and sub-Saharan area of supposedly anatomically modern origin. (1989, pp. 1–2)

At the south-west Asian sites of Kebara (Neanderthal site) and Qafzeh (AMH site), were found basically the same types of tool and the same types of activity – not even minor variations in tool use – which challenges the idea that these hominids constituted behaviourally different populations (Marshack 1989, p. 23). Marshack argues:

> Bit by bit, the accumulating data seem to be suggesting that despite morphological and historical cultural differences, the range of potential capacity for problem-solving and symboling among the two hominid groups was similar and comparable, if not precisely 'equal'. (1989, p. 24)

Achievements of Neanderthals

A number of writers have sought to correct the impression of Neanderthal deficiencies, pointing out their considerable achievements. They were among the most advanced humans of their time in 'capacities for planning, forethought, abstraction, kinaesthetic co-ordination, learning and other fundamental human characteristics' (Hayden 1993, p.137). They were the first to bury their dead, to use the technique of producing red ochre from yellow stones by fire. They used animal parts in ritual ways. They built shelters, using posts for construction, and possibly animal skins for the fabric.[7] They were probably specialised in the treatment of hides and in clothes-making (Campbell 1988, p. 413). They are said to have hunted large animals such as bison (Hayden 1993, p. 138). They hafted stone points on to handles (Marshack 1989, p. 11). They exchanged materials, such as stone, over long distances (Hayden 1993, p. 137). Their core-and-flake tool-making technique requires a high level of skill, as we have seen (p. 92).

Significantly, the last Neanderthals found at St-Césaire are associated with the Chatelperronian industry – recognisably modern forms of tools and body ornamentation,[8] evidence of the ability of Neanderthals to participate in the culture of AMHS (Mellars 1991, p. 72).

It is quite clear that the Neanderthals must have had a functioning language, enabling them to organise labour and social life. If it is borne in mind that they are part of the world population of archaic *Homo sapiens*, they are as well endowed linguistically as the humans described at the end of Chapter Five.

Could they speak?

In studies of Neanderthal capacities for speech we find a similar tendency to judge them from our viewpoint, looking backwards. Reconstructions of their vocal-tract anatomy have led to conclusions that it was very different from the modern human configuration, with a measure of basi-cranial flexion, outside the range for modern humans, that is said to be evidence for a high larynx position.[9] Lieberman argues that Neanderthal anatomy could not produce a modern human range of speech sounds and that their speech would be less distinct than that of modern humans, so that understanding might be reduced by as much as 30 per cent (Lieberman 1991, p. 65). Concerning the basicranium, Laitman, Heimbuch and Crelin's argument (1979) is that two lines of development led in one case to the Neanderthals and in the other to AMHS – with corresponding different facial anatomy. These measurements show that Neanderthal facial anatomy is different from that of humans and even from other archaic humans, perhaps not surprisingly, given the marked mid-facial projection noted above, related to very specific uses of their front teeth.

However, Lieberman's suggestion that the Neanderthal vocal tract was significantly different from the modern human was called into question by the discovery of the Neanderthal at Kebara, with a hyoid bone very similar in shape and position to the AMH hyoid (Arensburg *et al.* 1989). In fact it would be surprising to find the Neanderthals had their larynx high in the throat, given the energetic life they are said to have led. A lowered larynx is associated at least in part with mouth breathing (as Krantz (1988) argues), and the need to take in oxygen rapidly and effici-ently. Houghton suggests the degree of flexion of the La Chapelle individual appears to lie securely within the human range, and that some modern humans (Polynesians) may exhibit basicranial characteristics within the range of Neanderthals, yet speak perfectly well (Houghton 1993, p. 144). Schepartz considers it a mistake to assume that human speech can only be produced by anatomy exactly like modern humans. The human larynx and supralaryngeal arrangement is only one of a number of configurations that are capable of producing speech with the full array of human character-istics (Schepartz 1993, p. 103). Mynah birds and parrots, with very different anatomies from ours, are well known for their ability to produce very human-like sounds.

There is certainly no basis for proposing that Neanderthals became extinct because they were not efficient speakers, and if AMHS were speaking at this time, there is no reason to suppose that Neanderthals could not also learn to speak and communicate with them perfectly well.

What happened to the Neanderthals?

We still have no idea what happened to the Neanderthals, but there is no evidence for their physical liquidation by AMHS. The emergence of co-operative, egalitarian foraging society is hardly likely to have been based on mass slaughter. It is much more likely that Neanderthals became integrated with AMHS. The Chatelperronian finds indicate that they were able to adopt the latest technology, to start to take part in regional alliances and trade networks (Wolpoff 1989b, p. 124), in short, to live as part of the modern human world.

Wolpoff's solution to the puzzle (e.g. Wolpoff 1989a; 1992) is gene flow (interbreeding), with selection. He argues that the Aurignacians (the first European AMHS) are not just gracilised Neanderthals, nor are they simple descendants of Levant people. They have features of both, plus other features that are unique. Gene flow would produce a population with varied characteristics, both modern and archaic. As technology came more and more to carry out the tasks that had been previously required of anatomy, selection would favour the more gracile, and reduce the archaic characteristics, the mid-facial projections, the large teeth, the brow ridges, the heavy muscling and heavy bones.[10] Selection, mutation, gene exchange and drift are for Wolpoff the same features that govern evolution elsewhere.[11]

Reduction in robusticity is a form of selection for economy of energy in the organism (Frayer 1992, p. 220). Female AMHS showed reduction in robusticity somewhat earlier than Neanderthals did (Soffer 1992), though nobody talks about the disappearance of archaic *Homo sapiens* women.

Trinkaus' question, 'What were the selective advantages of the modern human adaptive pattern?'(1989a, p. 48) is easier to answer if reversed: 'What were the disadvantages of the archaic anatomy?' Simply, it was expensive to maintain. Gracility is cheap, easy to maintain. Why retain muscle that you do not use?

Many features of Neanderthal anatomy – brow ridges, flat skull shape, robust anatomy, heavy jaws and large teeth – are typical of archaic *Homo sapiens* across the world, and these features disappeared throughout the world. The explanation that they disappeared because they became redundant, and were expensive to maintain, once technology replaced anatomy as a way of achieving the same ends, is more convincing than a world-wide displacement by AMHS, or world-wide extinction.

WHAT HAPPENED AT THE TRANSITION?

If there really was a dramatic change prior to the Upper Palaeolithic in Europe,[12] the most likely explanation is that while the European Neanderthals, isolated among the glaciers, stagnated culturally and technically, AMHS humans elsewhere in the world advanced. When this new culture reached Europe, Neanderthals, or at least some of them, assimilated it, and underwent gracilisation.

A comparison can be made with a later stage of human history, when Africans, who had missed out on Bronze Age technology (McEvedy 1980, p. 26), proved quite capable of assimilating Iron Age technology when it was introduced.

All the significant achievements associated with modern humans – the cave art, body ornaments, the delicate stone tools, all the evidence of a higher form of culture – came long after the end of the Neanderthal period, between 5,000 and 10,000 years later. Therefore the argument that humans supplanted the Neanderthals by virtue of superior cognitive abilities does not hold up (Campbell 1988, pp. 394, 442; and Schepartz 1993, p. 117). Another factor in the artistic achievements of the period – the magnificent cave paintings and so on – may be a fortuitous abundance of game, the result of climatic conditions, that in fact disappeared in the later Mesolithic period, when cave paintings and many other forms of art similarly disappear from the archaeological record (as suggested by Gordon Childe 1965).

The language argument

There is an argument that the cultural and technical advances of the Upper Palaeolithic were the result of the creation of complex human language.[13] Binford argues that hunting techniques that were associated with the emergence of AMHS were at least in part the result of language and consequent ability to plan in depth (1989, pp. 35–6). However, Schepartz finds no evidence for the hypothesis that complex language is the condition for modern *Homo sapiens*, or that the Upper Palaeolithic explosion of symbolism is the result of a sudden arrival of human language, and he finds much more evidence for language abilities coinciding, if with any species then with the genus Homo – that is *Homo habilis* and *Homo erectus* (1993, p. 119). 'The capacity for complex language was part of the human adaptation for a very long time' (1993, p. 120).

Those who view the Upper Palaeolithic as witnessing a 'human revolution' have to explain how human language could suddenly appear, in evolutionary terms almost overnight. Such interpretation is almost forced to fall back on the explanation of language as the biological product of a new species of human. The argument is increasingly undermined as the period of the origins of modern anatomy is pushed further and further back, currently to around 200,000 BP, nearly 150,000 years before the 'human revolution'.[14]

It seems more convincing, in the light of evidence reviewed in Chapter Five for the gradual development of language, to view the Upper Palaeolithic as the culmination of a development of human social organisation and technology that had been going on for thousands of years. Assuming that spoken language, or a language combining gesture and speech had already emerged in the Mousterian period, then the best explanation of the flowering of the Upper Palaeolithic is technical or cultural.

Marshack finds time and again, in a whole range of activities – hafting, use of bone, use of red and black ochre – that there is no major leap or major invention across the Upper Palaeolithic; simply a change in technology and culture, and one which moreover did not persist, or spread very widely to other areas (Marshack 1989).

DEVELOPMENT OF THE FAMILY

It was suggested in Chapter 5 that the form of the family changes to fit in with ways of obtaining and distributing food at different historical stages. In the transition from ape to human society, organisation of foraging around a temporary home-base, may have led to division of the Australopithecine herd into two groups, on the basis of which a first incest taboo was established, prohibiting mating or marriage between parents and children.

According to Morgan/Engels, the next stage of kinship sees a division among children of the same generation, such that brothers and sisters do not marry (Engels 1954, p. 42). Morgan/Engels' scheme is simple, and quite elegant. In the herd, there are no divisions. Everybody belongs to everybody else; all children are the responsibility of the herd; all old people are regarded as the parents of all young people. The first division of the herd, by age, introduces the generation taboo. The second division, by gender, introduces the brother–sister taboo. We know that both these steps must have taken place at some point in human history, in order for the modern form of the family to have emerged. The only question is, when?

The brother–sister taboo may have been the eventual result of a development of the division of labour seen among modern foragers, when men and women started to specialise in their food-gathering – women gathering plants, and men foraging (either hunting live animals or scavenging). There are serious disagreements about when this division of labour and the consequent practice of sharing food might have been established. Binford (1985) suggests that it was really quite late, just before the appearance of modern humans. Others set the time much further back. It may not even have been the development of hunting that was the crucial development, but the discovery of the control of fire, which was certainly well established among archaic *Homo sapiens*, from 500,000 BP. If females were the ones to tend the fire, this would ensure that hunted or scavenged meat was shared.

Brother looks after sister

We know that kinship systems in foraging societies are generally organised around the obligation of a brother to feed his sister's children, rather than that of a husband to feed his wife's, and therefore their own, children, as in more recent societies. This obligation would seem to be a fundamental organising principle of the exchange of food, and must have a history as long as that of the family. The close relationship between brother and sister to which it attests suggests that brother–sister mating may indeed have been a feature of early human kinship, and that it may have been abandoned relatively late in the history of our species. What reason might be found to explain the gradual abandoning and eventual prohibition of this relationship?

Effect of marriage taboos

One practical effect of incest taboos is that they force individuals to seek mates outside their immediate family circle, encouraging alliances across groups and even across tribes. This is easily understood if you imagine the effect on a woman's children with and without the incest taboo. Suppose a woman has ten surviving children, five boys and five girls. Without any taboos, the children would simply form part of a large troop, travelling around, procuring food together, mating freely. Males would provide food for their sisters' children, and women's control of fire would help ensure that food continued to be brought back home by their brothers.

However, once the brother–sister taboo is established, the effect on social organisation would be dramatic. Instead of ten individuals in one group, we would have two groups, each of five children, plus five mates from other groups. Instantly you have not only twice the number of adults active, in two clans within the group, but also a series of links with up to ten other human groups, based on agreements by the husband to provide food to the wife's family, in addition to the traditional obligation of the brother to provide food for the sister's children. Each woman has now potentially doubled the supply of food for herself and her children, and each individual is for the first time part of a network of marriage-based alliances. The importance of alliances is not only their part in stimulating the collection and distribution of food, but also the fact that in bad times, you can turn to your in-laws for support, and vice versa. The more alliances a group has, the better chances it has of survival. It may have been this very practical consideration that led human groups slowly to abandon and finally forbid incestuous marriages.

If, as Hayden (1993) argues, recruitment is important to foragers, exogamy is the logical step to increase recruitment and alliances. The harder life is for a human community, the more taboos they are found to observe. For example, among aboriginal Australians in some arid areas, men may have to travel for hundreds of miles to find a women they are allowed to marry, because of the number of kinship taboos in operation. The more taboos, the more pressure on the individual to take part in forming alliances over long distances and the better insurance against hard times.[15] The smaller your group internally, the greater the need to build its alliances externally. Kinship systems thus provide a flexible means of responding to variable resources.

There is evidence just prior to the Upper Palaeolithic period in Europe, of the beginnings of regional trading networks, long-distance exchange of goods and so on (Binford 1989, p. 36). Interestingly they are first noticed among the Chatelperronians, the culture marked by the adoption of modern human technology by the resident archaic human population – the meeting, as it were, of two cultures:

> First established in the Chatelperronian . . . an industry associated with the latest Neanderthals of the region, these networks expanded to include extraordinarily broad areas that came to be characterized by singular cultural norms. (Wolpoff 1989, p. 124)

While this is not a conclusive argument for the establishment of the incest taboo at this time, it sets a final date for its establishment. Such a system of alliances is indeed what you would expect the incest taboo to produce. If it was contact with AMHs that led to this dramatic change in the culture of Neanderthals, then it would be reasonable to want to explore the possibility that the 'intangible difference' of the Neanderthals is the result of their kinship structure, transitional between apes and humans – where a generation taboo is established, but not yet the brother–sister taboo.

The picture that emerges of human society after the Upper Palaeolithic transition resembles that of today's foraging societies – small bands, whose members are allied by cross-marriages with neighbouring bands (Whallon 1989). O'Shea and Zvelebil note an extensive contact network in the foraging society of northern Russia in the much later Mesolithic, a period much poorer in resource terms than the European Upper Palaeolithic, in an environment of low population density (O'Shea and Zvelebil 1984, p. 37).

Headland and Reid (1989) suggest that the notion of isolated foraging societies, for example in the remote African or Amazon rain forests, is quite untrue, and that contact with neighbouring groups has been a characteristic feature of the foraging way of life from its inception.

ORIGINS OF FORAGING LIFE AT THE UPPER PALAEOLITHIC

One thing on which there is general agreement is that after the Upper Palaeolithic, certainly by about 20,000 BP, human beings in Europe, Asia and Africa, were living more or less as today's foraging societies today, perhaps without some of the more ingenious technology such as poisoned arrows or boomerangs (Harrold 1992, p. 224; Clark and Lindly 1989, p. 666). Whallon has shown that the foraging adaptation enables humans to live in a less resource-rich and more unpredictable environment than the primate model of dominance and limited co-operation would permit (Whallon 1989, p. 449), and for Lee and de Vore: 'the [foraging] way of life has been the most successful and persistent adaptation man has ever achieved' (1968, p. 3).

Features of foraging life

The three major principles of the foraging means of subsistence are defined by M. Power (1994), on the basis of studies of people in six parts of the world who live entirely by foraging: the Ju/'hoansi of the Kalahari; the Iñuit of Arctic Alaska; the original Australians; the Hadza of southeast Africa; the Fueguans of southern America; and the American Northwest Coastal Indians:
1. Immediate return feeding – in other words, food is eaten as soon as it is gathered.
2. Food is not stored or processed. There is no permanent wealth. Lee quotes a saying of the Dobe Ju/'hoansi: 'the environment is our wealth' (1979, p. 458).
3. Tools are simple and portable, easily made and easily replaced. The only personal property or equipment is what can be carried.
The effect of these techniques on social organisation can be summed up in general features of foraging societies.

Egalitarianism

The organising principle of every foraging society is distribution of food on the basis of complete equality of all. All food is shared, not consumed by a family but shared out within the band of 20 to 30 members so that every member gets an equitable share. This principle of generalised reciprocity within the camp is reported for foragers on every continent and in all kinds of environment (Lee 1979, p. 118). Exchange of goods is instituted in marriage. Egalitarian organisation is created and actively maintained by cultural mechanisms (Lee 1979, p. 460), for example, to discourage arrogance and stinginess (Lee 1979, p. 458; Whallon 1989; p. 448; Chance 1990, pp. 130–1). Insulting the meat, a practice with the function of preventing arrogance among successful hunters, is recorded among the Ju/'hoansi (Lee 1979, p. 220) and the Arctic Iñupiat (Chance 1990, p. 130); sharing arrows among Ju/'hoansi hunters similarly reduces opportunities for bragging, since the owner of the first arrow is owner of the animal killed, rather than the one who shot the arrow. This practice also strengthens bonds between men, such as brothers-in-law, reducing opportunities for disputes (Lee 1979, p. 247).

Women have a central role in production and in group discussions.

Relation between sexes is equal-but-different. For example, among the Ju/'hoansi, gathered food belongs to the woman who gathers it, and it is women who share out the meat obtained by men. Since the supply of hunted meat is not reliable, this gives women considerable economic importance.[16] Women exercise control over reproduction, birth, and so on.

No formal system of political organisation or control

Land ownership is vested in the collective, and all decisions are taken and carried out by the collective. Foraging group size tends to be about 30 people, on average 6 families, the ideal number for effective decision-making (Whallon 1989, p. 446; Lee 1979, p. 447). If there is any leadership it is 'charismatic', based on the personal qualities of the leader, and not inherited, nor reflected in unequal distribution of resources.

All problems are dealt with collectively

Everyone in the band is responsible for helping solve the problems of other band members, whether in sickness or interpersonal tensions. Healing, for example, is a social responsibility for all. When a member of the group is ill, it is seen, for example by Kalahari foragers, as an attack by ghosts or spirits, and it is then the responsibility of all present to unite to defend themselves, in ritual healing (Biesele 1993). The solidarity of the group is a key factor in this activity.

Mutual dependence across groups

Kinship and alliances are centrally important. There is reciprocal access to food resources, land, and water holes. People are in constant circulation. Strangers are generally welcomed, on the principle of recruitment rather than rivalry. Headland and Reid (1989) emphasise that contact with neighbouring peoples is a regular feature of modern foragers and, by implication, has been for a large part of human history.

Goods are exchanged in the giving of gifts, rather than in commercially based exchange. This acts as a way of establishing alliances between peoples, cementing social relationships, kinship and so on (Leach, Introduction to Malinowski 1966, vol. 1, p. xv). Part of the foraging life is extensive travelling, visiting, group ceremonies – activities which maintain the flow of information over wide distances. Large gatherings, usually seasonally timed, are a feature of most foraging societies. They are the occasion for establishing law, social regulation, marriage-arranging, and settling disputes, but also sacred rituals, reinforcing links with tradition, continuity with ancestors (Leakey and Lewin 1992; Lee 1979).

Group size and resources

Whallon shows how group size adapts to resources available, by means of social devices such as kinship taboos – not to the average but to the resource lows, so as to ensure that the group is always living within the carrying capacity of its environment (1989, p. 444).

LANGUAGE FOR SURVIVAL AMONG FORAGERS

Having seen that something similar to today's foraging way of life was established by the time of the Upper Palaeolithic period, it is worth considering the part played in this way of life by language. We have argued that language is associated not simply directly with labour, but with the function of planning for, and organising, labour. Even when individuals are apparently working alone, they are in reality engaging in collective labour, since the notions and concepts used to organise their labour are themselves social in origin. The grinder of corn, the hunter, the potter, all are using skills passed on from preceding generations, and understand the process of their work by means of internalised notions and concepts.

Oral traditions for survival

At a higher level, that of culture, socially created language forms also play a vital part in social life. Forms of oral tradition – myths, narratives – play a role in sustaining the social order, just as much as daily forms of social interaction. We have already noticed the range of speech-based activities among foragers designed to maintain egalitarian relations – insulting the meat, for example, prevents arrogance on the part of a successful hunter.

Whallon emphasises the importance of long-term, seasonal planning to foraging life. One important social activity that fulfils this function is story-telling. For example, Minc (1986), in a study of the Arctic Iñuit, shows how myths and narratives act to conserve vital information relevant to the movements of their source of food – caribou, or whales. Tales of how ancient ancestors behaved in times of crisis conserve these lessons well beyond the limit of what one generation might consider important to pass on to their children as practical advice. More generally, oral forms transmit values vital for survival. Another study of Arctic people by Chance shows how myths and narratives constantly stress the importance of co-operation, of making extensive social contacts and alliances to fall back on in hard times (Chance 1990, p. 131).

Magic as part of oral tradition

Magic, that appears to be the complete converse of rational thought, scientific analysis of the world, and practical technical skill, plays an important part in the social life of many human societies. It can be shown to be related to human efforts to transform the world. Magic has two aspects: on the one hand, observation of economically vital phenomena. So, for example, rain is associated with crop-growing; the moon with successful hunting. On the other hand, these associations are interpreted in terms of agency relations, as if rain and moon had human attributes. The agency is then addressed as a human with special powers – the spirit of rain, the moon god/goddess, and so on.

Magic is both a product of the power of language, and at the same time a result of the lack of power of human beings. Luria and Vygotsky explain magic as the necessary product of the desire to control both nature and one's own behaviour, from the primitive union of 'naive psychology and naive physics' (1992, p. 84).

Magic has to be understood as a special instance of oral tradition, with the function of transmitting information. Gordon Childe develops this point of the connection of magic with technical skills. The true relevance of magic to human progress may in fact be the converse of the role that science plays today. Whereas science is constantly pushing forward, transforming nature, magic plays the role of a conserving mechanism, keeping alive the technical knowledge that needs to be passed on from one generation to the next. This passage from Gordon Childe suggests as much:

> All the industries named, [garden culture, weaving, fishing, hunting, stock-breeding], have been rendered possible only by the accumulation of experience and the application of deductions therefrom. Each and all repose on practical science . . . Thus there grows up to be handed on a great body of craft lore – snippets of botany, geology and chemistry, one might say. If we may judge from the procedure of modern barbarians,[17] the legitimate deductions from experience are inextricably mixed up with what we should call useless magic. Each operation of every craft must be accompanied by the proper spells and the prescribed ritual acts. All this body of rules, practical and magical, forms part of the craft tradition. (Gordon Childe 1965, p. 96)

If the function of magic is here to help the memory, Malinowski's study of magic language in the Trobriand Islands shows how forms of language in spells and magic chants are made more memorable by what he calls 'weirdness': words that do not occur in everyday speech; particular grammatical forms; archaic forms; forms with no apparent etymology; abracadabras. The overall effect is to create a language of spells that cannot be confused with everyday speech. Verbal taboos prevent these special words from being integrated into everyday language. Magic language thus has a very powerful conserving force, transmitting the knowledge that is essential for survival.[18]

Magic in the Upper Palaeolithic

The art of the Upper Palaeolithic, in the Aurignacian and Magdalenian cultures, is generally agreed to have fulfilled magic functions. These artistic forms are seen by Marshack (1989) as having had forerunners in earlier periods, in simple forms of information processing among the Mousterians (simple lunar calendars of bone, and so on). The fully blown forms of magic continued to fulfil his function, alongside other social and ritual functions, enshrouded in mystical, psychologically extremely powerful forms.

SUMMARY

It is not speech that accounts for the Upper Palaeolithic explosion of symbolic activity. The conditions that favour the emergence of speech are not such as to allow an overnight transformation or 'human revolution'. The conditions that favoured speech are the hunting and gathering activities and the egalitarian practices of foraging society, activities that are foreshadowed among archaic *Homo sapiens*. Forms of kinship appear to develop early among *Homo erectus* or possibly archaic *Homo sapiens* groups. The division of labour that appears in social organisation around the home-base, and that must certainly have emerged by the time human groups learnt to control fire, is assumed to lead to a simple form of human kinship, based initially on a generation taboo. The culture and technology of late archaic *Homo sapiens* reaches a point where further progress is impossible within the group. Inbreeding may in any case have presented a genetic problem for the species. In isolated Ice Age Europe, humanity could not develop further, remaining in what was apparently a cultural backwater, in small, isolated groups. In Africa, south-west Asia, central and southern Europe, where human groups mingled and exchanged information, genes and technology, it is suggested that a new form of social organisation emerged based on the brother–sister taboo – what we would recognise as marriage. The result of the taboo was to encourage the formation of alliances between neighbouring groups, to stimulate production and techniques of food procurement, hunting, and so on. The Chatelperronian, where human met Neanderthal, apparently for the first time, sees the first evidence in western Europe for alliances and exchanges between groups. These alliances persisted even during the Mesolithic, when the spectacularly abundant resources of the Upper Palaeolithic in Europe receded.

There is no reason to suppose that spoken language was the fundamental factor in the cultural achievements of the European Upper Palaeolithic, many of which might be the accidental product of a period of temporary abundance of game.

At the Upper Palaeolithic, the foraging way of life was established in a form that we would recognise today. As a way of life it is still remarkably similar across the world. Its egalitarian principles are actively sustained by language – ideal forms that encapsulate social relations of kinship and family obligations, and cultural forms that transmit essential information.

NOTES

1. The Middle Palaeolithic is the term used in reference to Europe, and the Middle Stone Age elsewhere. There is no point in asking why.
2. These dates are constantly changing. For example, a recent find at Altamura, dating as far back as 400,000 BP, has been proposed as an early Neanderthal (Dorozynski 1993).
3. Shackley (1983) suggests that sightings of 'wildmen' in parts of the world may reflect survival of some Neanderthals.
4. This inference is drawn from observations of different cross-section of leg bones in Neanderthals and AMHS. For Trinkaus, their 'endurance- and strength-related locomotion was thus also poorly directed towards points in the land-scape' (1989a, p. 55).
5. Binford, cited by Mellars (1991, p. 70) referring not just to Neanderthals but to the Middle Palaeolithic generally.
6. Whallon (1989, p. 452), referring to the Middle Palaeolithic.
7. Marshack (1989, p. 9) stressing the conceptual advance implied by the use of holes in construction.
8. The Chatelperronian industry appeared sufficiently modern for some archaeologists to associate it with AMHS, though it is fairly certain it is associated with Neanderthals (Schepartz 1993, p. 117).
9. A high larynx position implies a shorter vowel tract, and therefore poor production of vowels like [i], [u] the quantal vowels – see Chapter Six, p. 99.
10. Interbreeding between humans and Neanderthals is not generally favoured, but should not be totally discounted. Simek finds it very hard to imagine that biological interaction did not occur between Neanderthal and modern (1992, p. 243).
11. Wolpoff (1989b, p. 139). Wolpoff's 'multi-regional hypothesis' of the origins of modern human populations, based on the merging or conveying of several different varieties of human populations from different regions is hotly contested, e.g. by Bräuer (1989), Stringer (1992). The alternative to Wolpoff is the 'out of Africa' or 'mitochondrial Eve' hypothesis.
12. This is disputed by Bednark, who sees the so-called Middle to Upper Palaeolithic transition as an invention of archaeologists, that can only really be sustained in Europe; elsewhere, there is no evidence for an abrupt transition (1994, p. 381).
13. Mellars (1991). Davidson and Noble (1989) argue that 'depiction' was the crucial factor in developing both language and art.
14. Some of the arguments about the origins of modern humans are based on studies of variation of mitochondrial DNA in modern human populations. Since this form of DNA is passed on down the female line it is claimed that it is relatively easy to trace its history, and hence the history of different human populations. However evidence from these studies, while extremely interesting and provocative, tends to shift its ground from one study to the next. Templeton (1993), reviewing some of the problems involved in these studies, argues that in general their conclusions do not support the 'out of Africa' hypothesis.

15. Whallon (1989). The importance of alliances for survival in the Arctic is emphasised by Chance (1990).
16. Male–female proportions in food-gathering are approximately, 66–33 in favour of women. When weight and calories are combined, 56% female, 44% male (Lee 1979, p. 452).
17. The term 'barbarian' which we now consider offensive, was widely used in the study of prehistory and anthropology to describe a stage of socioeconomic development, roughly that of early agriculture.
18. In this respect magic language can be compared to mnemonics, that have no meaning in themselves, no relationship between the memorising material and the phenomenon to be remembered. For example, *Richard Of York Gained Battles In Vain*, has no connection with colours of the rainbow except the initial letters, and the mnemonic is only memorisable because it calls upon knowledge that we already have.

8

The Social Formation of Grammar

At the start of this book arguments were put against the theory that grammar is a product of the human mind. In exploring alternatives to this theory, it will be necessary to consider possible factors that may have played a part in shaping human languages. These factors include speakers' perceptions; the tasks of language; factors of discourse; and speakers' values.

SPEAKERS' PERCEPTIONS OF THE WORLD

Chapter 2 criticised the ideas of linguistic determinism (pp. 35–37), the idea that forms of grammar will make speakers see the world in different ways. But what about the converse – the idea that the way we view the world governs the form of our grammar? For Searle, for example, 'the way that language represents the world is an extension and realisation of the way the mind represents the world' (1983, p. 197).

However there is a puzzle here, because if we look at the way that 'the mind represents the world', it seems that different minds represent the same world very differently, a point nicely illustrated by Ruwet's interesting cross-language study of weather terms (1991).

Even the most ordinary, everyday experiences of weather somehow do not quite fit into our syntactic patterns. Human syntax tends to be organised along the lines of two elements – subject and predicate (NP and VP).[1] But the experience of weather is usually one-dimensional. Rain, snow, wind and sunshine, are quite simple phenomena that just happen, and do not involve either agents or goals. In technical terms the utterance *It's raining* contains one argument, and no predicate, and we have therefore to strain syntax to accommodate it.

Ruwet notices a constant conflict in weather expressions between experience and syntax. To fit our subject–predicate model, we have to provide empty elements, like the *it* of *It's raining*; *It's hot*, or provide redundant verbs, as in *The wind blows*; *Rain is falling*; – what else could the wind do but 'blow', or the rain but 'fall'?

The weather is basically the same the world over – yet languages differ in the way they analyse it. One Chinese dialect, for example, represents rain as 'sky is dropping water' (Halliday 1985, p. 102). The Russian for *It's snowing* translates literally as 'Snow goes'. If language was shaped by representations of the world in the speaker's mind, we would expect similar experiences to result in similar forms of language. The study of weather expressions indicates that this is not so; grammar cannot simply be regarded as a representation or reflection of the world around us.

In starting with human perceptions of the world, cognitive syntax misses the important question of what shapes these perceptions. The assumption appears to be that we all perceive the world the same. Yet clearly not all minds do represent the world in the same way.

Luria and Vygotsky (1992) observe great contrasts between the perceptions of literate members of modern industrial societies and those of illiterate foragers with their vast memories, well-developed senses of vision, smell and hearing, but almost totally undeveloped skills of abstraction and generalisation. They compare such perceptions with the phenomenon of eidetic (detailed visual) memory, that we associate today with autism (p. 68). They then go on to draw a parallel between these aspects of perception and the concrete nature of languages spoken in pre-political societies – their large vocabularies, their wealth of lexical and grammatical devices for describing in detail appearances, shapes, movements and other sensual impressions of the environment.

The observation that differences in perception lead to differences in grammar leads to the further question of what is the underlying basis for these differences? Luria and Vygotsky argue that differences in perception, in individual psychology, and in language, have a very real basis in the socioeconomic existence of people. Thus foragers and modern city-dwellers not only live very different lives, and perceive the world around them very differently, but they also speak very different languages that reflect these lives and perceptions.

An interesting example of this relation between life, perception and language is found in Alpher's (1987) study of grammatical gender in the Amerindian language Iroquois. In this language the feminine gender is unmarked, that is, it is the norm to assign nouns to the feminine gender, and masculine items are specially marked by a special subject-prefix. This is the converse of most languages with a system of grammatical gender. Alpher's analysis of this system relates it to social relations among the Iroquois, who were traditionally a matrilineally organised society. Women held the land, passed it on to their heirs in the female line, organised agricultural production, held or withheld the food produced by themselves and by men, controlled the wealth, arranged marriages and selected and deposed chiefs. While men were the warriors, women could even veto wars (Alpher 1987, p. 183). Men might be absent, often for years at a time in periods of war.

> The semantics of the pronominal subject-prefixes strikingly mirrors the resulting spread of people over space: all-male groups at the periphery, mixed-sex groups of women and children and some men at the centre: one non-singular subject prefix for the former and another for the latter. (Alpher 1987, p. 183)

In other words, Iroquois grammar is organised from the viewpoint of those at the centre of society – the women. Alpher goes on to suggest that grammatical systems where feminine is the unmarked gender are more common than previously supposed.[2]

SYNTAX AS A RESULT OF HUMAN TASKS

When we examine reports of pre-political languages, we find that they have certain striking common characteristics, such as:
1. huge vocabularies, rich in details of the environment
2. focus on visual appearance and movement
3. a high incidence of names for topographical features – hills, rivers, woods, rocks
4. a lack of abstract or generic terms, and often few words for numbers
5. well-developed systems of gestural signing
6. two ways of expressing the relationship of possession – alienable and inalienable
7. the absence of the verb have
8. grammar based on classification of nouns.

Items (1) to (8) can be seen to form a set of properties that are a response to the tasks of languages in the particular ways of life of their speakers. Pre-political ways of life – foraging, horticulture, pastoralism – depend absolutely on resources available in the environment. Lee quotes the Ju/'hoansi saying : 'the environment is our wealth' (1979, p. 458). It is therefore essential that every member of the community should be aware which plants, animals and other sources of food are available; where, when and how to obtain them, cook them, preserve them. Encyclopaedic knowledge of the environment, and the way it changes with the seasons, follows naturally from this requirement. Reports such as the following, from Luria and Vygotsky, are representative:

> One of the Northern primitive peoples, for example, has a host of terms for the different species of reindeer. There is a special word for reindeer aged 1, 2, 3, 4, 5, 6 and 7 years; twenty words for ice, eleven for the cold; forty-one for snow in its various forms, and twenty-six verbs for freezing and thawing. It is for this reason that they oppose the attempt to make them change from their own language to Norwegian, which they find too poor in this regard. (1992, p. 63)

Along with this feature of language goes the high incidence of names for topographical features. Dixon mentions the value that Dyirbal speakers attach to detail in description: 'Vagueness is held to be a severe fault. All descriptions should be as specific as possible. This has often been misrepresented as a failure of the aborigines to develop generic thinking' (1972, p. 30).

The suggestion that these languages lack abstract or generic terms is worth examining in some detail. Lakoff (1987) comments on the often-quoted example of the many words for snow in Alaskan languages: 'when an entire culture is expert in a domain . . . they have a suitably large vocabulary. It's no surprise and it's no big deal' (1987, p. 308). He suggests a contemporary example would be our interest in cars, for which we could find hundreds of terms if we wanted to. In fact Lakoff is wrong here; there is a very real difference between the languages of industrial societies and pre-political societies. In the latter, a surprising fact is that although there may be hundreds of terms applying to important activities, the comment is found time and again in the literature, that there are few if any abstract or generic terms. It is as if we talked about cars by their names, their registration numbers, their colour, but did not have any general terms such as *car*, *convertible*, *family saloon*, *Ford*, *Toyota*, and so on.

Sometimes, as Malinowski argues, this is simply because a certain type of concept is not needed. Among the horticulturists of the Trobriand Islands everybody is engaged in gardening, so a general word for *gardening* is unnecessary, since everybody has a garden, and there are no people who do not garden at all (1966, vol. 2, p. 67). This has nothing to do with people's inability to think abstractly, but rather the result of a way of life where disinterested reflection and abstraction has no place.

Foragers, horticulturists, pastoralists, all are dependent on the vagaries of climate and unpredictable changes in resources. There is no point in developing the capacity to make plans, reflect, consider alternatives, when the technical means are not present to translate ideas into practice. This is nicely illustrated in Chance (1990), who shows that the culture of the Alaskan Iñupiat reflects an unwillingness to make firm predictions about the future. They have only one word that means both *if* and *when* in reference to the future, which annoyed the Christian missionaries in the community Chance was studying, as the phrase 'when Jesus comes' was consistently translated 'if Jesus comes' (1990, p. 127).

Many languages are from our point of view deficient in numbers, it being frequently reported that there may be only a few number terms – sometimes just *one*, *two* and *many*. Needless to say, the lack of counting in the language is not a result of mental inability to handle quantities. The same reports often comment on complex systems of counting, using fingers, the palm of the hand, the arm and other parts of the body. This contrast between elaborate counting systems and a lack of grammatical numerals is particularly telling. Because there is no need for abstract arithmetical operations in the life of these people, a grammatical system of numerals has not developed. Manual counting is accurate enough, so why develop further?

The emphasis of these languages on aspects of shape, movement, and other visual properties is widely reported, as in Miller's study of Delaware, where there are 'at least eight alternative classifications based on form, habitat, colour, movement, sound, use, relationship and appearance' (1975, p. 436).

Lévy-Bruhl's study of Klamath notes the variety of different expressions used to convey motion: in a straight line, motion to the side, along a curve, and so on. 'In a word, the spatial relationships that the Klamath language expresses so precisely may in particular be retained and repro-duced by the visual and muscular memory' (1928; quoted by Luria and Vygotsky 1992, p. 65), and Lévy-Bruhl goes on to suggest 'if verbal language, therefore, describes and delineates in detail positions, motions, distances, forms and contours, it is because gesture languages use exactly the same means of expression'. To refer back to the discussion of gesture theory in Chapter Six, if the focus of speakers is on visual aspects of phenomena and movement, then gestural signing may be equal to, and in some cases superior to, speech as a means of communication.

The tasks of a pre-political language

Luria and Vygotsky see the rationale of the above features in the two tasks that are the priority for a foraging people – the need to record accurately the environment, and to commit to memory the information required to survive in this environment (1992, p. 69). More generally, foraging and early agricultural ways of life are closely tied to concrete activity, where abstract thinking has little or no value, but a well-developed memory, sensitivity to changes in the environment, and a name for all relevant aspects of the environment relevant to food-gathering are essen-tials.

In sum, we see that these languages are dominated by activity, by immediate visual impressions of the physical environment, relevant to vital socioeconomic activities, and by the requirements of precise descrip-tion, accurate recording and memorising. Abstract, theoretical operations are absent from the lives of speakers, and therefore absent from the grammar of their languages.

Our focus on the tasks of languages has produced an adequate explana-tion, but is this simply because the tasks are so concrete? Not all languages can be so simply specified in terms of the tasks they carry out. We need to consider other factors that may shape syntax.

SYNTAX AS A PRODUCT OF DISCOURSE

Another view of syntax that seems at first sight to be based on practical common sense is that it arises naturally out of communication (or 'discourse'), that is, from the needs of speakers engaged in interaction.

Ingold sees syntax rising inevitably out of communication:

> Where an intelligent creature is placed in a developmental context which imposes a situational need for complex communication with similarly intelligent creatures in the social environment, syntactic structures are bound to emerge as necessary solutions to the communication problem. Thus language is no more given in the environment than it is in the organism; it emerges in the relational context of the organism in its environment, and is therefore a property of the developmental system constituted by those relations. (1993, p. 41)

The point is expanded by Savage-Rumbaugh and Rumbaugh (1993), who see syntax as a disambiguating device that becomes necessary when the content of messages grows too great for single words or compounds to suffice. In their example *Tickle Jane Sue*, for example, the number of potential relationships that can be assumed between Jane and Sue is too numerous to specify what the speaker (in this case a chimpanzee) wants to happen during a tickling bout. Some means is needed to specify agent and recipient; the listener must be told more about the way in which the nouns are to relate via the verb. A syntactical device must be invented if it does not exist. Whatever commonalties there are among grammars may well exist because only a limited number of solutions to the same problem are workable (Savage-Rumbaugh and Rumbaugh 1993, p. 105). They make the analogy with tools – shaped for and by the purpose for which they are made. But we have to wonder if this is really all there is to syntax. It all seems too easy.

Syntax and discourse

Givón (1979) prefers a more complex analysis, though along similar lines. His study of the transition from pidgin to creole in Hawaiian distinguishes two types of discourse, that are the product of distinct uses of language. In Givón's account, syntax is explained on the basis of communicative principles which underlie the structure of discourse (1979, pp. 207–8). His explanation shows how sociocultural factors produce quite dramatic differences in grammar.

For Givón, pidgin is the result of what he calls 'pragmatic' discourse, involving

1. communicative stress – a pressing need to exchange information, but with no common language
2. little shared information or background knowledge
3. immediately obvious context.

The resulting form of language has pragmatic characteristics: though its message is quite clear, its syntax is unstable, inconsistent and difficult to formalise (Givón 1979, pp. 224–6). Among other features it has a variable word order, where the element that is most important to the speaker is put first; clauses are loosely co-ordinated; there is a low ratio of nouns to verbs – typically one noun per verb; there are few grammatical words; little attention is paid to marking verbs for tense or aspect, marking nouns for plural, and so on.

Factors that cause such a pidgin to develop into a full grammatical creole would include many that are clearly non-linguistic, such as 'expanded geographical range', 'specialised sociocultural activities', 'increased size and variety of social units', 'contact with other bands' and 'slow dissolution of society of intimates and move towards the urban society of strangers' (Givón 1979, p. 297). These factors would lead to a shift from pragmatic to syntactic discourse, a shift that would be seen in the pidgin–creole transition but also may have taken place historically in the development of human syntax. In a fully syntactic language, characteristics would include the grammatical word order of subject–predicate; subordination of clauses in the sentence; a higher ratio of nouns to verbs; some grammatical marking of case; grammatical forms of noun plurals; verb tense, aspect and modality; and pronouns and demonstratives (Givón 1979, p. 305).

Contrary to theories putting forward innate programmes for syntacticisation (such as Bickerton 1984), Givón explains the growth of creole from pidgin as the result of rational, socially based principles:

> Years of living together have created an increasing body of common knowledge of members of the community, their personality and motivation. On this facilitating background, the syntactic mode of communication, with its condensation, time-saving and structuralised, automated coding procedures, can proceed. (1979, p. 226)

In short, a close-knit community, with a body of common knowledge, and a well-understood social life, produces a close-knit syntax, just as a loose conglomeration of individuals produces a loose type of syntax.

Givón's study of the pidgin–creole transition is a very interesting and important analysis of the relation between social factors and grammatical form. It is in the true sense a functional study. The only odd thing about it is Givón's description of the determining factors as 'discourse' principles, which is to give an extremely broad definition of discourse. Many of the factors that account for the transition he describes are obviously social factors, relating to the socioeconomic activity of speakers – that is to say, they are aspects of labour, rather than aspects of the autonomous linguistic phenomenon of discourse.

SYNTAX AS A SOCIAL METAPHOR

The factors considered so far are all partially adequate as explanations of the form of grammar. Consideration of speakers' perceptions may provide too passive a view of grammar. Consideration of discourse provides a seemingly simple, but perhaps too narrow a view. Givón's perceptive description of syntax succeeds only because he ignores his own definition. Consideration of the tasks of language provides a good explanation of grammars where tasks of language are closely related to activity, but may fall short with languages whose speakers are starting to engage in abstract thinking. One further factor is offered as a shaper of grammar – Halliday's concept of social metaphor (as in Halliday 1992).

Chapter Two referred to the centrifugal forces of language that seemed to arise from the proliferation of registers of language associated with new forms of activity. The centripetal tendencies that counteract those forces, are the great social themes or metaphors that predominate in a society at a given moment in time, that shape consciousness, and shape grammar.

Early philologists, such as Humboldt, talked about *Weltanschauung*, or world-view. While we would differ from Humboldt's mentalist view of folk psychology, we have to accept that it would indeed be strange if the organisation of society, the collective activities of its people, the exchange of ideas, concepts, notions among them, their sharing of experiences, did not finally create a shared system of values, the kind of system that finds its expression in mythology, religion, jokes, narratives, and so on. Social metaphors can be regarded as a realisation of the values, sometimes conscious, sometimes unconscious, of the speakers of a language.

Biesele's (1993) analysis of the culture and language of the Kalahari Ju/'hoansi reveals a systematic categorisation of experience that expresses a well-worked-out value system. Her description of their tales, folklore, mythology, shows that the Ju/'hoansi divide their world into the major categories of man's v. woman's; wet v. dry; herbivore v. carnivore. Food is divided into things that move, including meat *!ha* and things that stay put *'msi*, implying both plant food and food in general (1993, p. 86). *'msi* in fact stands for the general, unmarked category for food, which is of interest when we consider that a larger proportion of Ju/'hoansi subsistence is provided by gathering (and therefore by women) than by hunting (1993, p. 205 fn.).

Both kinds of food are cross-cut by a distinction between wet v. dry. Two important foods transcend this division. Both fat and honey can be either wet (drunk) or dry (eaten). As Biesele puts it, they are 'symbolic of the great mediation between men and women' (1993, p. 86). In this connection, it is interesting to note that euphemisms for sex include both 'drink fat', and 'eat honey'.

Another polarity which is symbolically mediated is carnivore v. herbivore. For the Ju/'hoansi, the sexual pursuit of women by men is expressed in the metaphor of the killing and eating of the herbivore by the carnivore. The symbolic classification of experience further groups together attributes of women – blood, milk, gathering utensils – separate from those of men – arrows, poison, semen.

The point about this classification is not just the world-view it reflects, but its close parallel with the needs of the Kalahari foraging way of life. The sexual division of labour, for example, is central to the system, as are the concepts with which people understand and interpret sexual activity: hunting, food-gathering. The production and distribution of food, the very basics of life, are expressed metaphorically in the system of classification.[3]

Malinowski's study of the Trobriand Islanders similarly identifies a common set of values, expressed in the terms *molu* and *malia*:

> The whole system of organised work and incentives is associated with the traditional handing on from generation to generation of stories of *molu* and *malia*, of success and failure, of the importance of magic, of work and discipline in gardening . . . [which] collectively serve to the building up of the moral tradition of the tribe. (1966, vol. 2, p. 47)

More importantly, as we shall see below (pp. 144–5), the importance of horticulture ('gardening') in Trobrianders' life is reflected in the grammatical system of the language, Kiriwinian.

Halliday discusses examples of the way social metaphors influence grammar. One is Martin's study of key motifs in Tagalog – where he identifies the social themes (he calls them 'grammatical conspiracies') of *family*, *face* and *fate*. Each of these themes is associated with grammatical forms. For example, the *fate* theme has to do with events taking place outside an individual's control – 'things simply happen; one cannot really determine one's fate'. Nine features of grammar can be found to sustain or express this fatalistic construction in the language (Martin 1988).

Utterance and Language

To conclude this section, it is worth drawing an analogy between an individual utterance and the language of a people. Any meaningful utterance represents an analysis by a speaker of some aspect of experience. This analysis depends on a number of factors – who you are, your social position, your interests, your current activity, your system of values, what you are trying to do with your utterance (persuading, praising, arguing), what your relationship to your language is (teacher, writer, entertainer, farmer, forager – all use their language in different ways).

We can also look at an entire language, in relation to its speakers, in the same way, seeing it as the result of the sum of its speakers' experiences, their activities, their system of values, their perceptions, the tasks they perform with language, their social organisation, their position in the world. At this most general level of analysis, a language is similarly an interpretation of the experience of all its speakers.

Syntax is socially constructed from thousands, millions of such utterances, varying according to their context, their speakers, their purpose, and so on. What unites them into a language is a collective analysis of experience, resulting in a single system of values, the product of the social themes that arise from the combined lives and utterances of all these speakers. These social themes, that themselves change as the lives of their creators change, shape grammar in a reflection and a record of life and labour (Jones 1991, p. 53).

NOUN-CLASS GRAMMAR

The part played by practical experience and social themes in shaping grammar can be seen in a grammatical feature characteristic of many pre-political languages, that of noun-class systems. A noun-class system is based on a grouping of nouns into grammatical classes, membership of which is indicated by markers or classificatory particles. With these particles the noun is linked to the verb or to other parts of speech.

In this example from Swahili, the particle *ki* links the noun and the numeral to the verb (Creider 1975, p. 128):

(1)   *ki*-dole *ki*-moja ha-*ki*-vunja chawa
      finger   one   not kill   louse
      'One finger cannot kill a louse.'

In languages of this type, spoken widely in Africa, but also in Melanesia, Australasia, and among American Indians (Breitborde 1975), the nominal class markers perform a variety of functions, linking noun–verb, noun–pronoun, noun–adjective, specifying numerals, demonstratives and so on. As Corbett says of Nunggubuyu – these markers are the glue that holds the language together (1991, p. 322).

The number of classes in languages is extremely variable. There may be as many as twenty in some languages.[4] It is widely accepted that nominal classes derive from what were originally semantically organised groupings of nouns (Corbett 1991, p. 49), and in many languages it is still possible to discern the principles on which nouns are grouped.

Proto-Bantu, the language from which the many Bantu languages of Africa are generally believed to have derived, had an elaborate system of noun classes. Creider's account suggests that the classes were based on the properties of:

   I. shape, including long, curved, round/protruded
  II. animate v. inanimate
 III. human v. non-human

IV. other properties of mass substances, including sticky, liquid, lumpy.
Hundreds of modern Bantu languages derive from this proto-language,
most of them retaining this characteristic of Bantu grammar.

The Trobriand language, Kiriwinian, described by Malinowski also
appears to have a system of at least five nominal classes:[5]

I. *tay/to/tau*   human
II. *na*   Female, animal
III. *kay*   trees, plants, wooden things, long objects
VI. *kway*   round or bulky objects, stones, abstract nouns
V. *ya*   flat thin objects, objects of fibre or leaf

What is the principle of the categories?

The Trobriand classification given above is a classic example. The classes
seem to encapsulate all the important aspects of the horticulturist or
'gardening' life of its people.[6] The same might be said of the Proto-
Bantu classifications, though it is hard to see why classes such as sticky,
lumpy should be so important.

However some classifications found in pre-political languages seem at
first sight quite bizarre. For example, the Australian language Dyirbal,
described by Dixon, has four classes that Lakoff found to 'boggle the
mind' (Lakoff 1987, p. 92).

I. (*bayi*) contains men, kangaroos, possums, bats, most snakes, most
fish, fishing equipment, insects, the moon, storms, rainbows, boomerangs, some spears, the willy wagtail bird

II. (*balan*) contains women, some snakes, some fish, most birds, the
sun, firefly, scorpion, crickets, the hairy Mary grub, fire, water and
things connected with them, shields, spears, some trees

III. (*balam*) contains all edible plant foods, the plants that bear them,
and honey

IV. (*bala*) parts of the body, meat, bees, wind, some spears, most trees
and vines, grass, mud, stones, noises, language and a jumble of
others (Dixon 1972, pp. 44 ff.).

This apparent jumble of nouns, becomes more consistent once related to
the beliefs of the Dyirbal, as Dixon's study does. For example, in myth,
the moon and the sun are married, so it is quite natural to classify the
moon with men and sun with women. The hairy Mary grub gives a sting
that feels like sun-burn, so it should be classified as *balan*. Similarly in
myth, birds represent the spirits of dead women,[7] so they are *balan*,
except for the willy wagtails, which are believed to be men (Dixon 1972,
pp. 308–12).

The classifications reflect a focus on the physical, concrete, spatial
properties of objects, plants, animals, cross-cut by categories from mythical
beliefs. Classifications according to role in mythology are found all over
the world (Corbett 1991, p. 10). For example, the classification of the sun

as feminine and the moon as masculine is very widespread.[8] Similarly, languages from widely separated parts of the world have classes of round things, of long thin things, and flat leafy things, which are clearly related to the interest people have in plants as sources of food.

Nevertheless these classifications are far from logical. To adopt the terminology of Vygotsky's work on children's thinking, they seem to show the characteristic of thinking in complexes or sets (Luria and Vygotsky 1992, pp. 62ff.) – in other words, arrangement of phenomena on the basis of accidental resemblances, the kind of associations that characterise children's early word meanings and associations. In line with Vygotsky's observations about complex thinking, the criteria for these categories, apart from the vital categories of living and human, are overwhelmingly visual – shapes, movements, physical properties – and reflect the dominance of immediate sense impressions in the perception of these speakers.

Where do noun classifiers come from?

Malinowski's explanation of the Kiriwinian particle is illuminating:

> The more important the term, the more pronounced is the tendency to use it over a wide range of meanings. *Ka'i*, for example, means anything from 'tree', 'plant', 'vegetable', 'wood as material', 'shrub', 'magical herbs', 'leaves', 'stick' to the abstract concept 'made of wood' or 'long object'; in this latter sense it also functions as a classificatory formative. (1966, vol. 1, p. 68)

– an explanation that relates the origins of a classificatory system to the centrality of gardening (growing yams and vegetables) in Trobriand Islanders' society.

Leakey on Kikuyu

Leakey's introductory grammar of Kikuyu (1959) suggests that the nominal class system in this Bantu language expresses a hierarchical view of the world, reflecting a belief in a hierarchy of spirits. The class of humans and spirits of humans is the highest class. Next in degree of importance are the 'second-class spirits' – of large trees and plants, epidemic diseases (which are spirit-borne), animals and certain reptiles. The third class of spirits includes birds, reptiles, insects, mammals, lesser plants, weeds and grasses, and demoted humans. A separate class includes religious and magical objects, and the remaining classes are categorised on semantic bases.

As with Dixon's account of Dyirbal, the linguist who has some knowledge of the material life, beliefs, values – and therefore the social metaphors – of a people[9] is able to give some explanation of the grammar of their language, rather than the mystified, 'mind-boggled' reaction expressed by Lakoff.

Becker's (1975) study of Burmese classifiers relates the system both to the real world and to the Buddhist view of the world. For example, one classifier is used to group together the sun, aeroplanes, the ocean and needles, among other things.

> Unless one knows that the traditional Burmese pictorial map of the cosmos has man located on an island, from the center of which flows a river in a spiral course to the sea, one may question why rivers and oceans are classified here along with arrows and needles, which move in circular orbits'. (Becker 1975, p. 118)

The Burmese classifier system is 'a linguistic image of speakers' world-view', but this world-view has no direct relation to speakers' material existence; it is mediated through a fairly elaborate ideological system.

These classification systems do not always represent a simple mechanical translation of important elements of life into language. It is rather a case of the incorporation into grammar of a system of values, values that work to keep society together, and in some societies have developed into a fairly elaborate ideological system. The Kikuyu system of ancestor spirits, the Burmese Buddhist world-view, Dyirbal beliefs and mythology – all clearly play a role in the lives, and also in the grammar of their speakers, though the connection with day-to-day activity is by now tenuous.

Decline of world-view

Further proof of this connection between life and language comes in the fact that when the socioeconomic life that gave rise to the system of values underlying classifications starts to disintegrate, these features of language correspondingly disappear or atrophy.

Recent generations of Dyirbal speakers, the children and grandchildren of Dixon's traditional Dyirbal speakers, have experienced marked changes in their lives, such that English is replacing Dyirbal, and the language is dying. In its later phases, the system of nominal classes is breaking down, into one resembling a simple gender system. Class III (*balam*), the class of edible foods, has disappeared. Only human females are now assigned to class II (*balan*). The mythical association of birds with spirits of dead women has been lost, and birds are now in *bayi* – the class of animate beings (Dixon 1991).

Burton and Kirk's study in modern Nairobi similarly finds that noun-class divisions of experience no longer correspond to the intuitions of native Kikuyu speakers (1976, p. 173). This is hardly surprising given the difference between the material existence of the original Kikuyu speakers and the residents of a cosmopolitan capital city.

FORMS OF POSSESSION

The argument that forms of social life result in different forms of grammar is furthered by a brief look at forms of property and their expression in language.

The relationship that we know as 'owning' is unique to latter-day humans. Among animals we may talk about animals possessing instincts, fur coats, caves, territory – but this is an anthropomorphic metaphor. Animals' possession of a territory is not a socially recognised right, it is rather the product of instinctive behaviour, and is established by fighting or aggressive display. Animals occupy territory; they do not own it. They cannot pass it on to their children and indeed may have to fight their children to continue living there. Among humans, by contrast, despite all that is said about human aggression, ownership rights are socially agreed and socially maintained over long periods of time.

Relationships that are labelled 'possessive' in languages may be of different types:

1. permanent relationship of whole to part (as in parts of the body, kinship relations, e.g. *my leg*; *my mother*; *my people*
2. locatives, places where things or people belong or are located, including location of bodily sensations, e.g. *my village*; *my country*; *pain in my leg*
3. relationship of product to its maker, e.g. *my basket*; *my arrow*
4. temporary attachment of an object to a person, e.g. *my drink*; *my meal*; *my money*
5. temporary attachment of a person to another person, e.g. *my friend*; *my husband*; *my boss*.

Notice that in modern English all these forms of possession are indicated in the same way. In many languages of pre-political societies however there are different forms for some of these relationships.

In pre-political society there is virtually no private property and things we treat as property – land, animals, weapons – are shared. Social practices, such as the Ju/'hoansi practice of sharing arrows, 'insulting the meat', and so on, promote sharing and egalitarianism. There are no land rights among foragers. Neighbouring groups share each other's land, waterholes, hunting grounds in co-operative, agreed fashion, and every so often come together to have a good time.

Most of these languages distinguish in their grammar two forms of possession – what linguists call alienable and inalienable possession.[10] Inalienable possession refers to items that are permanently attached or very close to an individual. In this class are not only body parts, but also kinship relationships such as mother, father, sister, uncle; the products of your own hand, such as arrows; items that stay with you throughout your life such as your home, your name, and so on. The class of alienable possession includes kinship relations that are not the result of birth; food; resources that are gathered or produced to be eaten or exchanged; goods that are exchanged.

For example, In the Melanesian language Mekeo we find the personal pronoun -*gu* placed after the noun for inalienable possession, and before the noun for alienable possession:

a manua-*gu*   'my wound'
a subana-*gu*   'remains of my meal'
hahin i-*gu*   'my sister'
anu-*gu* tunan   'my man (husband)'
anu-*gu* hahin   'my wife'

Interestingly, husband and wife are excluded from the class of close possessions, while wound and remains of meal are included. This distinction is in line with the social practice of exogamy (marrying outside your clan), as a result of which husband and wife belong to different clans. Accordingly husband and wife are not regarded as being related in the same way as brother and sister, and it is quite natural that the possessive pronoun should not be affixed after these nouns, while for example it is affixed to the noun 'sister' – *hahin i*-gu, because she is of the same clan (Lévy-Bruhl 1928, p. 73). Thus the individual is to the clan or family what the limb is to the living body. In thousands of other languages this relationship is observed, though through different grammatical forms, 'names of relationships and names of parts of the body make one in reality' (Lévy-Bruhl 1928, p. 76).

In many languages, the expression of the inalienable relationship may have no specific grammatical form, or else is performed very simply, using a personal pronoun in the possessive function. So for example, *my* in:

(2)   my house

and *I* in:

(3)   I take

would be the same grammatical form. On the other hand, alienable possession often gives rise to quite complex forms. Klimov concludes that in the so-called 'active' Amerindian languages, what we call a possessive relationship is not genuinely possessive, but rather expresses the relationship of whole to part (1974, p. 23).

An example from Dixon's account of Dyirbal illustrates the rather complex relation between social practices and the grammatical expression of possession:

> You need to understand that there is little spontaneous non-necessary giving among the Dyirbal, but a great deal of necessary giving, according to people's habits of sharing most things with relatives etc. In a sentence like 'man gave woman beans', the giver will be in the ergative

case, because it is subject; that which is given in the nominative case in this language, because it is object, and the recipient in the simple genitive case, as a possessive phrase qualifying that which is given. (1972, p. 237)

The Dyirbal sentence is literally translated as 'man gave beans of the woman', because the beans are being given to the person to whom they belong. Perhaps a better translation is 'The man gave the woman her share of the beans.'

In another example, the Trobriand language, Kiriwinian, Malinowski distinguishes four degrees of possession, (1) nearest is for parts of body and kin; (2) dress and food as owned, rather than (3) food to be eaten. (4) the class of furthest possession is 'really the most important class used with regard to such relationships as the full or legal ownership of land, houses, movable possessions' (1966, vol. 1, p. 183).

As previous sections have suggested, relationships between human beings and their physical environment in pre-political societies are quite different from those obtaining in our developed money economy, and these relationships find their way into their languages in a way that is not difficult to understand.

Absence of the verb have

In this connection too languages at the pre-political stage generally lack a verb resembling our modern *have*. Lehmann explains:

active languages lack a verb for *have*. They may express the meaning through use of a locative, comparable to the use of the dative in Latin, as in *mihi est liber* = 'I have a book'. Similarly, nouns may not be inflected for genitive or possessive case; juxtaposition of animate and inanimate nouns may indicate the relationship. (1992, p. 108)

Proto-Indo-European and some other early Indo-European languages such as Sumerian have been found to be of this type (Lehmann 1992, p. 248). We can regard this feature too as a result of the absence or relatively weak development of private property relations.

Marx and Engels show how property arose as a social institution when agricultural productivity was so great as to produce a consistent surplus. The question of who was to control this surplus led to struggles over a long period of time and eventually classes arose (on the basis of control of the surplus). Private property emerged as a social institution summing up the final arrangement of who should control the surplus, and the accumulation of wealth led finally to the development of cities and of class society.

It is interesting that even in early forms of Greek and Latin this verb was not strongly established. Vincent (1982) shows how forms of *habere*, the Latin for 'have', originally an active verb with the meaning 'hold', appeared in Latin first with lexical meaning and then with grammatical functions, establishing themselves in the Romance languages as they evolved from their original Latin forms. In this example from Vergil (Vincent 1982, p. 65):

(4)   Hostis *habet* mures.

'The army holds the walls.'

the verb is still used in its active sense.

A later form, in Vincent's example from Cicero is a precursor of the grammatical use of *habeo* as a verbal auxiliary. Interestingly the example has a very modern commercial feel (1982, p. 82):

(5)   in ea provincia pecunias magnas collocatas *habent*

'in that province they have large sums of money invested'

When we look at modern English we find, as we would expect, the use of *have* as a grammatical item firmly established and widespread. The use of the word as a grammatical form excites no interest. Most people would argue that there was little connection between the *have* in:

(6)   Have you finished?

and the same word in:

(7)   Do you have any children?

Linguists classify *have* in (6) as an auxiliary verb, and in (7) as a main verb, as if they were not really connected. Yet at one time they clearly were. How do we relate the two? One possible explanation is that the value placed on ownership in our world, leads to a widespread social metaphor of ownership, that causes us to view a wide range of experiences in terms of this relationship, even when the experience has little or nothing to do with ownership or property.

Every meaningful utterance is an interpretation of experience, seeing a relationship between events in the world about us. When we want to express a new experience, we probably turn first to familiar social metaphors. One of the social metaphors available to us to describe relationships between individuals and the world is that of ownership. So medical problems, social problems, technical problems, military problems, all fall easily and naturally into this form : *I've got a cold, I've got a problem, I've got a job to finish, We have a crisis situation, We have lift-off, We have a meltdown.*

The expressions *have, get, take, give*, are so central to social consciousness as to have become embedded in the grammar to the point where we do not even notice anything odd about it. So *have* is used to express the past tense, *I've eaten*; to express necessity, *I have to go*; to express the future, *I have some work to do*; to express agency, *Have a think about it*, and so on.

Halliday describes this use of *have* as a 'metaphor turned grammar' (1985, p. 327). The metaphor has become part of the system of English to such an extent that forms like *He bathed* are now archaic, and the standard form is *He had a bath.*

Interestingly although the possessive form in modern English is applied to nearly all the relationships listed on p. 147, products of labour do not generally take the possessive form *my* any more. Whereas the arrow made by the Ju/'hoansi hunter is 'my arrow', workers in car factories cannot talk about 'my car'. Once it has left the factory, the car no longer belongs to its makers. We only attribute ownership of product of labour to intellectual products – *my book*; *her film*.

Halliday would probably call the use of *have* as we have described it here a 'grammatical conspiracy' (e.g. Halliday 1992), suggesting that it leads us to view the world in a certain way, even when this is against our own interests. To counter this, we have to make clear that we see social metaphors as temporary, changeable phenomena, subject to the ebb and flow of opinion, of practical daily struggles going on in society, that can easily produce a re-evaluation and a change in the direction that social values take.

Summary

No animal society has anything like possession. In its fundamental forms possession represents human relationships, connections with each other, commitments, social obligations, people belonging to each other, especially in relations of kinship. The distinction between alienable and inalienable possession is a characteristic of many if not all pre-property societies, along with absence of the equivalent of a verb *have*. Once commodity exchange becomes an organising principle of social life, the relationship of ownership comes to dominate us, to take on a life of its own. In this process, it comes also to permeate our language, so subtly that we hardly notice it.

NOTES

1. In some descriptions of grammar, subject and predicate are described as Noun Phrase (NP) and Verb Phrase (VP), the verb phrase sometimes consisting of Verb and Noun Phrase.
2. Alpher (1987, p. 173). Corbett (1991) mentions a number of other languages where women occupy a favoured linguistic, if not social, position (1991, p. 30).
3. Biesele (1993) refers throughout to the Ju/'hoansi symbolic divisions of experience, based on their manifestations in oral narrative. It is not clear at the moment whether the divisions she is talking about are present in a formalised noun-class system. There is still no satisfactory grammar of the Ju/'hoansi's language.
4. E.g. in Fula (Corbett 1991, p. 45).
5. Malinowski (1966) initially says there are three genders, 'as in Slavonic languages' (vol. 2, p. 32), but later adds two further 'classificatory particles', and a possible sixth, that taken together strongly suggest a noun-class system (vol. 2, pp. 34–6).

6. A great many classifier systems in South-east Asia are based on the shapes: round (or fruit), rod (stick) and leaf (flat) (Becker 1975, p. 118).
7. This belief is reflected in many Australian languages (Alpher 1987, p. 178).
8. Indo-European languages with gender distinctions are unusual in marking the sun as masculine and the moon as feminine. There appears to be a connection here with the early Indo-European worship of a male Sun God (Gimbutas 1991). See pp. 168–9 below.
9. Based on Creider 1975, p. 129. Whether Leakey's account is correct is hard to assess; I have not been able to obtain the original textbook.
10. The terms 'organic' and 'inorganic' are also used. It may be easiest to think of alienable or inorganic possessions as transferable, with languages classifying what is transferable differently. The subject is rather complex, and the intention of this section is to do no more than give an idea of the extent of variation in the expression of possessive relations.

9

Language Evolution

VIEWS OF LANGUAGE CHANGE

The final chapter is concerned with the way languages change. Do they evolve in a generally progressive direction? Are the languages of today more advanced than those of historically earlier people, or does language change go round in cyclical movements?

The traditional three-stage view

In the nineteenth century the idea was put forward that languages passed through progressive historical phases – isolating, agglutinating and flexional. According to this theory, the original isolating languages consisted of nothing but roots. Some of these roots then took on grammatical functions, in the agglutinative stage, and in the flexional stage the grammatical words fused with roots as inflexions. This final stage corresponded with the highly inflected Greek and Latin, languages that were looked on as the high points of linguistic history, from which modern languages represent a decline.[1] This notion was gently deflated by Jespersen, who pointed out that the three language types are based on grammatical processes present to a greater or lesser extent in most languages, and the theory that these stages may correspond to stages of human society has little foundation. He replaced this idea with another, that modern languages are moving from synthetic (flexional) to analytic; that is, from a system with case endings and tense endings, to one where elements of grammar are relatively free of each other, a move that Jespersen claims enables languages to express ideas more flexibly (1922, p. 334). While this process is undoubtedly observed in many European languages as sex-gender and case endings decline in importance, Jespersen's observation is still rather localised in application. Chinese and Vietnamese, for example, have been synthetic languages in Jespersen's terms for hundreds, possibly thousands of years.

Views of cyclical change

We saw in Chapter 1 that many twentieth-century linguists tend to retreat from grand schemes. Even historical linguists are prone to deny that there is any historical progress in language, and to see 'historical linguistics' as moving in cycles, language simply undergoing the same processes time and time again. For example, Aitchison sees a process of ebbing and flowing, as languages grow complex and then 'tidy up'. In general, she agrees with Greenberg that 'the evolution of language has not been demonstrated' (Aitchison 1991, p. 216).

So it seems that mainstream linguistics has managed to get through almost the whole of the twentieth century studying languages without speakers, while historical linguistics has been studying language change without history.

Theories of language progress

The Japhetic Theory put forward by Marr and colleagues in the 1930s and 1940s in the Soviet Union, espoused the notion of progress in language, in a rather crude mechanical way relating stages of language to historical stages of society. They proposed that a historical development took place in the syntax of languages, with languages based on ergative constructions evolving into accusative types of language (Matthews 1950).

The theory was later revised in the light of more careful and detailed studies of data. While many western linguists are doubtful about historical progress in language, the evidence for historical evolution of syntactic form has won some support from, for example, Lehmann, who accepts Gamkrelidze and Ivanov's argument that proto-Indo-European must have gone through a stage when its syntax showed characteristics of the 'Active' typology (1992, p. 107–8).

Bichakjian's account of the evolution of linguistic form in Indo-European languages similarly sees language evolving in a more or less a straight line, from primitive to modern. Unfortunately he connects his study to a biological theory of paedomorphosis – that languages evolve in the direction of features that are acquired at an earlier stage by children. This prevents him looking for other reasons for linguistic evolution, such as pressures to adapt the language system, both internal and external. His picture is one of increasing simplification, in line with the observation that children learn easier, more generally applicable features first (Bichakjian 1987).

But while evidence from the comparatively short record of Indo-European languages may support a view of progressive simplification of inflexional endings, focus on inflexional endings gives a distorted picture of syntactic evolution. Morphology may well have simplified, but the functions of inflectional endings have in many cases been transferred to prepositions, verbal auxiliaries, modals, and so on. Simplicity in one area of the language may be countered by growing complexity in another (for example, in subordination). Ask anyone learning or teaching English today whether it really is a simple language.

Swadesh also believes that languages simplify over time, but he correlates simplicity with their range, the number of their speakers, and their role in the world. His developmental stages are eoglottic (= 'dawn tongue'), palaeoglottic, neoglottic, local (referring to relatively dispersed, pre-political languages, some of which survive today), classic (Latin, Greek, Sanskrit, Hebrew – the languages of city-states) and world languages, such as English, Russian, Spanish. Briefly his thesis is that as languages evolve their vocabulary grows, and their inflexions simplify (Swadesh 1971; see Bynon 1974 for a critical review). By implication, the farther back in time you go, the more complex languages grow.

All stages present in one language!

Halliday's position is interesting. He views evolution in languages in terms of a process of adjustments of the syntactic system, each new stage overlaying the last. So a language is not a simple system, but rather a system of systems. This position gets some support from Kibrik's (1985) finding that languages can contain subsystems that are nominative-accusative, ergative, active, neutral and contrastive – in other words, that there may be various strategies in one language. The implication of this notion is that when the rules or structure of languages change they are not quite across-the-board, but leave little bits of the old system that resist change.

Language and progress

Perhaps it is best to say that languages do not progress; it is human beings, organised in human society, that progress. While there are recognisably earlier (or more 'archaic') forms of language, no language can be seen as more primitive than another. Human languages are always good enough, if they carry out the tasks required by their speakers in their historic context. The human hand is the same, whether it is making a stone tool or typing a computer program. But the tasks differ – and so in the long run the form of activity will differ. An analogy might be made with different forms of bridge – the stone arched bridge and the steel suspension bridge. The arch is the best form if you are using stone, the suspension bridge the appropriate form if you are using high-tensile steel. It is only because the steel bridge will cross a wider span than a stone arch, that there is progression.

What has advanced in the course of prehistory and history is human knowledge, technical skill, and with it our ability to control our environment. There is no doubt that this may well have affected the languages we now speak. The functional view of language as the product of tasks and the expression of social values, means we have to look to human history for external explanations of language change, without ruling out internally motivated reorganisations of the linguistic system.

Those who seek to explain language change on the basis of the abstracted language system will always have a problem in discerning a clear historical line of development. Language change appears to go round in circles, an illogical and haphazard pattern of ebbs and flows. However, look at language from the point of view of speakers engaged in socially organised activity, and it then becomes possible to trace a clear line of development based on the needs imposed by human beings' social existence at different historical periods: needs that rise from activity, forms of communication, and forms of thinking.

LANGUAGE AND ACTIVITY: A HISTORICAL VIEW

Linguists today appear to assume that grammar was shaped from the beginning in terms of the syntactic relations subject, verb and object. However many pre-political languages are not of this type. Noun-class and active languages represent grammars based on semantic principles. These languages seem to have been shaped by the need to describe visual and spatial impressions of the world, to handle notions that are predominantly concrete and sensual.

The history of grammar may represent the slow emergence of syntactic relations from what were originally semantic roles. Syntactic relations differ from concrete semantic relations. They are oriented less on immediate sense impressions, and more on relations between phenomena. In this sense syntactic relations are abstract, though not in the sense of being divorced from the world. The abstraction of syntax is like the abstraction of a triangle or a square. It is an abstraction that can be visualised and made concrete, an abstraction that resides in its quality of relating two or more phenomena.

How to explain the creation of these new relational structures in language? Biological changes in the physical composition of human beings have to be ruled out, as have unmotivated changes in the mental life of human groups. The only possible explanation remaining, is that of changes in human activity that might give rise to new notions, new concepts. In other words, in response to new types of cognitive content, human beings have created new forms to express this content.

The following sections focus on the transition from the semantic roles of agent, action and patient, to the syntactic functions subject, verb and object.

THE ACTIVE LANGUAGE TYPE

Linguists working in the field of language typology have identified a class or type of active languages, associated with people living in pre-political societies in many parts of the world today,[2] particularly the original Americans. The principle of organisation in such languages is semantic, in that the role a word plays in an utterance is directly related to its meaning.

1. Nouns are divided into an active (animate) and an inactive (inanimate) class, for example, in Navaho: proper names, animals, trees, plants are active; and all else, including 'water', 'snow', 'cloud', 'stone', 'steam' are inactive. This division is not marked by any kind of classifier, unlike a noun-class system, but is noticed in the restriction on which verbs can occur with which nouns. Active nouns may only occur with active verbs, and inactive with stative verbs. There is a third class of verbs – affective verbs such as 'see', 'hear', 'like'. Some verbs show one form for active nouns and another for inactive, for example, 'lie', 'move'. Where the same verb is used with active and inactive subjects, its meaning undergoes a change, for example 'lead' (active); 'go' (inactive); 'drag' (active); 'crawl' (inactive).

2. In the formation of an utterance, the verb is the central, dominant element. Numerous particles are added to modify the meaning of the verb, adding details such as person, number, manner of action, various adverbial and instrumental affixes, visual aspects of the action and modal force such as subjunctive (Klimov 1974, p. 16). Nouns are less important, and are mirrored in particles of the verb in a way reminiscent of class languages, for example, 'I-saw-him Bobby'.

Example (1) from Tlingit, consists of a single verb, with a number of particles (Klimov 1974, p. 18):[3]

(1)   *i-q!A-xa-wuː-s!în* –
      'I asked you'
      i-   2nd person inactive affix
      q!A   the so-called nominal prefix with instrumental function (literally 'mouth')
      xa-   1st person active affix
      wuː   aspect marker
      s!în the root morpheme 'to ask'

3. There is no class of adjectives; their functions are fulfilled by stative verbs ('be white'; 'be long', and so on).

4. There are no verbs of possession and no special form of pronouns for possession.

How do we explain the features of the active type of language? It would appear to be a language type that is oriented towards the description of action and appearance – the recording of visual phenomena in the environment seems to be the priority, as we saw in the previous chapter. The speaker of an active grammar appears to interpret events in the world in terms of either action carried out by an animate agent, or a state with an inanimate entity involved. A reason for this was suggested in Chapter 8 (p. 136) – the importance to foraging people of describing the environment accurately, of sensitivity to the slightest change that might mark the seasons, changes in the habits of animals that you hunt or trap – these are life-and-death issues. Active grammar also makes it possible to describe the behaviour and appearance of fellow humans, on whose co-operation life also depends.

Antiquity of active grammar

Not only are active languages geographically associated with foraging and pre-political societies, but the antiquity of the grammatical type is suggested by the recent discovery that Proto-Indo-European was probably an active language (Gamkrelidze and Ivanov 1995, pp. 233–76; Lehmann 1992, p. 248). Evidence for this stage of the language is found, for example, in the existence of two forms for the words *fire* and *water* – the animate forms that became Latin *ignis* and *aqua*, and the inanimate forms that led to Germanic *Feuer* and *Wasser* (Lehmann 1992, p. 248).

Two points are particularly important about these languages: that the emphasis is on the verb, on action as the principle element round which the sentence is organised; and that the organising principle is almost completely semantic, based on the tangible distinction between living and non-living things.

Ergative syntax

The grammar of today's European languages can be characterised as Accusative[4] – based on the distinction between nominative marking of subjects and accusative marking of objects. Verbs are divided into two classes, but whereas the active language divides them on the semantic principle of whether they are active, stative or affective, accusative languages divide verbs into transitive and intransitive on the basis of whether they can take an object. While many transitive verbs represent actions – *take, eat, kiss*, and so on, others are not – *consider, own* – and many intransitive verbs are actions – *run, go, arrive*. The sentence is now organised on quite different autonomous principles, the principles of its own internal structure.

If you combine this division of verbs into transitive and intransitive, with the Active principle of dividing nouns into animate and inanimate, the result is what linguists identify as ergative syntax. While there is no general agreement as to which languages should be classified as ergative or not (see, e.g. Jake 1978), it is agreed that many languages have within them features of ergative syntax.

Ergativity can be demonstrated in certain registers of English today. For examples:

cooking
(2) a.   The meat's roasting in the oven.
    b.   The coffee's percolating right now.
Commercial transactions
(3) a.   Government bonds sold briskly.
    b.   Interest rates rose; prices have fallen.
scientific processes
(4) a.   The metal is cooling.
    b.   Water freezes at 0° C.
children's speech
(5)   The lamp just broke.
In each of these examples, the subject of the sentence is not an active responsible agent, but a patient, an item that is acted upon. Ergativity is seen in situations which minimise the role of the active agent. In an ergative system inflexions distinguish the elements appearing as subject and object of the verb. The patient is usually in the unmarked absolutive case (abs.), and agents are marked with the ending of the ergative case (erg.). The absolutive case is both the object of a transitive verb and subject of an intransitive verb, giving the same unmarked form for *rabbit* in:
(6) a.   The hunter (erg.) caught a rabbit (abs.).
    b.   The rabbit (abs.) is sleeping.
There are other features of the ergative typology, but the identity of the intransitive subject and the transitive object in the absolutive case is the key one.

The reason why ergativity is important in discussions on language evolution is that it seems to be a hybrid form of syntax, transitional between the totally semantic system of Active grammar type, and the syntactic system of accusative grammar (as Klimov (1974; 1979) argues).

The division of verbs into transitive and intransitive means a partial break with the semantic system and the introduction of a grammatical distinction. But subject and object still behave according to semantic principles – the ergative subject of the intransitive verb has to be an agent, an animate being, while the absolutive subject of the intransitive verb/object of the transitive verb has to be a patient, an inanimate or non-human being. There are really no true subjects and no objects, only agents and patients (Bichakjian 1987, p. 218). The rabbit in example (6) is a patient. Grammar, in other words, might be said to be still related in quite a direct way to human activity in the world, and to processes that are of importance to human life.

The exact status of the ergative typology is still questionable (see, e.g. Dixon 1987; Plank 1979a). It is tempting to see a straightforward transition from active or class languages, via ergative, to accusative, as Klimov (1974; 1979) suggests. However things may not be that straightforward.

While ergative grammar may develop into accusative, Accusative languages can develop ergative features (Bichakjian 1987, p. 123), though there are no known cases of ergative or accusative languages developing Active grammar. Many languages show combinations of different grammatical systems, with traces of earlier stages, overlaid one on another (as Halliday 1992 suggests).

Plank suggests that what seems to distinguish ergative and accusative systems is the feature of primary responsibility: 'In accusative systems, the participant primarily responsible for the successful execution of an action is typically the agent; in ergative systems it is typically the patient' (Plank 1979a, p. 18). There is a tradition of attempts to explain ergativity as the mode of expression of people whose life is relatively at the mercy of external forces – less in control of events. Plank contrasts the attitude of the 'agent' in foraging and agricultural societies: farmers see themselves as responsible for success and for failure; foragers see themselves as subject to the vagaries of nature, events not being due to their own volition (1979a, p. 20). As we saw in Chapter 8, the Iñupiat express their future not in terms of 'when' but 'if' (see Chance 1990).

Sasse suggests that ergativity might also be the result of a less anthropo-centric world-view, or of sociocultural conditions that taboo a linguistic emphasis on man as a wilfully responsible agent – in other words, the presence of ergative syntax in the language of egalitarian, foraging peoples could be a reflection of a cultural restraint on self-promotion (Sasse 1978, cited in Plank 1979a, p. 16). In many such societies there is a convention against utterances such as 'I killed that rabbit', permitting only utterances like 'That rabbit got caught' (see Dixon 1972; Lee 1984).

Kuryłowicz, focusing on the linguistic system alone, argued that ergative and accusative constructions are merely superficial morphosyntactic vari-ants, entirely equivalent in semantic and pragmatic respects (Kuryłowicz 1973, cited in Plank 1979a, p. 21). This leaves unanswered the question of what social factors led to these 'superficial morphosyntactic variants' in so many of the languages of the world, and why these same variants do not occur in the major languages of advanced industrial societies today.

Many of the above 'explanations' of ergativity focus on the fact that it is different from the more prevalent accusative system – and 'different' can easily lead to the implication of inadequate. Because the grammatical system places more emplasis on patients than agents, the implication is that the role of agency is 'less developed'. However, if we look at the way content might influence form, and consider what content would pro-duce a form of grammar of this type, we see that a focus on the environment – plants, animals, natural processes, and so on – might lead to exactly this type of syntax: where all events in the world are interpreted in terms of two processes – the agent acting, successfully or unsuccessfully, on the world, or the world undergoing some change of state (moving, growing, dying), in situations where humans cannot affect the outcome. In other words, the role of the agent may be very well perceived – but recognised to be simply ineffective in some situations.

One of the difficulties of establishing the historical position of 'ergative languages' or 'ergative grammar' is that these grammatical relations might be produced by a number of different factors at different historical periods. Ochs (1988) notes two quite distinct uses of the ergative in different societies – in Samoan to express social distance; in Kaluli for interaction with small children. We find features of ergativity in modern English, and Halliday suggests that all so-called transitive systems are in reality a combination of two means of representing processes – the transitive and the ergative, and that the ergative may have been growing in functional importance over the last 500 years (Halliday 1985, p. 149).

To simplify the discussion the term 'transitivity' will continue to be used to describe the syntactic relation between subject, verb and object, and rather than try and account for ergativity we shall focus on the transition from active to accusative syntax.

HOW DID TRANSITIVITY RELATIONS EVOLVE? ACCUSATIVE SYNTAX

The accusative typology characterises the Indo-European languages, such as classical Greek, Latin, the modern Romance, Germanic and Slavonic languages. In accusative languages any noun, in fact almost any expression, can be subject of the sentence; whether it is animate, inanimate, abstract noun, item of value or numerical expression.

This is a purely syntactic principle of organisation, based on the internal structure of the sentence, that may also be related to the logical structure of propositions *argument–predicate*. It enables ideal forms and abstract entities, such as families, governments, companies, theories, laws, concepts to enter the same kind of relations as human beings, and verbs of action metaphorically express relationships between these entities.

(7)   The theory of X depends on/gives rise to/is supported by/leads to Y.

(8)   Gold fell/rose to four hundred dollars an ounce.

The rise of civilisation and transitivity

It is not enough, however, to merely observe that the transition from active to ergative or accusative syntax involves a replacement of a semantic system with a more abstract syntactic system. We need to also try and offer some explanation of how this change came about. Was it merely the result of a slow inevitable drift from semantic to grammatical principles, as in the gradual loss of semantic value (loss of iconicity) that accounts for the transformation of lexical words into grammatical items?[5] Or can we suggest a materially based motivation for the move from semantics to syntax? Further, is such a motive to be sought in the intellectual needs of expressing abstract thoughts, or in the practical needs of material existence?

The explanation must, as we have argued throughout, be sought on material grounds, in the material existence of human beings, at a certain time and place, in certain historical conditions. We suggest that it was in the rise of civilisation, with the dramatic expansion in activities that accompanied the growth of cities, that we find the explanation for this historical transition.

When cities arose, on the basis of a surplus of food sufficient to sustain the administrators, priests, or kings, simple exchange came to be regulated and institutionalised, with tributes, taxes and the start of systematic distribution of goods. The development of the activities of weighing, measuring and recording transactions, must have become important, in fact, central to the organisation of life.

Schmandt-Besserat shows how a system of recording agricultural products developed from about 8,000 BP in Mesopotamia, based on shaped clay tokens, each shape representing a different commodity. For example, 1 sphere = 1 bushel of grain; 1 lenticular disk = 1 flock of sheep; 1 large tetrahedron = one week's work or the work of a gang; 1 small tetrahedron = one day's work (Schmandt-Besserat 1992, p. 162).

The practice developed over time of enclosing the tokens in clay envelopes, marked on the outside with symbols representing the tokens. Later, tokens were omitted, and a flat tablet was marked with cuneiform shapes, derived from the shape of the token, and other symbols representing numbers (Schmandt-Besserat 1992, p. 192).

By the third millennium, this system of record-keeping had developed into what we now know as cuneiform writing. By 3500 to 2500 BC the civilisation of Sumer had a redistribution economy involving the production of surplus goods by commoners that were surrendered to the temple. An élite administered the communal property, and the temple conferred meaning and pomp on the act of giving.

> In sum, the plain tokens of the 8th to 5th millennium BC made possible the rise of a rank society, preparing the background for the powerful 4th to 3rd millennium bureaucracy. I also postulate that, vice versa, the development of political power was based on the development of reckoning technology and could not have occurred in the same way without it. According to Lévi-Strauss, the first use of writing was, ultimately, a control on the production of real goods – but so were the first tokens. (Schmandt-Besserat 1992, p. 178)

Here we have evidence that both writing and counting systems developed at the same time, not out of the heads of writers and mathematicians, but from the organisation of a vital administrative activity, centrally connected to the distribution of goods.

The collection of temple tributes must have entailed a system of weights and measures, for commodities such as oil, grain and so on. Stone weights dated to the Uruk period showed that goods were being weighed and measured (Schmandt-Besserat 1992, p. 181).

The syntax of weights and measures

Is it possible to trace a connection between the activity of weighing and measuring and the changes in grammar that characterise a transition from grammar based on semantic roles to one based on syntactic functions? The first point to make here is that weighing and measuring, although apparently practical activities, introduce into human life the requirement to handle abstract relations such as weight, measure and value. These phenomena are ideal forms in Ilyenkov's sense, as discussed in Chapter Two. Like any other activity, weighing and measuring will carry with them a wealth of new terms that will establish themselves in the language. More significantly, however, the requirement to express forms of value will start to have an effect on the shape of utterances, introducing new forms of grammar.[6] This point can be illustrated first by looking at the very specific ways of handling weights and measures in modern English.

(9) a.   The woman weighed the chicken.
    b.   The chicken was weighed by the woman.
    c.   The chicken weighs four pounds.

but not

(9) d.   *The chicken weighs.
    e.   *Four pounds is weighed by the chicken.

The verb *weigh* in these examples is both an action and an expression of value. In (9a), as an action it has an agent as a subject, and patient as object. The sentence is still organised on semantic lines. In (9c), as a value expression, the verb has a patient as subject, and a value in 'object' position. That the verb in (9c) is transitive is shown by the unacceptability of (9d); the verb has to have some kind of object. The object in (9c) is not a patient, and as (9e) shows, it cannot become the subject of a passive.

The verb in (9c) is not a verb of action, nor is it a stative verb, expressing a property. It appears that this verb would not fit into a semantically-based system of grammar such as Active grammar. The fact that (9c) cannot be turned into a passive form, suggests that here we have an utterance that is no longer a simple representation of action or state of affairs in the world, but the expression of a relation, specifically between a commodity and a value. As a verb expressing a value relation it must be followed by an item – normally a numerical item.[7]

It appears that the institutionalised activity of exchange must lead inevitably to abstraction and to syntactic rather than semantic grammar. When a horse, chicken, even a slave, can be exchanged for goods on the same basis as a roll of cloth or a bag of wheat, it is clear that some kind of generalisation or abstraction is taking place. In expressions of value such as weighing, measuring or valuing, there is some measure of value that makes the items to be exchanged equivalent. As we have seen in Chapter 2 (pp. 29–32), this value is not a physical phenomenon, but a form of ideality. It is an abstract relation that may be given concrete form in a weight, or a yardstick, or a coin; but its essence as an ideal form is that it is a relation – which is why the verb cannot appear in its relational function without both subject and (object) value expression.

While it is quite possible that a semantically-based grammar, such as an Active or noun-class language, might find a way of handling activities such as weighing, measuring, and later the more abstract expressions of value represented by money, it seems most likely that the functional requirements of such tasks would compel speakers to create specific language forms for them – registers characterised by new linguistic forms, and therefore in some tension with established forms of the language. Now all would depend on the question of how central to the life of the society these new activities are. In a city, where forms of exchange and distribution of goods are vital to all individuals, such activities as weighing and measuring would certainly come to assume a central importance – as central, for example, as money in our own lives. The linguistic forms associated with these activities would tend to diffuse across the rest of the grammar, eventually leading to new, more abstract forms of syntax.

This example does not tell the whole story of how abstract syntax came about[8] – but offers a suggestion of the kind of factors that would lead eventually to a syntax based on relations between phenomena, rather than the direct representation of visual or physical form, and would incidentally lead to abstract relational thinking.

Gordon Childe observes that between 6000 and 300 BC humans learnt to harness the force of oxen and of winds; invented the plough, the wheeled cart and the sailing boat; discovered the chemical processes involved in smelting copper ores and the physical properties of metals; and began to work out an accurate solar calendar. They thereby equipped themselves for urban life, and prepared the way for a civilisation which required writing, processes of reckoning and standards of measurement – instruments of a new way of transmitting knowledge and of exact sciences. In no period of history until the days of Galileo was progress in knowledge so rapid or far-reaching discoveries so frequent (Gordon Childe 1965, p. 105).

This period of the rise of cities saw an enormous expansion in the range of activities undertaken by individuals and in the number of distinct social roles (priests, administrators, tax collectors and soldiers); and the number and range of language registers, each with their specific vocabulary, systems of classification and unique linguistic forms. Many of these registers would further the process of adapting active verbs to new relational roles.

Here it is important to recall Vygotsky's observation that abstract thinking is not merely something that developed by accident over thousands of years, nor is it a result of genetic mutations, but a cultural achievement, involving the skill of understanding and manipulating ideal forms.

We have seen that the classifications underlying noun-class systems are reminiscent of the associative systems (complexes or sets) that characterise children's thinking. A history of syntactic development has to explain how thinking progressed beyond such associations to the stage of generalisation, thinking at least in notions if not in concepts.

Interestingly, the rise of the state and political organisation would have a part to play in this development too. Kinship relations that govern foraging and pre-political life are based on essentially arbitrary factors – they are simply a matter of birth. In the city, social relations are based on functional categories – priest, farmer, soldier, tax payer or tax collector, and so on. In social terms, this shift of relations is equivalent to the shift from organising in sets or complexes to organising in notions, classes of phenomena that are categorised not simply by accidental visual resemblance but on the basis of more abstract functional properties.

Language shaped by social needs: the English modal verbs

The way that social needs shape syntax may be further illustrated by the historical development of the English modal system. The modern English modal auxiliary verbs *can, could, shall, should, will, would, may, might, must,* derive from verbs that behaved in Middle English like main verbs. They could stand alone as the verb of a sentence. They could take objects, they could be combined with verbal auxiliaries such as *have* and *be*. In modern English, however, these verbs cannot normally stand alone: they are auxiliary to a main verb. Their meaning, or cognitive function is a fairly complex one, which can be roughly described as expressing a speaker's judgement or evaluation of the proposition in the predicate. Many uses of modal auxiliaries in modern English are so conventional that their function is hard to detect, but in a contrasting pair of sentences like:

(10) a.   He tells the truth.

      b.   He might tell the truth.

it is fairly clear that (10b) expresses a judgement of probability on the part of the speaker.

Lightfoot (1976; 1979) suggests that the system of modal verbs first emerged in English, quite clearly and suddenly, at the end of the fourteenth century. A series of changes in the system took place over the next two centuries, and when these changes were completed, in the sixteenth century, the modal verbs 'no longer occurred with *-ing* or after *to*, they were no longer found with *have*, and they were limited to one per sentence. In the seventeenth century, ordinary verbs stopped undergoing inversion, and no longer preceded the negative *not*' (Aitchison 1991, p. 99). The modals had become, in other words, a class of verbs that behave in a fashion quite distinct from ordinary verbs.

Described in this fashion, the change appears to be simply an adjustment of the grammatical system. This is how some linguists might treat the matter. However, two facts of history should prevent the discussion from ending at this point. One is the matter of other developments in the English language in this period. Many other changes were taking place, among them a rapid growth in vocabulary as the upsurge in scholarship and learning associated with the Renaissance led to an influx of Latin and Greek vocabulary into the language. There were changes associated with new activities in science and the growth of new areas of scholarship, as the next section will show. Since the sixteenth century the rate of change appears to have slowed. There was a relatively conservative period of consolidation in the late seventeeth and eighteenth centuries, for example. As a result, early modern English, the language of Shakespeare, is still relatively easy to read after four hundred years, whereas Middle English seems, at first sight, like a foreign language.

The second fact of history is that the period in which these changes took place led up to and included the English Revolution of 1640, a period at the end of which 'The state power protecting an old order that was essentially feudal was violently overthrown, power passed into the hands of a new class, and so the freer development of capitalism was made possible' (Hill 1955, p. 11).

The movements that led to the overthrow of this old order were shaped long before the Revolution itself. The key period may have been 1350 to 1500, the late Middle Ages. In this period there was the Hundred Years War, when the English monarchy lost all its French possessions except Calais. There were a number of recurrences of the Plague from 1348 on, that decimated the population, loosened the ties of the feudal order and led to increased social mobility and a shortage of labour. The resulting reaction of the ruling class, to tighten up laws governing labour on the land, and to introduce a poll tax, led ultimately to the Peasants' Revolt. At the same time, towns were growing in importance, especially in the East Midlands and the North. A new class of merchants and family household manufacturers arose. Their voice seems to have been found initially among the supporters of Wyclif. Discontent and dissent were channelled into religious debates, reaching a crescendo after the abolition of censorship in 1640. The old feudal order was destroyed, as a new social class struggled to take political control.

The question that arises here is whether there is any connection between these two sets of facts – social turmoil and a revolution in social relations, on the one hand; and a dramatic series of changes in the language on the other. It seems plausible that there was such a connection. In this period of English history the whole people were for the first time able to take part in a debate over their own future, and it seems fitting that the grammar of English should respond with the creation of the new system of modal verbs. Modality is the aspect of grammar that provides speakers with a flexible means of expressing interpersonal relations, values and judgements. It would appear to be an essential feature of argumentation, theorising, speculation, and so on. There seems to be a strong case for proposing that this change in the grammar of the language was a response to the requirements of speakers, to the cognitive tasks of considering and debating possible future actions, alternatives and outcomes. Such an approach to the study of changes in grammatical systems would, I suggest, throw new light on facts that have until now been considered exclusively linguistic phenomena.

Scientific registers

Halliday (1992) argues the development of writing, of mathematics and philosophy, and of experimental science has produced lasting changes in syntax. There is no doubt that scientific language has also shaped our language since its rise in the sixteenth and seventeenth centuries. Halliday shows how scientific language has taken particular linguistic forms, related to the tasks of science as an activity. In the first stage, concrete actions are transformed into nouns, such as *action*, *movement*, *force*, *process*, and so on. Then these nominalised actions become part of a subject–predicate construction, in other words, are put into sentences in the role of subject, object, complement, and so on, as in Newton's:

> That the flux and reflux of the sea arises from the actions of the sun and moon. (1686, p. 435)

> [A]ll bodies by percussion excite vibrations in the air. (1730, p. 280)

> The extension, hardness, impenetrability, mobility and inertia of the whole, result from the extension, hardness, impenetrability, mobility and inertia of the parts. (1686, p. 399)

A number of other features of scientific English can be enumerated. Halliday notes that Biaggi's study of the language of Newton and of Galileo shows the same grammatical features in scientific English and scientific Italian of the seventeenth century (Biaggi 1989; see Halliday 1992, p. 77).

> Neither Galileo nor Newton was inventing new forms of language. Probably all the grammatical features of their discourse already existed in Italian, or English. What they did was to reconstruct the probabilities; and in doing so, to create a new register – not alone, of course, but in conjunction with others taking part in the activity of science.

Perhaps the most important feature of scientific language noted by Halliday is the newly emerging clause type 'happening (a) caused happening (x)' (Halliday 1992, p. 78), two nominalised processes linked by a verb expressing logical relationship between them. What scientific language achieves, in Halliday's view, is that

> experience is first construed in the form of clauses, as a world of happening which can be experimented with; and then reconstrued in the form of nominals . . . as a world of things, symbolically fixed so that they can be observed and measured, reasoned about, and brought to order. (1992, p. 78)[9]

We can argue that this register is shaped partly by its content, partly by the intellectual tasks that it has to carry out.

What scientific language has to do is to manipulate the highly abstracted phenomena of concepts. However, it was not science that started the process of shaping a language capable of handling abstractions. This task probably had been carried out by communication associated with the exchange of goods at a much earlier stage.

The effect of the trend that started in scientific language of converting actions and processes into things can be seen in today's techno-bureaucratic language, where the process has reached a fairly extreme form, and new nouns such as *spend*, *savings*, *return*, *throughput*, and *overspend* are rapidly created and equally rapidly discarded. Similar tendencies are found in a whole number of registers such as scientific writing, journalism, social science, administration, and political discourse, indicating a general trend towards what Halliday calls 'thinginess' (1992, p. 68).

However this trend is not a one-way process. Verbs can also be formed from nouns, and other linguistic forms can be more and more freely interchanged. Aitchison mentions such 'conversions' as a feature of modern English: 'If this trend continues, the eventual result may be complete interchangeability of items such as nouns and verbs which were once kept rigidly apart' (1991, p. 118).

As an example of such conversions, here is an extract from the scientist Stephen Rose writing in the *Guardian* (17 November 1994):

> The competitive nature of the grant system and its 3–year cycle means that *short-termism* is endemic and safety essential, so research *bandwagons* as anxious *me-tooers* chase the market leaders who have developed this year's fashionable model.

In one sentence there are three creative uses of innovative forms – *short-termism*, an ideology noun formed from the adjectival phrase *short-term*; *bandwagon*, a noun converted into a verb; *me-tooers*, an agentive noun formed from a phrase.

SEX-GENDER

One final example of the way that social life might influence grammar arises from a detail of language history that has long puzzled linguists –

the rise of sex-gender marking in Indo-European languages,[10] which would repay study, in the light of its historical emergence at a time when matrilineal society was giving way to patrilineal in Old Europe.

Brosman suggests sex-gender was introduced into Indo-European shortly after the separation of Anatolian languages from the main Indo-European language family. The Anatolian language Hittite had only two genders – common and neuter. In the non-Anatolian branch some words with female associations started to take the ending -*a* and eventually a dual system dividing originally common nouns into masculine and feminine forms was established (Brosman 1982; Corbett 1991, p. 309). The separation of Anatolian is dated by Gamkrelidze and Ivanov between 6,000 and 5,000 BP.[11]

At this time, the Indo-Europeans' culture seems to have included cattle-breeding, agriculture, horse-riding and wheeled transport. Their culture is associated historically with the displacement of matrilineal systems by patrilineal. For Gimbutas, the invasions of the Indo-European people associated with what she calls Kurgan culture into Europe were instrumental in the replacement of the original matrilineal civilisation of Old Europe by a patrilineal culture based on horse-riding warriors, originating from the steppes of southern Russia. These invasions started around 4400 to 4300 BC continuing sporadically till 3000 BC (Gimbutas 1991, p. 352).

Is it just by chance that the introduction into the grammar of consistent distinctions between male and female, expressed in the gender system, started after this cultural shift in social organisation and in relations between the sexes? The topic is one that would well repay further study, though unfortunately it is not one we can pursue here.

DIFFUSION

To summarise this model of language change, language form can be related to the predominant activities that taken together constitute social existence. New activities bring with them new communicative demands, forming new registers, and new forms of language that are rationally explicable in terms of the new tasks of communication.

Depending on the value of a register to the life of the community, new forms may or may not subsequently extend throughout the language, resulting in a gradual but thorough readjustment of the whole system.

Social metaphors that predominate in a society at a given historical, economic or political stage of development similarly derive from the activities around which social life is organised, though the connection may be indirect, and values, beliefs, myths, oral traditions, and so on, are all relevant to the creation of social metaphors. Social metaphors, varying over time, may play an important part in language change at every level, from vocabulary to grammatical function words. The transition of individual words from lexical to grammatical, or to arbitrary form, is an expression of the way social themes shape grammar. The more important a meaning is to a community, the more likely it is that its linguistic form will be used in the grammar. The Trobrianders' widespread use of the classifying particle *ka'i* (see p. 145), from the word for tree, shows just how important to their lives are trees and plants. The widespread use of forms of *have* as a grammatical formative in modern European languages similarly indicates the importance to our societies of the property relationship. To the early Indo-Europeans differences between men and women came at a certain point to assume a significance they had never had before, and it was after that point that sex-gender may have started to play an important role in grammar.

The ideology or world-view of a society can be discerned and excavated from deep inside grammar – a point that linguists as far apart as W. von Humboldt (1767–1835), F. Boas (1858–1942), B. Whorf (1897–1941) and M. Halliday have made, though their deterministic notion that grammar shapes the world-view of speakers should be rejected. Even complex social relationships, such as exchange of commodities, can be buried deep in the grammar of a language.

If we can understand the importance of social value in the process of grammaticisation of signs, the movement from iconic to arbitrary, we may be able more successfully to reconstruct from apparently unimportant little bits of grammar the history of social metaphors that caused them to be pressed into grammatical service in the first place. Today's conventional form may at one time have represented to the speakers of the language highly significant distinctions.

Finally we should turn from details of grammatical change to the more general question that was put at the start of this chapter, of whether there is progress in language. Just as the history of human society is a freeing of the species from dependency on its environment, and a freeing of the individual from the life of the herd, so there is a historical movement in language, in the sense of syntax becoming progressively free of the practical, activity-related forms which dominated the language of pre-political societies.

The form of languages associated with foraging and other pre-political societies is, as we have argued, related to the needs of people to describe and record the close relationship between human beings and their environment, to organise and record human activities in this environment. A semantically-based grammar – active, noun-class, or even ergative-based grammar – may represent a logical solution to this task. The basic semantic relations, such as agent–action–patient, are those of practical human beings actively attempting to transform the world around them. These are the fundamental relations of the labour process.

However, the syntax of modern languages is more complex than this. This is not the result of the simple addition of more and more transformations on an original base, but rather a fundamental transformation in the base, in response to the content of human activity. Language evolution is not a case of the transformation of form, but transformation in the relation between form and content. The relational activities associated with civilisation – first, counting and measuring, then buying, selling, writing, science, perhaps also philosophy and logic – have reshaped languages as their speakers apprehend and express the general rules and principles by which the world operates. While weighing and measuring are thoroughly practical tasks, they involve the mental handling of abstract forms – ideal forms of value.

Other activities have produced additions to knowledge, and have reorganised human thinking. Luria and Vygotsky's studies (1992) suggest that historical forms of thinking first took the form of association along quite accidental lines – thinking in sets or complexes, based on immediate sensory impressions, with the organisation of grammar along the same lines. Subsequently, human beings started to deal with more abstract notions, with ideal forms that arose from social activity. These led the way, ultimately, to higher forms of thinking in concepts, the material of logic, philosophy and science. The creation of relational forms of language, that is, of syntax, has provided the means for humans to manipulate notions and concepts. In turn, these concepts and new, related forms of intellectual activity, have shaped and will continue to reshape, today's urban and international languages. We conclude: language changes are progressive, not in the sense that today's languages are any better than those that preceded them, but in the sense that, historically, humans have more and more to say about the world, and continue to expand the means to say it.

NOTES

1. This was argued strongly by August Schleicher (1850; 1863), Max Müller (1861) and Dwight Whitney (1875) (see Jespersen 1922, pp. 76–8).
2. Active languages, have been identified among the Amerindian NaDene language family; the Sioux group of families; the Gulf group, and the South American Tupi-Guaraní family (Klimov 1974). Active languages as a 'typology' differ from Class languages discussed in the previous chapter, though sharing some properties. Class and active languages may possibly be distributed according to language family, with Class languages found in Africa, and Active types in America and other parts of the world (cf. Lehmann 1992, p. 108).
3. The sounds represented *q!* and *s!* are not clicks but ejectives, and can be represented in IPA symbols as [q'] [s']. The transcription in the text is taken from Klimov (1974).
4. Also termed 'nominative' or 'nominative-accusative' languages.
5. For example, the modal auxiliary *can* that derives from a Middle English verb meaning 'know'.
6. Special grammatical features for value are widespread. In Kiriwinian, a bundle

of yams, the measure of value in Trobriand society, is the only item that may be counted without special numerical classifiers (Malinowski 1966, vol. 1, p. 90). In Pima-Papago, money also has unique features of grammar. Money is the only non-food item that takes the alienable possession suffix -*ga* (Bahr 1986).

7. For further discussion of the syntactical peculiarities of value expressions, see Jones (1991).

8. In fact value expressions cannot be seen as a route to 'transitivity', a term often used to characterise 'modern' syntax. Sentences such as (9c) are not transitive, because they cannot be made passive. Nor are they intransitive, because they must have a value after the verb. They are a unique form of syntax. The argument here is about their importance in breaking down a purely semantic organisation of grammar.

9. Halliday (1994) explores the historical development of the language of science in greater detail.

10. The subject goes back to the work of Brugmann in the nineteenth century (see Brugmann 1891).

11. Or 4000 to 3000 BC (Hayward 1989, p. 74).

Bibliography

ABBREVIATIONS

Adv. Inf. Res.	Advances in Infancy Research
Afr. Lang. Sts	African Language Studies
Afr. Sts	African Studies
Am. Anth.	American Anthropologist
Am. J. Phys. Anth.	American Journal of Physical Anthropology
Am. Sp.	American Speech
Anim. Beh.	Animal Behaviour
Anth. Ling.	Anthropological Linguistics
Arch. Ling.	Archivum Linguisticum
Aus. J. Ling.	Australian Journal of Linguistics
Beh. & Br. Sci.	Behavioral and Brain Sciences
CA	Current Anthropology
Cam. Arch. Jnl	Cambridge Archaeological Journal
Cog. Neur.	Cognitive Neuropsychology
Hist. Ling.	Historical Linguistics
IJAL	International Journal of American Linguistics
J. Anth. Arch.	Journal of Anthropological Archaeology
J. Ch. Lang.	Journal of Child Language
J. Exp. Psych.	Journal of Experimental Psychology
J. I.-E. Sts	Journal of Indo-European Studies
J. Ling.	Journal of Linguistics
J. Mind & Beh.	Journal of Mind and Behavior
J. Morph.	Journal of Morphology
J. Pidg. & Cre. Lang.	Journal of Pidgin and Creole Languages
J. Theor. Bio.	Journal of Theoretical Biology
JASA	Journal of the Acoustic Society of America
JHE	Journal of Human Evolution
Lang. & Comm.	Language and Communication
Lang. in Soc.	Language in Society
LOS	Language Origins Society
Lang. Sci.	Language Sciences
Psych. Rev.	Psychological Review
Sci. Am.	Scientific American
St. Afr. Ling.	Studies in African Linguistics
Trans. Phil. Soc.	Transactions of the Philological Society
Yrbk of Phys. Anth.	Yearbook of Physical Anthropology

REFERENCES

Aiello, L. C. (1993) 'Encephalization and gut size', Paper presented at the Palaeontological Anthropology meeting, Toronto, April.

Aiello, L. C. (1994) 'The fossil evidence for modern human origins in Africa', *Am. Anth.* 95: 73–96.

Aiello, L. C. (forthcoming) 'Hominine preadaptations for language and cognition', in P. Mellars and K. Gibson (eds), *Modelling the Early Human Mind*. Cambridge: McDonald Inst. Monograph Series.

Aiello, L. C., & C. Dean (1990) *An Introduction to Human Evolutionary Anatomy*. NY: Academic Press.

Aiello, L. C., and R. I. M. Dunbar (1993) 'Neocortex size, group size and the evolution of language', *CA* 34: 184–93.

Aitchison, J. (1989) 'Spaghetti junctions and recurrent routes: some preferred pathways in language evolution', *Lingua* 77: 151–71.

Aitchison, J. (1991) *Language Change, Progress or Decay*? Cambridge: Cambridge University Press.

Allott, R. (1992) 'The motor theory of language; origin and function', in Wind *et al.* 1992; 105–19.

Allott, R. (1994) 'Gestural equivalence (equivalents) of language', Paper read at the tenth LOS conference, 'Social and Cultural Origins of Language', July, Berkely, Calif.

Alpher, B. (1987) 'Feminine as the unmarked grammatical gender: buffalo girls are no fools', *Aus. J. Ling.* 7: 169–87.

Arensburg, B., A. M. Tillier, B. Vandermeersch, H. Duday, L. A. Schepartz and Y. Rak (1989) 'A middle Palaeolithic human hyoid bone', *Nature* 338: 758–60.

Armstrong, D. F., W. C. Stokoe & S. E. Wilcox (1994) 'Signs of the origin of syntax', *CA* 35: 349–68.

Armstrong, D. F., W. C. Stokoe & S. E. Wilcox (1995) *Gesture and the Nature of Language*. Cambridge: Cambridge University Press.

Bahr, D. M. (1986) 'Pima-Papago -*ga* "alienability"', *IJAL* 52: 161–71.

Bakhtin M. (1986) *Speech Genres and Other Late Essays*. Austin, Tex.: University of Texas Press.

Barnard, A. (1988) 'Kinship language and production: a conjectural history of Khosian soial structure', *Africa* 58: 29–50.

BBC Horizon (1992) *Before Babel*. Tapescript of programme transmitted 6 April 1992. London: BBC.

BBC Horizon (1993) *Chimp Talk*. Tapescript of programme transmitted 13 December 1993. London: BBC.

Becker, A. L. (1975) 'A linguistic image of nature: the Burmese numerative classifier system', *Linguistics* 165: 109–21.

Bednark, R. G. (1994) 'Comment' on Byers 1994, *CA* 35: 381–2.

Bellugi, U. and E. S. Klima (1976) 'Two faces of sign: iconic and abstract', in Steklis and Harnad 1976; 514–38.

Bender, M. L. (1973) 'Linguistic indeterminacy', *Lang. Sci.* 26: 7–12.

Biaggi, M. L. A. (1989) 'The Evolution of Scientific English', Paper presented to workshop at University of Bologna, 22–3 May 1989.

Bichakjian, B. H. (1987) *Evolution in Language* (Linguistica Extranea Studia 18). Ann Arbor, Mich.: Karoma.

Bichakjian, B. H. (1988) 'Neoteny and language evolution', in Landsberg 1988; 113–36, 145–8.

Bickerton, D. (1984) 'The language bioprogram hypothesis', *Beh. & Br. Sci.* 7: 173–221.

Bickerton, D. (1990) *Language & Species*. Chicago: University of Chicago Press.
Biesele, M. (1993) *Women Like Meat*. Johannesburg: Wiwatersrand and Indiana University Press.
Binford, L. R. (1985) 'Human ancestors: changing views of their behavior', *J. Anth. Arch.* 4: 292–327.
Binford, L. R. (1989) 'Isolating the transition to cultural adaptations: an organizational approach', in Trinkaus 1989b; 18–41.
Bloom, L., and M. Lahey (1978) *Language Development and Language Disorders*. New York: J. Wiley.
Boas, F. (1911) *The Mind of Primitive Man*. New York: Macmillan, 1934.
Boehm, C. (1992) 'Vocal communication of *Pan troglodytes*: "triangulating" to the origin of spoken language', in Wind *et al.* 1992; 323–50.
Boesch, C. (1991) 'Teaching among wild chimpanzees', *Anim. Beh.* 41: 530–3.
Boesch, C. (1993) 'Aspects of transmission of tool-use in wild chimpanzees', in Gibson and Ingold 1993; 171–84.
Brace, C. L. (1979) 'Krapina, "classic" Neanderthals and the evolution of the human face', *JHE* 8: 527–50.
Braitenberg, V., and A. Schüz (1992) 'Basic features of cortical connectivitiy and some consideration on language', in Wind *et al.* 1992; 89–102.
Bräuer, G. (1989) 'The evolution of modern humans: a comparison of the African and non-African evidence', in Mellars and Stringer 1989; 123–54.
Bräuer, G., and F. H. Smith (eds) (1992) *Continuity or Replacement*. Rotterdam: Balkema.
Breitborde, L. B. (1975) 'Communicating insults and compliments in Jacaltec', *Anth. Ling.* 17: 381–403.
Brosman, P. W. (1982) 'The development of the PIE feminine', *J. I.-E. Sts* 10: 253–72.
Brown, R. (1973) *A First Language: The Early Stages*. Cambridge, Mass.: Harvard University Press.
Brugmann, K. (1891) *Elements of the Comparative Grammar of the Indo-Germanic Languages: A Concise Exposition of the History of Sanskrit*, vol. 2, *Morphology*, trans. R. S. Conway and W. H. D. Rouse. Strasburg: Trübner.
Bruner, J. S. (1981) 'Intention in the structure of action and interaction', *Adv. Inf. Res.* 1: 41–56.
Bühler, K. (1934) *The Mental Development of the Child*. London: Kegan Paul.
Burke Leacock, E. (1981) *Myths of Male Dominance*. New York and London: Monthly Review.
Burling, R. (1993) 'Primate calls, human language, and non-verbal communication', *CA* 34: 25–53.
Burr, D. B. (1976) 'Neandertal vocal tract reconstructions: a critical appraisal', *JHE* 5: 285–90.
Burton, M., and L. Kirk (1976) 'Semantic reality of Bantu noun classes: the Kikuyu case', *St. Afr. Ling.* 7: 157–74.
Byers, M. (1994) 'Symboling and the Middle-Upper Paleolithic Transition', *CA* 35: 369–80
Bynon, T. (1974) Review of *The Origin and Diversification of Language* by M. Swadesh (1971), *J. Ling.* 10: 153–61.
Byrne, R. W. and A. Whiten (eds) (1988) *Machiavellian Intelligence: Social Expertise and the Evolution of Intellect in Monkeys, Apes and Humans*. Oxford: Oxford University Press.
Callaghan, C. A. (1993) 'Comment' on Burling 1993, *CA* 34: 25–53.

Calvin, W. H. (1983) 'A stone's throw and its launch window: timing precision and its implications for language and hominid brains', *J. Theor. Bio.* 104: 121–35.

Campbell, B. (1988) *Humankind Emerging* (5th edn). Glenview, Ill.: Scott, Foreman.

Cavalli-Sforza, L. L. (1991) 'Genes, people and languages', *Sci. Am.* 265, 5: 72–8.

Cavalli-Sforza, L. L., A. Piazza, P. Menozzi and J. Mountain (1988) 'Reconstruction of human evolution: bringing together genetic, archaeological and linguistic data', *Proc. Nat. Acad. Sci. USA* 85: 6002–6.

Chance, N. A. (1990) *The Iñupiat and Arctic Alsaka: An Ethnography of Development*. Fort Worth: Holt, Rinehart & Winston.

Cheney, D. L., and R. M. Seyfarth (1990) *How Monkeys See the World: Inside the Mind of Another Species*. Chicago: University of Chicago Press.

Chomsky, N. (1964) 'Formal discussion' in U. Bellugi and R. Brown (eds) *The Acquisition of Language*, reprinted in J. P. B. Allen and P. van Buren *Chomsky: Selected Readings*. Oxford, OUP: 129–34.

Chomsky, N. (1965) *Aspects of the Theory of Syntax*. Cambridge, Mass.: MIT Press.

Chomsky, N. (1968) *Language and Mind*. New York: Harcourt.

Chomsky, N. (1979) *Language and Responsibility*. Hassocks: Harvester.

Chomsky, N. (1980) *Rules and Representations*. Oxford: Blackwell.

Chomsky, N. (1981) *Lectures on Government and Binding*. Dordrecht: Foris.

Chomsky, N. (1988) *Language and Problems of Knowledge: The Managua Lectures*. Cambridge, Mass.: MIT Press.

Clark G. A., and J. M. Lindly (1989) 'The case of continuity: observations on the biocultural transition in Europe and western Asia', in Mellars and Stringer 1989; 626–76.

Clark, R. A. (1978) 'The transition from action to gesture', in Lock 1978; 231–59.

Clarke, G. (1969) *World Prehistory* (2nd edn). Cambridge: Cambridge University Press.

Comrie, B. (ed.) (1987) *The World's Major Languages*. Beckenham: Croom Helm.

Corballis, M. (1994). 'Comment' on Armstrong *et al.* 1994, *CA* 35: 349–68.

Corbett, G. (1991) *Gender* Cambridge: Cambridge University Press.

Cowan, W. M. (1979) 'The development of the brain', *Sci. Am.* (Sept.): 107–17.

Creider, C. A. (1975) 'The semantic system of noun classes in Proto-Bantu', *Anth. Ling.* 17: 127–38.

Darwin, C. (1859) *The Origin of Species*. London: Murray.

Darwin, C. (1872) *The Expression of the Emotions in Man and Animals*. London: Murray.

Davidson, I., and Noble, W. (1989) 'The archaeology of perception: traces of depiction and language', *CA* 30: 125–55.

Deacon, H. J. (1989) 'Late Pleistocene palaeoecology and archaeology in the southern Cape, South Africa', in Mellars and Stringer 1989; 547–64.

Delson, E. (ed.) (1985) *Ancestors: The Hard Evidence*. New York: Liss.

Dixon, R. M. W. (1972) *The Dyirbal Language of North Queensland*. Cambridge: Cambridge University Press.

Dixon, R. M. W. (ed.) (1987) *Studies in Ergativity*. Amsterdam: Elsevier.

Dixon, R. M. W. (1991) 'A changing language situation: the decline of Dyirbal, 1963–1989', *Lang. in Soc.* 20: 183–200.

Donald, M. (1991) *Origins of the Modern Mind: Three Stages in the Evolution of Culture and Cognition.* Cambridge, Mass. and London: Harvard University Press.

Dorozynski, A. (1993) 'Possible Neanderthal ancestor found', *Science* 262: 991.

Dreyfus, H. L., and N. Rabinow (1982) *Michel Foucault: Beyond Structuralism and Hermeneutics.* Hassocks: Harvester Press.

Duchin, E. L. (1990) 'The Evolution of articulate speech: comparative anatomy of the oral cavity in Pan and Homo', *JHE* 19: 687–97.

Dunbar, R. I. M. (1988) 'Darwinizing man: a commentary', in L. Betzig, M. B. Mulder and P. Turke (eds), *Human Reproductive Behaviour: A Darwinian Perspective.* Cambridge: Cambridge University Press: 161–9.

Dunbar, R. I. M. (1992) 'Neocortex size as a constraint on group size in primates', *JHE* 22: 469–3.

Ellis, J., and R. Davies (1951) 'The Soviet linguistics controversy', *Soviet Studies* 3: 209–64.

Engels, F. (1942) *The Origins of the Family, Private Property and the State.* Beijing: Foreign Languages Press.

Engels, F. (1954) 'The part played by labour in the transition from ape to man', in his *The Dialectics of Nature*, Moscow: Foreign Languages Publishing House.

Englefield, R. (1977) *Language: Its Origin and Relation to Thought*, ed. G. A. Wells and D. R. Oppenheimer. London: Pemberton.

Falk, D. (1980a) 'Language, handedness and primate brains: did the australopithecines sign?', *Am. Anth.* 82: 72–8.

Falk, D. (1980b) 'Hominid brain evolution: the approach from paleoneurology', *Yrbk of Phys. Anth.* 23: 93–107.

Falk, D. (1990) 'Comment' on Pinker and Bloom 1990, *Beh. & Br. Sci.* 13: 707–84.

Fodor, J. A. (1983) *The Modularity of Mind.* Cambridge, Mass.: MIT Press.

Foley, R. (1989) 'The ecological conditions of speciation: a comparative approach to the origin of anatomically modern humans', in Mellars and Stringer 1989; 298–320.

Foley, R. (1994) 'Speciation, extinction and climatic change in hominid evolution', *JHE* 26: 275–89.

Foley, R., and P. C. Lee (1989) 'Finite social space, evolutionary pathways, and reconstructing hominid behaviour', *Science* 243: 901–6.

Foster, M. L. (1983) 'Solving the insoluble: language genetics today', in de Grolier 1983; 455–80.

Foster, M. L. (1989) 'Symbolic origins and transitions in the Palaeolithic', in Mellars and Stringer 1989; 517–39.

Foucault, M. (1970) *The Order of Things*, trans. A. Sheridan from *Les Mots et les choses.* London: Tavistock.

Frayer, D. W. (1992) 'The persistence of Neanderthal features in post-Neanderthal Europeans', in Bräuer and Smith 1992; 179–88.

Gamkrelidze T. V., and V. V. Ivanov (1995) *Indo-European and the Indo-Europeans* (new edn), trans. J. Nichols. Berlin: Mouton de Gruyter.

Gardner, R. A., and B. T. Gardner (1969) 'Teaching sign language to chimpanzees', *Science* 165: 664–72.

Gardner, R. A., and B. T. Gardner (1992) 'Early signs of language in cross-fostered chimpanzees', in Wind *et al.* 1992; 351–84.

Gellner, E. (1989) 'Culture, constraint and community: semantic and coercive compensations for the genetic under-determination of *Homo sapiens sapiens*', in Mellars and Stringer 1989; 514–28.

Gibson, K. R. (1991) 'Tools, language and intelligence: evolutionary implications', *Man* 26: 255–64.

Gibson, K. R. (1993) 'Tool use, language and social behaviour in relationship to information processing capacities', in Gibson and Ingold 1993; 251–70.

Gibson K. R., and T. Ingold (eds.) (1993) *Tools, Language and Cognition in Human Evolution*. Cambridge: Cambridge University Press.

Gimbutas, M. (1991) *The Civilisation of the Goddess: The World of Old Europe*. San Francisco: HarperCollins.

Givón, T. (1979) *On Understanding Grammar*. New York: Academic Press.

Givón, T. (1994) 'On the co-evolution of language, cognition and neurology', Paper read at the tenth LOS conference, 'Social and Cultural Origins of Language', Berkeley, Calif., July 1994.

Goodall, J. (1988) *In the Shadow of Man* (revised edn), intro. S. J. Gould. London: Weidenfeld & Nicholson.

Gordon Childe, V. (1965) *Man Makes Himself* (4th edn). London: Watts.

Gould, S. J. (1977) *Ontogeny and Phylogeny*. Cambridge Mass.: Belknap.

Gould, S. J. (1988) 'Introduction' to Goodall 1988; v–viii.

Greenberg, J., and M. Ruhlen (1992) 'Linguistic origins of native Americans', *Sci. Am.* (Nov.): 60–5.

Greenfield, P. M. (1991) 'Language, tools and brain: the ontogeny and phylogeny of hierarchically organised sequential behaviour', *Beh. & Br. Sci.* 14: 531–92.

de Grolier, E. (ed.) (1983) *Glossogenetics: The Origin and Evolution of Language* New York: Harwood.

de Grolier, E. (1989) 'Glossogenesis in endolinguistic and exolinguistic perspective: palaeoanthropological data', in Wind *et al.* 1989; 73–138.

de Grolier, E. (1990) 'Towards a tentative reconstruction of Homo sapiens sapiens language(s)?', in W. Koch (ed.), *Geneses of Language*. Bochum: Brookmeyer; 135–63.

Halliday, M. A. K. (1978) *Language as Social Semiotic*. London: Arnold.

Halliday, M. A. K. (1985) *An Introduction to Functional Grammar*. London: Arnold.

Halliday, M. A. K. (1990) 'New ways of meaning: the challenge to applied linguistics', in M. Pütz (ed.) *Thirty Years of Linguistic Evolution*. Amsterdam and Philadelphia PA: Benjamin; 59–95.

Halliday, M. A. K. (1994) 'The construction of knowledge and value in the grammar of scientific discourse, with reference to Charles Darwin's *The Origin of Species*', in M. Coulthard (ed.), *Advances in Written Text Analysis*. London: Routledge; 135–56.

Harrold, F. B. (1992) 'Palaeolithic archaeology, ancient behaviour, and the transition to modern *Homo*', in Bräuer and Smith 1992; 219–30.

Hayden, B. (1993) 'The cultural capacities of Neanderthals: a review and re-evaluation', *JHE* 24: 113–46.

Hayes, C. (1951) *The Ape in our House* New York: Harper & Row.

Hayes, J., and C. Hayes (1951) 'The intellectual development of a home-raised chimpanzee', *Proceedings of the American Philosophical Society* 95: 105.

Hayward, K. M. (1989) 'The Indo-European language and the history of its speakers: the theories of Gamkrelidze & Ivanov', review article, *Lingua* 78: 37–86.

Headland, T. N., and L. A. Reid (1989) 'Hunter-gatherers and their neighbors from prehistory to the present', *CA* 30: 43–66.

Hewes, G. W. (1973) 'Primate communication and the gestural origin of language', reprinted in *CA* Supplement 33 (1992): 65–84.

Hewes, G. W. (1975) *Language Origins: A Bibliography*. The Hague: Mouton.

Hewes, G. W. (1976) 'The current status of the gestural theory of language origin', in Steklis and Harnad 1976; 482–504.

Hewes, G. W. (1983) 'The communicative function of palmar pigmentation in man', *JHE* 12: 297–303.

Hewes, G. W. (1988) 'Ways to accelerate progress in glottogonic research', in Landsberg 1988; 79–88.

Hewes, G. W. (1989) 'The upper Paleolithic expansion of supernaturalism and the advent of fully developed spoken language', in Wind *et al.* 1989; 139–57.

Hill, C. (1955) *The English Revolution 1640* (3rd edn). London: Lawrence and Wishart.

Hockett, C. F. (1978) 'In search of Jove's brow', *Am. Sp.* 53: 243–319.

Hockett, C. F., and R. Ascher (1964) 'The human revolution', *CA* 5: 135–47.

Holloway, R. L. (1976) 'Paleoneurological evidence for language origins', in Steklis and Harnad 1976; 330–47.

Hopkins, W. D. and E. S. Savage-Rumbaugh (1991) 'Vocal communication as a function of differential rearing experiences in Pan paniscus: a preliminary report', *International Journal of Primatology* 12: 559–83.

Houghton, P. (1993) 'Neandertal supralaryngeal vocal tract', *Am. J. Phys. Anth.* 90: 139–46.

Humboldt, W. von (1836) *On Language: The Diversity of Human Language Structure and its Influence on the Mental Development of Mankind* (trans. P. Heath). Cambridge: Cambridge University Press. 1988.

Hunt, K. D. (1994) 'The evolution of human bipedality: ecology and functional morphology', *JHE* 26: 183–202.

Hurford, J. R. (1989) 'Biological evolution of the Saussurean sign as a component of the language acquisition device', *Lingua* 77: 187–222.

Hurford, J. R. (1991) 'The evolution of the critical period for language acquisition', *Cognition* 40: 159–201.

Ilyenkov, E. V. (1982) *The Dialectics of the Abstract and the Concrete in Marx's Capital*. Moscow: Progress Publishers.

Ingold, T. (1993) 'Introduction(s)' and 'Epilogue', in Gibson and Ingold 1993; 449–72.

Irsigler, F. J. (1989) 'Language origin and the Island of Reil (insula reilli)', in Wind *et al.* 1989; 233–56.

Isaac, G. L. (1976) 'Stages of cultural elaboration in the Pleistocene: possible archaeological indicators of the development of language capabilities', in Steklis and Harnad 1976; 275–88.

Isaac, G. L. (1979) 'The food sharing behavior of Proto-human hominids', in *Human Ancestors*, readings from *Scientific American*. San Francisco: Freeman; 100–23.

Jake, J. (1978) 'Why Dyirbal isn't ergative at all', *Studies in the Linguistic Sciences* 8: 97–110.

Jaynes, J. (1976) 'The evolution of language in the late Pleistocene', in Steklis and Harnad 1976; 312–25.

Jespersen, O. (1922) *Language: Its Nature, Development and Origin*. London: Allen & Unwin.

Jolly, K. (1988) 'Lemur social behaviour and primate intelligence', in Byrne and Whiten 1988; 27–33.

Jones, P. E. (1991) *Marxism, Materialism and Language Structure, Part 1: General Principles*. Sheffield: Centre for Popular Culture Series No. 6.

Jones, P. E. (1994) 'Biological determinism and epistemology in linguistics: some considerations on the "Chomskyan Revolution"' (unpublished paper).

Jones, P. R., and A. Cregan (1986) *Sign and Symbol Communication for Mentally Handicapped People*. London: Croom Helm.

Kelemen, G. (1948) 'The anatomical basis of phonation in the chimpanzee', *J. Morph.* 82: 229–56.

Kendon, A. (1988) 'Parallels and divergences between Warlpiri sign language and spoken Warlpiri: analyses of spoken and signed discourses', *Oceania* 58: 239–54.

Kendon, A. (1989) *Sign Languages of Aboriginal Australia*. Cambridge: Cambridge University Press.

Kendon, A. (1991) 'Some considerations for a theory of language origins', *Man* 26: 199–221.

Kendon, A. (1993) 'Human gestures', in Gibson and Ingold 1993; 43– 62.

Kibrik, A. E. (1985) 'Towards a typology of ergativity', in J. Nichols and A. Woodbury (eds), *Grammar Inside and Outside the Clause: Some Approaches to Theory from the Field*. Cambridge: Cambridge University Press; 268–323.

Kidder, J. H., R. L. Jantz and F. H. Smith (1992) 'Defining modern humans: a multivariate approach', in Bräuer and Smith 1992; 157–78.

Klein, R. G. (1989) *The Human Career: Human Biological and Cultural Origins*. Chicago: University of Chicago Press.

Klima, E. S., and U. Bellugi (1979) *The Signs of Language*. Cambridge Mass.: Harvard University Press.

Klimov, G. A. (1974) 'On the character of languages of active typology (translation of K xarakteristike jazykov aktivnogo stoja)', *Linguistics* 131: 11–25.

Klimov, G. A. (1979) 'On the position of the ergative type in typological classification', in Plank 1979b; 327–32.

Knight, C. (1991) *Blood Relations. Menstruation and the Origins of Culture*. New Haven and London: Yale University Press.

Knight, C. (1994) 'Ritual and the origins of language', in C. Knight and C. Power, *Ritual and the Origins of Symbolism*. Dagenham: University of East London; 16–32.

Köhler, W. (1925) *The Mentality of Apes* (2nd edn). London: Gollancz.

Kortlandt, A. (1973) 'Comment' on Hewes 1973, *CA* Supplement 33 (1992): 65–84.

Kortlandt, A. (1986) 'The use of stone tools by wild-living chimpanzees and earliest hominids', *JHE* 15: 72–132.

Kozulin, A. (1990) *Vygotsky's Psychology: A Biography of Ideas*. New York: Harvester Wheatsheaf.

Krantz, G. S. (1988) 'Laryngeal descent in 40,000 year old fossils', in Landsberg 1988; 173–80.

Kuryłowicz, J. (1973) 'Ergativeness and the stadial theory of linguistic development', *The Study of Man* 2: 1–21.

Kyle, J. G., and B. Woll (1985) *Sign Language: The Study of Deaf People and Their Language*. Cambridge: Cambridge University Press.

Labov, W. (1972) 'The transformation of experience in narrative syntax', in *Language in the Inner City: Studies in the Black English Vernacular*. Philadelphia: University of Pennsylvania Press; 354–96.

Ladefoged, P. and A. Traill (1994) 'Clicks and their accompaniments', *J. Phon.* 22, 1: 33–64.

Laitman, J. T. (1983) 'The evolution of the hominid upper respiratory system and implications for the origin of speech', in de Grolier 1983: 63–90.

Laitman, J. T., R. C. Heimbuch and E. S. Crelin (1979) 'The basicranium of fossil hominids as an indicator of their upper respiratory systems', Am. J. Phys. Anth. 51: 15–33.

Laitman, J. T., J. S. Reidenberg and P. J. Gannon (1992) 'Fossil skulls and hominid vocal tracts: new approaches to charting the evolution of human speech', in Wind *et al.* 385–97.

Lakoff, G. (1987) *Women, Fire and Dangerous Things. What Categories Reveal about the Mind.* Chicago: Chicago University Press.

Landsberg, M. E. (ed.) (1988) *The Genesis of Language: A Different Judgment of Evidence.* Berlin: Mouton de Gruyter.

Leakey, L. B. (1959) *First Lessons in Kikuyu.* Nairobi: East African Literature Bureau.

Leakey, R., and R. Lewin (1992) *Origins Reconsidered: In Search of What Makes us Human.* London: Little Brown.

Lee, R. B. (1979) *The !Kung San: Men, Women and Work in a Foraging Society.* Cambridge: Cambridge University Press.

Lee, R. B. (1984) *The Dobe !Kung.* New York: Holt, Rinehart & Winston.

Lee, R. B., and I. de Vore (1968) 'Problems in the study of hunter-gatherers', in R. B. Lee and I. de Vore (eds), *Man the Hunter.* Chicago: Aldine; 3–12.

Lehmann, W. P. (1992) *Historical Linguistics.* London: Routledge.

Lenneberg, E. (1967) *Biological Foundations of Language.* Cambridge, Mass.: MIT Press.

Leontiev, A. N. (1978) *Activity, Consciousness and Personality.* Englewood Cliffs, NJ: Prentice Hall.

Leroi-Gourhan, A. (1993) *Gesture & Speech*, trans. A. B. Berger. Cambridge Mass.: October Books, MIT Press.

Leutenegger, W. (1972) 'Newborn size and pelvic dimensions of Australopithecus', *Nature* 240: 568–9.

Lévy-Bruhl, L. (1928) *The 'Soul' of the Primitive*, trans. L. A. Clare. London: George Allen & Unwin, 1965.

Lightfoot, D. (1976) 'Diachronic syntax: exposition and deep structure re-analyses', *Folia Linguistica* 9: 1–4.

Lightfoot, D. (1979) *Principles of Diachronic Syntax.* Cambridge: Cambridge University Press.

Lieberman, P. (1991) *Uniquely Human: The Evolution of Speech, Thought and Selfless Behaviour.* Cambridge, Mass.: Harvard University Press.

Lieberman, P. (1992) 'On the evolutionary biology of speech and syntax', in Wind *et al.* 1992; 399–419.

Linden, E. (1976) *Apes, Men and Language.* Harmondsworth: Penguin.

Livingstone, F. B. (1973) 'Did the Australopithecines sing?', *CA* 13: 25–9.

Lock, A. (ed.) (1978) *Action, Gesture and Symbol: The Emergence of Language.* New York: Academic Press.

Lock, A. (1983) '"Recapitulation" in the ontogeny and phylogeny of language', in de Grolier 1983; 255–74.

Luria, A. R., and L. S. Vygotsky (1992) *Ape, Primitive Man and Child* (trans. E. Rossiter). Hemel Hempstead: Harvester Wheatsheaf.

Luria, A. R., and F. I. Yudovich (1959) *Speech and the Development of Mental Processes in the Child.* Harmondsworth: Penguin.

Lyons, J. (1988) 'Origins of language', in A. C. Fabian (ed.), *Origins: The Darwin College Lectures*. Cambridge: Cambridge University Press; 141–66.

McEvedy, C. (1980) *The Penguin Atlas of African History*. Harmondsworth: Penguin.

McHenry, H. (1993) 'Behavioral and ecological implications of early body size', *Am. J. Phys. Anth.* Supplement 16: 143.

MacLarnon, A. (1993) 'The vertebral canal', in A. Walker and R. E. Leakey (eds), *The Nariokotome Homo Erectus Skeleton*. Cambridge, Mass.: Harvard University Press; 359–90.

MacLean, P. D. (1988) 'Evolution of audiovocal communication, as reflected by the therapsid-mammalian transition and the limbic thalamocingulate division', in J. D. Newman (ed.), *The Physiological Control of Mammalian Vocalisation*, New York: Plenum; 185–201.

MacNeilage, P. (1992) 'Evolution and the lateralization of the two great primate systems', in Wind *et al*. 1992; 281–300.

McNeill, D. (1985) 'So you think gestures are non verbal?', *Psych. Rev.* 92: 350–71.

Maisels, C. K. (1993) *The Emergence of Civilisation: From Hunting and Gathering to Agriculture, Cities and the State in the Near East*. London: Routledge.

Malinowski, B. (1966) *Coral Gardens and their Magic*, Vol. 1: *Soil-tilling and Agricultural Rites in the Trobriand Islands*, intro. E. R. Leach, Vol. 2: *The Language of Magic and Gardening*, intro. by J. Berry (2nd edn). London: Allen & Unwin.

Manessy, G. (ed.) (1967) *La Classification nominale dans les langues négro africaines*. Paris: Colloques internationaux du Centre National de la Recherche Scientifique.

Marshack, A. (1989) 'Evolution of the human capacity', *Yrbk of Phys. Anth.* 32: 1–34.

Marshack, A. (1992) 'The origin of language: an anthropological approach', in Wind *et al*. 1992; 421–48.

Martin, J. R. (1988) 'Grammatical conspiracies in Tagalog: family, face and fate – with regard to Benjamin Lee Whorf', in J. D. Benson, M. J. Cummings and W. S. Greaves (eds), *Linguistics in a Systemic Perspective*. Amsterdam: Benjamin; 243–300.

Marx, K. (1857) *Grundrisse* (The Pelican Marx Library). Harmondsworth: Penguin, 1973.

Marx, K. (1887) *Capital: A Critique of Political Economy*, trans. S. Moore and E. Aveling, ed. F. Engels. London: Lawrence & Wishart, 1970.

Matthews, W. K. (1950) 'The Soviet contribution to linguistic thought', *Arch. Ling.* 2, pt. 1: 1–23 and pt. 2: 97–121.

Mehler, J., J. Morton and P. W. Jusczyk (1984) 'On reducing language to biology', *Cog. Neur.* 1: 83–116.

Mellars, P. (1991) 'Cognitive changes and the emergence of modern humans in Europe', *Cam. Arch. Jnl* 1: 63–76.

Mellars, P., and C. Stringer (eds) (1989) *The Human Revolution: Behavioural and Biological Perspectives on the Origins of Modern Humans*. Edinburgh: Edinburgh University Press.

Menzel, E. W., Jr (1979) 'Communication of object-locations in a group of young chimpanzees', in D. A. Hamburg and E. R. McCown (eds), *The Great Apes*. Menlo Park: Benjamin/Cummings; 357–71.

Menzel, E. W., Jr (1988) 'A group of young chimpanzees in a 1–acre field: leadership and communication', in Byrne and Whiten 1988; 155–9.

Miles, L. L. (1990) 'The cognitive foundations for reference in a signing orang-utan', in S. T. Parker and K. R. Gibson (eds), *'Language' and Intelligence in Monkeys and Apes*. Cambridge: Cambridge University Press; 511–39.

Miller, G. A. (1956) 'The magical number seven, plus or minus two: some limits on our capacity for processing information', *Psych. Rev.* 63: 81–97.

Miller, J. (1975) 'Delaware alternative classifications', *Anth. Ling.* 17: 434–44.

Milo, R., and D. Quiatt (1993) 'The evidence for and implications of a late origin of vocal language', *CA* 34: 569–98.

Minc, L. (1986) 'Scarcity and survival: the role of oral tradition in mediating subsistence crises', *J. Anth. Arch.* 3: 159–89.

Morgan, L. H. (1877) *Ancient Society*, intro. E. B. Leacock. Cleveland and New York: Meridian, 1963.

Müller, F. M. (1861) *Lectures on the Science of Language*, 2 vols. London: Longmans Green.

Müller, F. M. (1887) *The Science of Thought*. London: Longmans Green.

Nauta, W. J. H., and M. Feirtag (1979) 'The organization of the brain', *Sci. Amer.* (Sept.): 78–105.

Negus, V. (1949) *The Comparative Anatomy and Physiology of the Larynx*. London: Heinemann.

Newman, J. D. (1992) 'The primate isolation call and the evolution and physiological control of human speech', in Wind *et al.* 1992; 301–21.

Newmeyer, F. J. (1991) 'Functional explanation in linguistics and the origins of language', *Lang. & Comm.* 11: 3–28.

Newmeyer, F. J. (1992) 'Iconicity and generative grammar', *Language* 68: 756–96.

Newton, I. (1686) *Philosophiae naturalis principia mathematica*, trans. Motte, *The Mathematical Principles of Natural Philosophy* (1729), rev. F. Cajori. Berkeley, Calif.: UCLA.

Newton, I. (1730) *Opticks, or a Treatise of Reflections, Refractions, Inflections and Colours of Light* (4th edn). New York: Dover, 1952.

Noble, W., and I. Davidson (1991) 'The evolutionary emergence of modern human behaviour: language and its archaeology', *Man* 26: 223–53.

Noiré, L. (1917) *The Origins and Philosophy of Language*. Chicago: Open Court.

Ochs, E. (1988) *Culture and Language Development: Language Acquisition and Language Socialisation in a Samoan Village*. Cambridge: Cambridge University Press.

Ohala, J. (1983) 'Cross-language use of pitch: an ethnological view', *Phonetica* 40: 1–18.

Ohala, J. (1984) 'An ethnological perspective on common cross-language utilization of F^0 of voice', *Phonetica* 41: 1–16.

O'Shea, J., and M. Zvelebil (1984) 'Oleneosrovski mogilnik: reconstructing the social and economic organization of prehistoric foragers in northern Russia', *J. Anth. Arch.* 3: 1–40.

Paget, R. A. S. (1944) 'The origin of language', *Science* 99: 14–15.

Parker, S. T. (1994) 'Comment' on Armstrong, Stokoe and Wilcox, 1994, *CA* 35: 349–68.

Passingham, R. E. (1982) *The Human Primate*. Oxford: Freeman.

Patterson, F. G. P. (1981) *Conversations with a Gorilla*. New York: Holt, Rinehart & Winston.

Patterson, F. G. P., and R. H. Cohn (1990) 'Language acquisition by a lowland gorilla. Koko: ten years of vocabulary development', *Word* 41: 97–121.

Pavlov, I. P. (1957) *Selected Works*. Moscow: Foreign Languages Publishing House.

Pedersen, H. (1931) *The Discovery of Language*, trans. J. W. Spargo. Cambridge, Mass.: Harvard University Press.

Penfield, W., and L. Roberts (1959) *Speech and Brain Mechanisms*. Princeton: Princeton University Press.

Piaget, J. (1955) *The Child's Construction of Reality*. London: Routledge and Kegan Paul.

Piaget, J. (1959) *The Language and Thought of the Child* (3rd edn), trans. J. Gabain. London: Routledge and Kegan Paul.

Pinker, S. (1994) *The Language Instinct*. Harmondsworth: Allen Lane.

Pinker, S., and P. Bloom (1990) 'Natural language and natural selection', *Beh. & Br. Sci.* 13: 707–84.

Plank, F. (1979a) 'Ergativity, syntactic typology and Universal Grammar: some past and present viewpoints', in Plank (1979b): 3–36.

Plank, F. (1979b) *Ergativity: Towards a Theory of Grammatical Relations*. London: Academic Press.

Plooij, F. X. (1978) 'Some basic traits of language in wild chimpanzees', in Lock 1978; 111–31.

Porter, A. M. W. (1993) 'Sweat and thermoregulation in hominids: comments prompted by the publications of P. E. Wheeler 1984–1993', *JHE* 25: 417–23.

Power, C. (1994) 'Cosmetic manipulation of reproductive signals: a preadaptation to ritual in archaic Homo sapiens', in C. Knight and C. Power (eds), *Ritual and the Origins of Symbolism*, Dagenham: University of East London.

Power, M. (1994) 'The mutual dependence system of undisturbed chimpanzees and human foragers', Paper read at the Tenth LOS conference, 'Social and Cultural Origins of Language', Berkeley, Calif., July 1994.

Premack, D. (1988) ' "Does the chimpanzee have a theory of mind" revisited', in Byrne and Whiten 1988; 160–79.

Premack, A. J., and D. Premack (1972) 'Teaching language to an ape', *Sci. Am.* 227: 92–9.

Pulleyblank, E. G. (1983) 'The beginnings of duality of patterning in language', in de Grolier 1983; 369–410.

Quiatt, D., and V. Reynolds (1993) *Primate Behaviour: Information, Social Knowledge, and the Emergence of Culture* (Cambridge St. in Bio. Anth.). Cambridge: Cambridge University Press.

Ragir, S. (1985) 'Retarded development: the evolutionary mechanism underlying the emergence of the human capacity for language', *J. Mind & Beh.* 6: 451–68.

Ragir, S. (1993) 'Comment' on Milo and Quiatt, 1993, *CA* 34: 588–9.

Ragir, S. (1994) 'Toward an understanding of the relationship between bipedal walking and encephalisation', Paper read at the Tenth LOS conference, 'Social and Cultural Origins of Language', Berkeley, Calif., July 1994.

Richman, B. (1976) 'Some vocal distinctive features used by gelada monkeys', *JASA* 60: 718–24.

Richman B. (1993) 'On the evolution of speech: singing in the middle term', *CA* 34: 721–2.

Rightmire, G. P. (1985) 'The tempo of change in the evolution of mid-Pleistocene Homo', in Delson 1985; 255–64.

Rightmire, G. P., and H. J. Deacon (1991) 'Comparative studies of late Pleistocene human remains from Klasies River Mouth, South Africa', *JHE* 20: 131–56.

Rolfe, L. H. (1992) 'Gesture and deixis', in Wind et al. 1992; 25–31.

Rose, S. J., R. C. Lewontin and L. J. Kamin (1990) *Not in our Genes*. Harmondsworth: Penguin.

Rouhani, S. (1989) 'Molecular genetics and the pattern of human evolution: plausible and implausible models', in Mellars and Stringer 1989; 47–61.

Ruhlen, M. (1987) *A Guide to the World's Languages*, Vol. 1: *Classification*. Stanford, Calif.: Stanford University Press.

Ruwet, N. (1991) *Syntax and Human Experience*, ed. and trans. Goldsmith. Chicago: Chicago University Press.

Sapir, E. (1929) 'A study in phonetic symbolism', *J. Exp. Psych* 12: 225–39.

Sasse, H.-J. (1978) 'Subjekt und Ergativ: zur pragmatischen Grundlage primärer grammatischer Relationen', *Folia Linguistica* 12: 219–52.

Saussure, F. de (1974) *Course in General Linguistics*. trans. W. Baskin. London: Fontana.

Savage-Rumbaugh, E. S. (1986) *Ape Language: From Conditioned Response to Symbol*. New York: Columbia University Press.

Savage-Rumbaugh, E. S., and K. MacDonald (1988) 'Deception and social manipulation in symbol-using apes', in Byrne and Whiten 1988; 224–37.

Savage-Rumbaugh, E. S., and D. M. Rumbaugh (1993) 'The emergence of language', in Gibson and Ingold 1993; 86–108.

Savage-Rumbaugh, E. S., J. Murphy, R. A. Sevcik, K. E. Brakke, S. L. Williams and D. M. Rumbaugh (1993) *Language Comprehension in Ape and Child* (Mon. Soc. Res. Ch. Dvpt no. 223, vol. 58). Chicago: Chicago University Press.

Savage-Rumbaugh, E. S., B. J. Wilkerson and R. Bakeman (1977) 'Spontaneous gestural communication among conspecifics in the pygmy chimpanzee (Pan paniscus)', in G. Bourne (ed.), *Progress in Ape Research*. New York: Academic Press; 97–116.

Schaller S. (1991) *A Man without Words* New York: Summit.

Schepartz, L. A. (1993) 'Language and modern human origins', *Yrbk of Phys. Anth.* 36: 91–126.

Schleicher, A. (1850) *Die Sprachen Europes in Systematischer Ubersicht: Linguistiche Untersuchunger*, intro. K. Koerner. Amsterdam Studies in the Theory and History of Linguistic Sciences, Vol. 4, 1983.

Schleicher, A. (1863) *Darwinische Theorie und die Sprachwissenschaft: Offenes Sendschreiben an Herrn Dr Ernst Häckel*. Weimar: H. Böhlau.

Schleicher, A. (1865) *Uber die Bedeutung der Sprache für die Naturgeschichte des Mensches*. Weimar: H. Böhlau.

Schmandt-Besserat, D. (1992) *Before Writing*, Vol. 1: *From Counting to Cuneiform*. Austin, Tex.: University of Texas Press.

Searle, J. (1983) *Intentionality: An Essay in the Philosophy of Mind*. Cambridge: Cambridge University Press.

Senut, B., and C. Tardieu (1985) 'Functional aspects of Plio-Pleistocene limb bones: implications for taxonomy and phylogeny', in Delson 1985; 193–201.

Sept, J. M. (1992) 'Was there no place like home?', *CA* 33: 187–96.

Shackley, M. (1983) *Wildmen, Yeti, Sasquatch and the Neanderthal Enigma*. London: Thames and Hudson.

Shaywitz, B. A., S. E. Shaywitz, K. R. Pugh, R. T. Constable, P. Skudlarski, R. K. Fulbright, R. A. Bronen, J. M. Fletcher, D. P. Shankweiler, L. Katz and J. C. Gore (1995) 'Sex differences in the functional organization of the brain for language', *Nature* 373(6515): 607–9.

Simek, J. F. (1992) 'Neanderthal cognition and the Middle to Upper Palaeolithic transition', in Bräuer and Smith 1992; 231–46.

Skelly, M. (1979) *Amer-Ind Gestural Code Based on Universal American Indian Hand Talk*. New York: Elsevier N. Holland.

Smerken, M. J. (1992) 'Bickerton and the sociobiologists', *J. Pidg. Cre. Lang.* 7: 111–14.

Snyman, J. W. (1983) 'Zu/'hoasi, a Khoisan dialect of S. W. Africa', in I. R. Dihoff, *Current Approaches to African Linguistics*. Dordrecht: Foris; 115–25.

Soffer, O. (1992) 'Social transformations at the Middle to Upper Palaeolithic transition: the implications of the European record', in Bräuer and Smith 1992; 247–59.

Staal, F. (1994) 'Is syntax adaptive for cognition or communication?', Paper read at the Tenth LOS conference, 'Social and Cultural Origins of Language', Berkeley, Calif., July 1994.

Steklis, H. D. (1988) 'Primate communication, comparative neurology and the origin of language re-examined', in Landsberg 1988; 37–61.

Steklis, H. D., and S. R. Harnad (eds) (1976) *Origins and Evolution of Language and Speech*. Annals of N. Y. Acad. Sci., vol. 280.

Steklis, H. D., and M. J. Raleigh (1973) 'Comment' on Hewes 1973, *CA* Supplment 33 (1992): 65–84.

Stern, W. (1924) *The Psychology of Early Childhood*. London: Allen and Unwin.

Stevens, K. N. (1972) 'Quantal nature of speech', in E. E. David Jr, and P. B. Denes (eds), *Human Communication*. New York: McGraw-Hill; 51–66.

Strauss, L. C. (1989) 'On early hominid use of fire', *CA* 30: 488–91.

Stringer, C. (1989) 'The origin of early modern humans: a comparison of the European and non-European evidence', in Mellars & Stringer 1989; 232–44.

Stringer, C. (1992) 'Replacement, continuity and the origin of Homo sapiens', in Bräuer & Smith 1992; 9–24.

Susman, R. L. (ed.) (1984) *The Pygmy Chimpanzee: Evolutionary Biology and Behaviour*. New York: Plenum.

Susman R. L., J. T. Stern, W. L. Jungers (1985) 'Locomotor adaptations in the Hadar hominids', in Delson 1985; 184–92.

Swadesh, M. (1971) *The Origin and Diversification of Language*. London: Routledge.

Tanner, N. M. (1981) *On Becoming Human*. Cambridge: Cambridge University Press.

Tanner, N. M., and A. Zihlman (1976a) 'Discussion paper: the evolution of human communication: what can primates tell us?', in Steklis and Harnad 1976; 467–80.

Tanner, N. M., and A. Zihlman (1976b) 'Women in evolution pt 1: innovation and selection in human origins', *Signs* 1: 585–608.

Teleki, G. (1973) 'The omnivorous chimpanzee', *Sci. Am.* 228: 33.

Templeton, A. R. (1993) 'The "Eve" hypothesis: a genetic critique and reanalysis', *Am. Anth.* 95: 51–72.

Terrace, H. S. (1979) *Nim: A Chimpanzee who Learned Language*. New York: Knopf.

Terrace, H. S. (1986) introduction to Savage-Rumbaugh 1986.

Terrace, H. S., L. A. Pettito and T. G. Bever (1979) 'Can an ape create a sentence?', *Science* 206: 821–901.

Thomson, G. (1975) 'Speech and thought', in D. Craig (ed.), *Marxists on Literature: An Anthology*. Harmondsworth: Penguin; 25–46.

Tobias, P. V. (1987) 'The brain of *Homo habilis*: a new level of organisation in cerebral evolution', *JHE* 16: 741–61.

Toth, N. and K. Schick (1993) 'Early stone industries and inferences regarding language and cognition', in Gibson and Ingold 1993; 346–62.

Trinkaus, E. (1989a) 'The Upper Pleistocene transition', in Trinkaus 1989b; 42–66.

Trinkaus, E. (ed.) (1989b) *The Emergence of Modern Humans*. Cambridge: Cambridge University Press.

Trinkaus, E. (1992) 'Cladistics and later Pleistocene human evolution', in Bräuer and Smith 1992; 1–8.

Uemlianin I. A. (1994) 'The development of the subject category in first language acquisition', Ph.D. thesis, University of Edinburgh.

UNESCO (1981) *General History of Africa 1: Methodology and African Prehistory*. Berkeley, Calif.: Heinemann.

Vincent, N. (1982) 'The development of the auxiliaries *habere* and *esse* in Romance', in N. Vincent and M. Harris (eds), *Studies in the Romance Verb*. London: Croom Helm; 71–96.

Vincent, N. (1988) 'Latin', in N. Vincent and M. Harris (eds), *The Romance Languages*. London: Croom Helm; 26–78.

Voloshinov, V. N. (1973) *Marxism and the Philosophy of Language*, trans. L. Matejka and I. R. Titunik. New York: Seminar Press.

Vrba, E. S. (1985) 'Ecological and adaptive changes associated with early hominid evolution', in Delson 1985; 63–71.

Vygotsky, L. S. (1962) *Thought and Language*, trans. E. Haufman and G. Vakar. New York: Academic Press.

de Waal, F. (1988) 'The communicative repertoire of captive bonobos (*Pan paniscus*) compared to that of chimpanzees', *Behaviour* 106: 183–251.

de Waal, F. (1989) *Chimpanzee Politics: Power and Sex among Apes*. Baltimore: Johns Hopkins.

Wallace, R. (1989) 'Cognitive mapping and the origin of language and mind', *CA* 30: 518–26.

Wallace, R. (1993) 'Comment' on Burling 1993, *CA* 34: 25–53.

Wallace, R. (1994) 'Comment' on Armstrong *et al.* 1994, *CA* 35: 349–68.

Wallman, J. (1993) 'Comment' on Burling 1993, *CA* 34: 25–53.

Wenner, A. M. (1994) 'On the question of "language" among bees'. Paper read at the Tenth LOS conference, 'Social and Cultural Origins of Language', Berkeley, Calif., July 1994.

Wenner, A. M., & P. H. Wells (1990) *Anatomy of a Controversy: the Question of a 'Language' among Bees*. New York: Columbia University Press.

Wenner, A. M., D. Meade and L. J. Friesen (1991) 'Recruitment, search behavior and flight ranges of honey bees', *American Zoologist* 31: 768–82.

Wertsch, J. V. (1985) *Vygotsky and the Social Formation of Mind*. Cambridge, Mass.: Harvard University Press.

Whallon, R. (1989) 'Elements of cultural change in the later Palaeolithic', in Mellars and Stringer 1989; 433–54.

Wheeler, P. E. (1990) 'The significance of selective brain cooling in hominids', *JHE* 19: 321–2.

Wheeler, P. E. (1992) 'The thermoregulatory advantages of large body size for hominids foraging in savannah environments', *JHE* 23: 351–62.

Whitcombe, E. (1994) 'Rearranging the head furniture.' Talk given at Research in progress seminar on the origins of language, University of East London, Stratford, 7 July 1994.

Whitcombe, E. (forthcoming) *The Power of Speech: An Essay in Anatomy*. Oxford: Oxford University Press.

Whitney, W. D. (1873–4) *Oriental and Linguistic Studies*, 2 vols. New York: Scribner, Armstrong.

Whitney, W. D. (1875) *The Life and Growth of Language*. London: Henry S. King.

Whorf, B. L. (1956) *Language, Thought and Reality: Selected Writings*. Cambridge, Mass.: MIT Press.

Williams, R. (1977) *Marxism and Literature*. Oxford: Oxford University Press.

Wilson, E. O. (1975) *Sociobiology: The New Synthesis*. Cambridge, Mass.: Harvard University Press.

Wind, J. (1976) 'Phylogeny of the human vocal tract', in Steklis and Harnad 1976; 612–30.

Wind, J. (1983) 'Primate evolution and the emergence of speech', in de Grolier 1983b; 15–36.

Wind, J. (1989) 'The evolutionary history of the human speech organs', in Wind *et al.* 1989; 173–97.

Wind, J. (1992) 'Speech origin: a review', in Wind *et al.* 1992; 21–37.

Wind, J., B. Chiarelli, B. Bichakjian and A. Nocentini (eds) (1992) *Language Origin: A Multidisciplinary Approach*. Dordrecht: Kluwer.

Wind, J., E. G. Pulleybank, E. de Grolier and B. H. Bichakjian (eds) (1989) *Studies in Language Origins*, vol. 1. Amsterdam: John Benjamin.

Wolpoff, M. H. (1989a) 'Multiregional evolution: the fossil alternative to Eden', in Mellars and Stringer 1989; 62–108.

Wolpoff, M. H. (1989b) 'The place of the Neandertals in human evolution', in Trinkaus 1989b; 97–141.

Wolpoff, M. H. (1992) 'Theories of modern human origins', in Bräuer and Smith 1992; 25–63.

Wolpoff, M. H., and A. Nkini. (1985) 'Early and early middle Pleistocene hominids from Asia and Africa', in Delson 1985; 202–5.

Woolfson, C. (1982) *The Labour Theory of Culture*. London: Routledge.

Wright, R. (1991) 'Quest for the mother tongue', *The Atlantic Monthly* 267 (4): 39–68.

Wynn, T. (1981) 'The intelligence of Oldowan hominids', *JHE* 10: 529–41.

Wynn, T. (1988) 'Tools and the evolution of human intelligence', in Byrne and Whiten 1988; 271–84.

Wynn, T. (1993) 'Layers of thinking in tool behaviour', in Gibson and Ingold 1993; 389–406.

Youssef, V. (1988) 'The language bioprogram hypothesis revisited', *J. Ch. Lang.* 15: 451–8.

Zihlman, A. L. (1978) 'Women in evolution pt 2: subsistence and social organisation among early hominids', *Signs* 4: 4–20.

Zihlman, A., J. E. Cronin, D. L. Cramer and V. M. Sarich (1978) 'Pygmy chimpanzee as a possible prototype for the common ancestor of humans, chimps and gorillas', *Nature* 275: 744–6.

Name Index

Subject Index

138-9 orig. by
synd of

140 given —
But this was
1st 2 lst to
whe pidgeon.

61, K & Wall Sts?
  Skelly - Amend?

68!?!
  p. 129 stories